THE DAILY DAD

The
DAILY
DAD

366 MEDITATIONS ON PARENTING, LOVE, AND RAISING GREAT KIDS

RYAN HOLIDAY

PORTFOLIO · PENGUIN

Portfolio / Penguin
An imprint of Penguin Random House LLC
penguinrandomhouse.com

Copyright © 2023 by Ryan Holiday
Penguin Random House supports copyright. Copyright fuels creativity, encourages
diverse voices, promotes free speech, and creates a vibrant culture. Thank you for
buying an authorized edition of this book and for complying with copyright
laws by not reproducing, scanning, or distributing any part of it in any form
without permission. You are supporting writers and allowing Penguin
Random House to continue to publish books for every reader.

Most Portfolio books are available at a discount when purchased in quantity for
sales promotions or corporate use. Special editions, which include personalized
covers, excerpts, and corporate imprints, can be created when purchased in
large quantities. For more information, please call (212) 572-2232 or e-mail
specialmarkets@penguinrandomhouse.com. Your local bookstore can also
assist with discounted bulk purchases using the Penguin Random House
corporate Business-to-Business program. For assistance in locating a
participating retailer, e-mail B2B@penguinrandomhouse.com.

Library of Congress Cataloging-in-Publication Data

Names: Holiday, Ryan, author.
Title: The daily dad : 366 meditations on parenting, love and
raising great kids / Ryan Holiday.
Description: [New York, NY] : Portfolio/Penguin, [2023]
Identifiers: LCCN 2022051010 (print) | LCCN 2022051011 (ebook) |
ISBN 9780593539057 (hardcover) | ISBN 9780593539064 (ebook)
Subjects: LCSH: Parenting. | Parenting—Quotations. | Fathers. | Parent and child.
Classification: LCC HQ755.8 .H6345 2023 (print) | LCC HQ755.8 (ebook) |
DDC 649/.1—dc23/eng/20230209
LC record available at https://lccn.loc.gov/2022051010
LC ebook record available at https://lccn.loc.gov/2022051011

Printed in the United States of America
1st Printing

Book design by Daniel Lagin

First say to yourself what you would be;
and then do what you have to do.

—EPICTETUS

CONTENTS

INTRODUCTION

A lot of people have kids. Not enough people are parents. It might seem like having a kid is what makes you a mother or a father, but we all know it isn't. There are plenty of people who take their kids to school, buy them clothes, put food in their bellies, give them a warm bed to sleep in . . . but who are not really parents. They act more like legal guardians, checking boxes to get through the day . . . and the first eighteen years.

That is not parenting. *That is the minimum.*

It's a sad fact that some don't even manage to get there. They seem to think that their obligation ends at conception or birth or the day their divorce papers are signed.

Procreating is biological. Parenting is psychological. It's a decision. A conscious choice. A commitment—commitment to actually change who you are and what your priorities should be for the benefit and betterment of your children. Commitment to sacrifice and service and the real work of making hard decisions, of *loving*, not just *having*.

Being a parent is the choice to make your children if not the center of your life, then *central* to your life, embracing the fact that bringing these little people into the world has changed everything about who you are, what you value, what your duties are.

A person with kids does enough to stay on the right side of Child Protective Services . . . or to avoid the raised eyebrows of their neighbors. A parent makes a commitment to a set of timeless principles that can feel like clichés but are rare enough in practice to be noticed when someone actually lives by them. You know, *put your family first, love unconditionally, be present, help them be who they're meant to be, lead by example, take nothing for granted, live with gratitude.*

Let's be clear: this is a modern choice. It's not an exaggeration to say that just a few generations ago, keeping your kids *alive* was about all that was expected. A child was seen as a future asset that began as a liability, another set of hands to help work the land on the family farm or a warm body to slot in on the line at the local factory and draw wages to help make ends meet.

Even the early years of the twentieth century were still a gauntlet of obstacles defined by mortality and infirmity. If all your kids made it through, it was a bona fide miracle. That you had a responsibility to care for them emotionally? To love them unconditionally? Please, who had the time? Or the ability?

There is a story about Winston Churchill, who was by no means a perfect father but had been raised by two self-absorbed and preoccupied aristocratic parents, themselves products of Victorian England. One evening, while talking to his son, Randolph, late into the night during a school holiday, a thought struck Churchill. "You know, my dear boy," he said with a kind of forlorn amusement, "I think I have talked to you more in these holidays than my father talked to me in the whole of his life." It was not only not an exaggeration but far from uncommon—and for many years after continued to be common. It may well be relatable to you and your own childhood.

How sad that is! Not just for the children but for the parents too.

For generations and generations, parents—especially fathers—were deprived of the most rewarding and beautiful thing in the world: being involved in the lives of their children. Loving them not just generally but actively, on a daily basis. The flip side of a patriarchal culture that burdened women with the whole of domestic life has been the soft bigotry of low expectations for men at home and with their children. Loving and being loved? Understanding and being understood? Nobody taught it to men. Nobody demanded it of fathers.

Again, think about how different history might have been if more parents had been *parents*. If [insert villain] had been raised better. If [insert greedy businessman] had been made to feel enough. If [insert heartbreaking victim] had been protected. If [insert anonymous nobody] had been equipped to fulfill their potential. If somebody had told [insert powerful person] they were proud of them.

While we can't change that traumatic past, we can write a better future.

That's the philosophy that underpins this book.

Despite the flaws of generations past, parenting is one of those beautiful experiences that links us, in an unbroken chain, back thousands and thousands of years. One of the most beautiful passages in the writings of Lucretius, the Roman poet, captures the joy of a father bending down as his children race each other to jump into his arms. One of the oldest pieces of evidence of humans in America is the footprints of a parent, probably a mother, walking in what is now White Sands National Park, carrying and then setting down, carrying and then setting down, carrying and then setting down, a young child.

This thing we're doing, our wild, chaotic daily existence—the one filled with joy and difficulty, love and labor—is a timeless one. The ancient world was unfathomably different from our world today—those footprints in New Mexico are intermixed with those of giant sloths and ancient camels and an extinct species of mammoth—yet somehow that experience is one you've had yourself countless times, at the park, walking back to the car after dinner, at the beach on a vacation.

Parents have always worried about their kids. Parents have always played games with their kids. Parents have always made plans for their kids. Parents have always tried to be a model for their kids. Parents have always tried to support and encourage their kids. Parents have always questioned and doubted and wondered if they are doing enough, if they're providing enough, if the school is good enough, if the sport is safe enough, if the kid's future is secure enough. They were doing the same stuff you're doing, and it's the same thing people are going to be doing fifty generations from now.

We are a part of something timeless and eternal, something very small and very large at the same time. This should humble and inspire us. It should give us purpose . . . and perspective.

And practical advice. Parenting is a topic that every philosophy and religious tradition has spoken about. We can find lessons on how to control our temper in front of our kids from Plato. Lessons on how to cultivate a peaceful home for our kids from Marcus Aurelius. Lessons on how to not spoil our kids from Seneca. Lessons on how to support our kids from Queen Elizabeth II. Lessons on how to inspire our kids from Florence Nightingale. Lessons on how to cultivate curiosity in our kids from Sandra Day O'Connor. Lessons on how to cherish time with our kids from Jerry Seinfeld. Lessons on how to balance our careers and our kids from Toni Morrison. Lessons on how to believe in our kids from the life of Muhammad Ali. Lessons from mothers who survived the Holocaust, fathers who led the civil rights movement, sons who became war heroes, and daughters who won Nobel Prizes . . . the Stoics and the Buddhists, the moderns and the ancients. We can learn from them all.

Like my previous book, *The Daily Stoic*, this book is built around accessing that advice—one piece at a time, one day at a time. I recommend that you begin on the page with the date you are presently holding this book. (Don't wait until January 1! Start today!) Wherever you begin, the power of the book resides in your picking it up daily, consistently engaging with the material—because even though the pages stay the same, your kids will change, the world will change, and you too will change.

My book *The Daily Stoic* is now well into the second half of its first decade. With more than a million copies in print in forty languages, there are people who have read it every day for *years*. Even though the book is the same as it was when I submitted it to the publisher in the fall of 2015, it continues to connect with and be of service to people all over the world. There's a Stoic observation about how we never step into the same river twice, for both we and the river are in a constant state of change.

This metaphor holds true for parenting too, and *The Daily Dad* was designed around that very idea. It's not a book for expecting parents or parents with adult children; it's a book for *anyone* at *every* stage in their journey. Each day's entry will strike the single parent of young twins differently from the new empty nester, just as that same entry will strike that same parent differently if they pick it back up the subsequent year. And let us linger on that idea of "picking it back up" for a second, as it is a critical theme in the philosophy of this book, as well as good and present parenting.

Parenting, like the pursuit of wisdom, is a lifelong affair. No one is expecting you to magically "get it." In fact, that is the fundamental flaw of far too many parenting books. You're supposed to read some book, be it in the scramble before they're born, in the sleep-deprived toddler years, or in some crisis when they're older, and then be *good*? That's not how it works. On a minute-by-minute basis, your kids and life put you in situations you could never have imagined on your own (and that none of the books seem to anticipate). So while there is no sudden transformation in parenting, there is still a process, a *working at it*, that you must take up. That's what this book—one page per day—is built around. Not a one-time thing but a morning or an evening ritual, a checking in, a continual process.

We will fall short. We will lose our tempers, get distracted, prioritize the wrong things, even hurt ourselves and the people we love in the process. What then? Just as with the pages of this book, we must pick back up where we left off. We must accept the fact that we are flawed humans while doing our best to learn from our errors and to not make the same mistakes twice . . . or any more times than we already have.

Dust yourself off. Recommit. Do better.

That journey—*The Daily Dad* as a book and as an idea—is, of course, not just for men. Our daily email, which has been free at dailydad.com, is received by thousands of women each morning. It's called *The Daily Dad* because I happen to be a father—of two boys—and that's about all you need to read into the name.

Whether your kids are old or not yet born, whether you're a stepparent, a coparent, an adoptive parent, gay or straight, whatever gender, this book is about the journey to become the parent you're capable of being, that your children deserve you to be . . . that the world *needs* you to be. It is not a short journey either—from birth to legal adulthood, as culture sometimes defines it. No, being a great parent begins long before that and ends, well, never. For even after we leave this life, our children will carry with them, good and bad, the lessons we taught them by word and deed.

Raising children—or, as I heard a parent once correct an interviewer, *raising adults*, since that's the goal—is the hardest thing you will ever do. It will also be the most rewarding and important thing you ever do.

That's what this book—and the hard-won wisdom of generations past—is about.

You are a parent. You are every parent who has ever lived or will ever live.

We are in this together.

Now let's go do our best, *together*.

THE DAILY DAD

JANUARY

TEACH BY EXAMPLE

(THE ONLY METHOD THAT WORKS)

January 1

A Little Fellow Follows You

In 1939, nine years before John Wooden would be hired to coach the UCLA men's basketball team, a friend sent him a picture with a poem on it to celebrate the birth of Wooden's first child. The picture is a man on a beach whose son is running behind him, playing in his footsteps in the sand. Wooden hung the picture in his home so he might see it every day. The poem, which he memorized and liked to give as a gift, went as follows:

> A careful man I want to be—
> a little fellow follows me.
> I do not dare to go astray,
> for fear he'll go the self-same way.
> I cannot once escape his eyes.
> Whatever he sees me do he tries.
> Like me he says he's going to be—
> that little chap who follows me . . .

You don't have to memorize these words as Wooden did, but you better internalize their message. Your children follow behind you. They see everything you do. If you go astray, so too will they.

January 2
Never Let Them See You Act Like This

> I think of myself as a philosopher only in the sense of being able to set an example.
>
> —FRIEDRICH NIETZSCHE

There is a story in Seneca's famous essay "On Anger" about a boy who at a very young age went to live in the house of Plato to study under the famous philosopher. Returning home to visit his parents, the boy witnessed his father lose his temper and yell at someone. Surprised by this violent outburst, and with the simple innocence of a child are capable of, the boy said, "I never saw anyone at Plato's house act like that."

However we conduct ourselves in front of our children—particularly at home, in private—they will come to see as normal. If we are rude or unkind to our spouse, they will assume that is an appropriate way to treat people they love. If we are anxious and overly worried, they will come to think that the world is a scary place that must be feared. If we behave unethically or cynically, they too will begin to cheat and lie.

January 3
Their Faults Are Your Faults

Don't worry that children never listen to you; worry that
they are always watching you.

—ROBERT FULGHUM

Your kids can drive you nuts. The way they can push your buttons. The way they can ask an interminable number of questions. The way they can mimic you.

"I love him very dearly I guess because of his faults which are my faults," the novelist John Steinbeck writes of his son. "I know where his pains and his panics come from."

Our kids have our virtues *and* our vices. That's what makes this whole crazy parenting thing such a wonderful opportunity. Because we are here to help them become the best possible versions of themselves. One of the ways we do that is to help them become like us in all the good ways. But one of the other ways is to prevent them from becoming too much like us in all the bad ways.

It can be an incredibly difficult balancing act if we aren't honest or self-possessed, if we let our egos get in the way. We can't let that happen. This is our chance, our time! To help them. To bolster them. To help them overcome flaws that maybe we never quite got over ourselves. To seize this second chance—to give what we didn't get.

More than that, it's a chance to understand.

January 4
Show Them How to Keep Their Cool

In 1952, Margaret Thatcher's father was driven out of office when a rival political party won a majority in the election. He was upset. He was hurt. And he could have allowed those emotions to drive how he reacted. But he didn't.

Instead, Thatcher's father made a statement of incredible restraint and dignity: "It is now almost nine years since I took up these robes in honor, and now I trust in honor they are laid down." He added later, "Although I have toppled over I have fallen on my feet. My own feeling is that I was content to be in and I am content to be out."

We could say that what he was doing was showing his daughter how to lose with grace. But it was much more than that. He was showing her that external circumstances don't define us, only how we respond to them. He was showing her how to bear adversity and how to never surrender your poise or self-control. These would all be lessons that Thatcher would use throughout her tumultuous life as a public servant, a prime minister, and a mother.

Your kids will need them too. So show them. Show by example, not just with words. Show them, when you've been screwed over and it really hurts, that still your personal code of conduct matters more. Because it does. Because it will.

January 5
Which Will It Be?

In his Broadway show, Bruce Springsteen explained the choice presented to all parents:

> We are ghosts or we are ancestors in our children's lives. We either lay our mistakes, our burdens upon them, and we haunt them, or we assist them in laying those old burdens down, and we free them from the chain of our own flawed behavior. And as ancestors, we walk alongside of them, and we assist them in finding their own way and some transcendence.

Will you be a ghost or an ancestor to your children? Will you haunt them or guide them? Will you curse them or inspire them?

Of course, we all know which of those two we *want* to be, just as Bruce's flawed father surely did. But then our demons, our issues, the ghosts of our own parents, get in the way.

That's why we go to therapy and read good books. That's why we stay up at night before bed talking to our spouse about how hard this parenting thing is, to exorcise those demons by bringing them into the light. It's why, wordlessly, when we hold our kids, we promise ourselves to do better, to try harder, to not repeat the mistakes we endured growing up.

This isn't going to be easy. We're not going to be perfect. But we're going to keep trying. We're going to be an ancestor—someone who guides them and inspires them. We're not going to haunt their future selves like a ghost.

January 6
Hang Their Pictures on Your Wall

He could not have known what the future would hold. He could not have known how he and his country would soon be tested. But in 2019, Volodymyr Zelenskyy gave a twenty-minute presidential inaugural address to the people of Ukraine that foreshadowed how he would respond.

Despite being one of his country's greatest success stories, making a fortune in the entertainment business and then holding its highest office, Zelenskyy asked not to be celebrated or held up as a model. "I really do not want my pictures in your offices, for the president is not an icon, an idol, or a portrait," he said. "Hang your kids' photos instead, and look at them each time you are making a decision."

Then, in February 2022, in an act of brutal illegality and avarice, Russia invaded Ukraine. Zelenskyy stood and fought, refusing opportunities to be rescued. What could be motivating him? His own advice. He has two children, ages eighteen and ten, whom he fights for. The Ukrainian military and its citizen-soldiers were similarly motivated—fighting valiantly alongside him against incredible odds for the chance that their children might live in freedom and live proudly, knowing that when it counted, their parents were prepared to sacrifice everything on their behalf.

Each of us should be inspired and humbled by this example. But as Zelenskyy said, we don't need to put pictures of heroes on our wall. Instead, we can hang up pictures of our children and strive to make them proud, and this should inspire and fortify us when we have to make tough decisions for their future, for their safety, for their freedom.

It is our kids who compel us to do the right thing . . . because they are always watching.

January 7
They Learn from Home

It is constantly reiterated that education begins in the home, but what is often forgotten is that morality begins in the home also.

—LOUIS L'AMOUR

You tell them to be good. To be honest. To follow the law. To care about other people. That safety comes first.

You say these things, but what do you *do*?

You can't say that you care about other people and then speed through stop signs because you're late. You can't tell your kids that honesty is important and then lie to get out of the ticket. What's worth more to you, avoiding a fine or living your values? That's what you have to ask yourself in every situation, particularly the ones where your kids are watching. Is getting what you want worth teaching the wrong lesson and undermining the values you are trying to instill?

Those kids buckled in behind you—they are absorbing your example and assimilating the lessons that will shape them in the smallest and biggest of ways. From the kind of driver they are going to be to the kind of *person* they are going to be. They are watching you as you go through the world. *Right now.* They're watching you break traffic laws, break promises. They hear you when you lie. They feel it when your actions don't match your words.

Kids learn from home. They learn in the car. They learn from Mom and Dad. You set the standard, so *be* the standard.

January 8
How Are You Embodying Your Values?

On April 1, 1933, shortly after coming to power in Germany, the Nazis held a boycott of all Jewish businesses. It was the first small persecution of many to come. But too many mothers and fathers who had talked to their kids about doing the right thing simply went along with it.

Not everyone, of course. Dietrich Bonhoeffer's ninety-nine-year-old grandmother, for instance. On that day, she was out shopping and she refused to be told whose businesses she could support. She ignored or dodged the Nazi troops stationed in front of stores and shopped wherever she liked. Their grandmother "marching past Nazi gorillas" came to be seen in the Bonhoeffer family as "an embodiment of the values they sought to live by."

That embodiment wasn't lost on Dietrich, who ten years later would lose his life plotting to assassinate Hitler. Even though he was a pastor, even though he had plenty of opportunities to escape Germany and live in peace and freedom in London or America, he stayed. His grandmother's example guided him, showed him how to *live* by his values.

Let the same be true for you and your children, whatever the future holds, big or small.

TEACH BY EXAMPLE

January 9
Protect This Great Invention

The author, educator, and cultural critic Neil Postman points out in *The Disappearance of Childhood* that childhood is a social construct. Genetic expression makes no distinction between who is a child and who isn't. Children, as we understand them, have existed for less than four hundred years. "The idea of childhood is one of the great inventions of the Renaissance," he writes, because it allowed children to develop, to learn, to have a safe space to play and explore and discover themselves.

Like any invention, childhood can disappear. How? With *the disappearance of adulthood*. Childhood, as both a social structure and a psychological condition, works when things like maturity, responsibility, literacy, and critical thinking mark an adult. But when things like long-form writing and reading decline, the gap between child and adult shrinks; the line between them blurs and then dissolves.

As parents, we have to protect this great invention. We have to increase the gap between childhood and adulthood. Let them be kids . . . but also make sure that you are being an adult. Be a leader. Be responsible. Be an example, a model they have to strive toward. Let them see you with a book they can't yet comprehend. Let them be around adult conversations they can't quite understand. Let them see you working and sweating and providing.

Let them see an adult—so they have something not just to look up to but to look forward to as well.

January 10
Your Living Is the Teaching

Example is not the main thing in influencing others. It is the only thing.

—ALBERT SCHWEITZER

Socrates's students said of their teacher that for all the genius he possessed, Plato and Aristotle and all the other sages who learned from him "derived more benefit from [his] character than [his] words." So it was for Zeno and Cleanthes, the two earliest Stoic philosophers. "Cleanthes could not have been the express image of Zeno," Seneca wrote, "if he had merely heard his lectures; he shared in his life, saw into his hidden purposes, and watched him to see whether he lived according to his own rules."

Is there a better description—a better bar to set—for a parent than this? If you want to teach your kids, it's not going to be with words. It's not going to be with lectures. It's going to be through showing them that you live according to the rules you set and the values you are trying to tell them are important.

January 11
We Can Be That Gift

Marcus Aurelius's father died when he was young. But then this young boy who was cursed by tragedy received a great gift. A gift that all children who have received it know to be one of the most incredible things in the world: a loving stepfather.

Ernest Renan wrote that, more than his teachers and tutors, "Marcus had a single master whom he revered above them all, and that was Antoninus." All his adult life, Marcus strived to be a disciple of his adoptive stepfather. While he lived, Marcus saw him, Renan said, as "the most beautiful model of a perfect life."

What were the things that Marcus learned from Antoninus? He learned the importance of compassion, hard work, persistence, altruism, self-reliance, cheerfulness; keeping an open mind and listening to anyone who could contribute; taking responsibility and blame, and putting other people at ease; yielding the floor to experts and heeding their advice; knowing when to push something or someone and when to back off; being indifferent to superficial honors and treating people as they *deserved to be treated*.

It's quite a list, isn't it? These lessons impacted Marcus so deeply, he remembered them far into adulthood and recorded them for his own reference in what would become *Meditations*. What made the lessons so powerful was that they were *embodied* in Antoninus's actions rather than written on some tablet or scroll.

There is no better way to learn than from a role model. There is no better way to judge our progress than in constant company with the person we would most like to be one day.

January 12
Don't Talk About It. Be About It.

Tim Duncan is likely the greatest power forward in the history of the NBA. Five titles. Three NBA Finals MVPs. Fifteen All-Star appearances. Fifteen All-NBA Team selections. Fifteen NBA All-Defensive Team selections. The most devastating turnaround jumper off the glass that basketball has ever seen. And he did it with a selflessness and poise that are almost unmatched.

Almost is the operative word, of course, because Duncan was helped along on this journey to greatness by his predecessor and teammate David Robinson. How did these two superstars connect? How did one mentor the other? In his NBA Hall of Fame induction speech, Duncan explained:

> People always ask, "What did he tell you? What did he show you?" I don't remember one thing we sat down and talked about specifically. But what he did was he was a consummate pro, he was an incredible father, he was an incredible person, and he showed me how to be a good teammate, a great person to the community, all those things. Not by sitting there and telling me how to do it, but by being that.

We're better off *embodying* our philosophy rather than talking about it. As the Stoics said, it's a waste of time to speculate or argue about what makes a good man, a good athlete, a good teammate. Our job, they said, is *to be one.* This is how it goes, in sports, in life, and for parents. Sure, we can talk all we want. We can have great conversations. But what matters is what we do, who we are, how we act

January 13
Here's How to Have Lasting Impact

To be in your children's memories tomorrow, you have to be
in their lives today.

—BARBARA JOHNSON

Whether you know it or not, whether you knew them or not, your grandparents have had a significant impact on your life. They did that through the values they instilled in their children—your parents. And now you're passing many of those lessons on to your own kids.

That's one person having an impact on three generations. When you think about it like that, it's not an exaggeration to say that your grandparents quite literally changed the world. And they did it in the smallest of ways—with just a few conversations, with how they went to work every day, with the books they read in the evening and the manners they displayed at dinner. They did it in the conversations they had when their kids made mistakes. They did it in how they treated their neighbors and mowed their lawns and plowed their driveways.

There are lots of things we can do to change the world. We should try to do all of them. But we have to know—and we can never forget—how much impact we can have on the world right here at home. Through our children, their children, and their children's children, we have profound multigenerational legacy.

That's an incredible power. Don't neglect it.

January 14
Where Do They Learn to Judge?

I have a two-year-old son. Know what he hates? Naps. End of list.

—DENIS LEARY

We wonder where our kids learn to judge or, worse, where they learn to be biased or to think less of this group or that one. There is only one answer: they learn it from us.

It was a comment under your breath about your brother's spending habits. It was a joke about a celebrity's weight. It was a complaint about the way your neighbor parks in their driveway. It was the conversation between you and your spouse over dinner about what's wrong with the *other side*, with *them*.

You didn't mean anything by it. You don't *really* care. But your kids heard it. And they can read only your lips, not your mind.

We want kids who are open-minded, who give people the benefit of the doubt. But are you showing yours what this looks like day to day? Sure, you're not a bigot, but are you always kind? You would never say something cruel to someone's face, so why are you saying it behind their back? Especially when your kids can hear you.

The world needs less judgment, less bullying, fewer opinions, period. Can you start this trend at home? Can you teach your kids what that looks like, instead of letting the same old rumor mill spin round and round, grinding their goodness to dust?

January 15
If You Want Your Kids to Respect You

> You will earn the respect of all men if you begin by earning the respect of yourself.
>
> —MUSONIUS RUFUS

Every parent wants to be listened to. We want our advice to be taken seriously. We want to be looked up to. Most of all, we want to be respected.

Well, if you want your kids to respect you, be *worthy* of respect.

Just think about it for a second: Why would they respect advice that you don't live by? Why would they admire you when you're not living up to your own potential? Why would they look up to you when you yourself are dealing (poorly) with self-esteem issues, when you have accepted the lies of impostor syndrome and allowed them to affect how you act as a parent?

Get your stuff straight. Be the parent you know you can be—be the *person* you know you can be. The rest will follow. And if it doesn't? Then at least you'll be strong enough to deal with whatever comes.

January 16
Don't Let Your Kids Down

> The Warrior Ethos . . . rests on the will and resolve [of Spartans] to defend their children, their home soil and the values of their culture.
>
> —STEVEN PRESSFIELD

I f you don't know the story of the three hundred Spartans at Thermopylae, here's what happened: The ancient Greek king Leonidas led some seven thousand men, three hundred of whom were Spartan warriors, into a battle against the invading army of Xerxes the Great and more than three hundred thousand Persian soldiers. The Spartans held the front line for two days, but on the third, they were finally overrun. Leonidas ordered the three hundred Spartans to remain and fight, sacrificing himself and his men to allow Greece to live and fight another day.

How did Leonidas choose the three hundred warriors he would lead out to the Hot Gates to battle an overwhelming enemy? They were all "fathers of living sons," according to Plutarch. You might think it would have been the opposite, that parents would be allowed to sit out a potential suicide mission—but that's not how it worked in Sparta. These warriors were chosen because *parents would never want to let their kids down*. These fathers would fight most bravely, most fiercely, not only to protect what they had back at home but to protect the reputations of their family names, which might be all their children had left if they were to fall in battle. To abandon their comrades or behave in a cowardly way would be to risk great shame and the possibility of letting down the family that so looked up to them.

Our kids are whom we should want to impress. They're the ones we should never want to let down. They're not only the ones we're fighting for but also the ones whose standards—whose natural admiration and love—we should always be fighting to live up to.

January 17
You Can't Be a Hypocrite

The only thing worse than a liar is a liar that's also a hypocrite.

—TENNESSEE WILLIAMS

A few years ago, the Emmy-winning actor William H. Macy was asked
for the best piece of advice he had ever been given. "Never lie," he
answered. "It's the cheapest way to go. Lies cost you a lot and they're never
worth what they cost."

But as the authors of *Unacceptable: Privilege, Deceit & the Making of the
College Admissions Scandal* noted, precisely as Macy was giving this interview, he and his wife, Felicity Huffman, were fabricating their daughter's
SAT scores (without her knowledge, as it happens, and they were planning
to do the same for their youngest daughter). The worst part? His daughter
wanted to go to a theater school that didn't even require high SAT scores!

It was the cheapest way to go and yet not remotely worth the cost. Macy's
wife would briefly go to jail for her role in the fraud scheme. His daughter
was crushed. Not only was the whole scandal a massive embarrassment,
but she also had to bear witness to the hypocrisy of her parents, who had
talked so much about being good people and then done such a bad thing,
the motivation for which was that they didn't believe in her!

No child deserves that. At the very least, they deserve parents who live
up to what they say. Give your kids that. Don't be a hypocrite.

January 18
Teach Them to Be Particular

Kids are picky. They don't like this. They don't like that. They need *those* to be exactly like *them*. But that can't possibly be what John Lewis's mother meant to encourage when she repeated her motto to her kids as they grew up. "Be particular," she'd tell them.

What she meant, David Halberstam would write in his powerful book on the civil rights movement, *The Children*, was, "be careful, and be responsible for yourself, and always be well prepared." This was a set of standards that she tried to hold her kids to not only when they were little but all their lives. In the 1990s, when her son John had become *Congressman* John Lewis and was well into his fifties, she was still reminding them of her motto. When John faced off in a series of political fights with Newt Gingrich, Willie Mae Lewis called her son and said, "I want you to be particular with that man." Meaning again, as Halberstam writes, that, "he was to be careful in his criticism of Gingrich; any attack had better be factually accurate."

Not picky but particular. Not peculiar but particular. Be exacting. Get your facts straight. Do your job. Don't let anyone or anything excuse you from it. Do it well.

These are wonderful reminders to give our kids . . . but as always, it's much more important *that they see us living these lessons.* Show them the difference between picky and particular, between factual and fatuous, between compromise and *compromising your standards.*

Show them what responsibility looks like. Show them how to be careful and how to always be prepared. Because someday you won't be here, and they will have kids of their own who will need to learn these very *particular* lessons from them.

January 19
Where Did You See That?

Without a ruler to do it against, you can't make crooked straight.

—SENECA

Your daughter gets mad, so she slams the door and screams. Your son makes himself a snack and leaves the kitchen a disaster for someone else to clean up. You hear them say something rude to a waiter. You see them write something offensive on social media.

Before you get mad, before you condemn their actions, just take them aside. Ask them, kindly and openly, a question that the bodybuilder Mark Bell says he always asks his teenage kids: "Hey, when have you seen *me* do that?"

This is a great question. Because it may well be that you have been inadvertently modeling behavior you find repugnant in others. And while that's no excuse for bad behavior, it's useful to know if we've been tacitly condoning the wrong things to our kids. But if you haven't, then they have even *less* of an excuse.

January 20
Do the Things You Want Them to Do

You want your son to be strong and to be honest. You want your daughters to be those things too. You want them to work hard, to help other people, to be respectful to their parents and the people they meet on the street. You want them to be clean and organized, to laugh and to be resilient.

Of course you want those things. Everyone does. The question is, how do we raise good kids? The answer is staring you in the mirror.

The bestselling author and father of two Austin Kleon talks about how this is the hardest part of parenting: You have to be the kind of human being you want your children to be. You have to do the things you want your kids to do. "I find this with parents all the time," he said. "They want their kids to do things that they don't do themselves." He wants his kids to be readers, so he makes sure they see him reading. He wants them to explore different hobbies and interests, so he makes sure they see him practicing an instrument or tinkering in a sketchbook. He wants them to work hard and find work they care about, so he makes sure they see him working in his studio. He wants them to treat others with respect and kindness, so he makes sure they see him giving their mother something he made for her.

Who you are forms who they will be. So be who you want them to be. Do what you want them to do. It's hard, but it's the only way.

January 21
What Are They Learning from How You Carry Yourself?

That's what we're all doing. . . . We're setting examples, . . .
and our conduct will have a great bearing on our youth, certainly, and our youth are our future.

—JOHN WOODEN

From his dad, Bruce Springsteen learned about shame, broken pride, and struggling with demons that you can't quite conquer. You can hear the pain it caused Bruce in many of his songs.

As unlucky as Springsteen was to be dealt that hand, he was also incredibly lucky to have a mother who set a very different example. In his memoir, *Born to Run*, Bruce writes about visiting his mom at her job as a legal secretary. "I am proud, she is proud," he writes, recalling how it felt to see her in her element, away from their house, doing her job. Bruce could see himself in her, and it called him to be better. "We are handsome, responsible members of this one-dog burg pulling our own individual weight, doing what has to be done. We have a place here, a reason to open our eyes at the break of day and breathe in a life that is steady and good." Think what he felt seeing her do her job.

What are your kids learning from how you carry yourself? Are you showing them, as Bruce's dad did, how to be angry and bitter and lost? Or, as Bruce's mom did, are you showing them how to be brave and tough and find their niche? Is your example calling them to be better or worse?

January 22
They Are Always Listening

> Children have never been very good at listening to their elders, but they have never failed to imitate them.
>
> —JAMES BALDWIN

Have you ever heard your kids say something that just stops you cold? One of those remarks that makes you instinctively do a double take? Like that scene in *A Christmas Story*? Ralphie is holding a hubcap full of lug nuts as his father changes a tire on a snowy night. Old Man Parker knocks the hubcap and the lug nuts go flying. "Oh, fuuuuuuuuuudge," Ralphie says. "Only I didn't say *fudge*," Ralphie's voice-over explains. "I said *the* word, the big one, the queen mother of dirty words, the *F*-dash-dash-dash word!"

Old Man Parker's jaw drops and his eyes go wide. *Where did that come from?* he must be thinking. Where did he hear *that*?

Of course, he knows. Ralphie heard it from his father, famous for the "tapestry of obscenities" he could weave with his words when he was upset. The little fellow was simply following in the old man's profane footsteps.

The point is this: Kids are always watching, eyes, ears, and heart open. They absorb everything. What will they hear? What is going to pour out of you that will soak into them? That's the question.

January 23
You Gotta Live Up to It

There are some very basic parenting laws that we all know and we all try to get our kids to follow. They involve hard work, sportsmanship, effort, manners, respect, and boundaries. You know the ones; they're the basic rules that every parent knows.

There are a million others that we believe are essential to growing up. Some have become clichés, others are simple truisms, but they got that way because we have found virtue in repeating them, day after day, child after child, generation after generation. What we think less about is whether we're actually following those rules ourselves, whether we are abiding by the laws we seek to enforce. As the billionaire Charles Koch once explained of the main lesson he learned from his father's very hands-on parenting: *you can't lecture your kids on anything you don't live up to.*

You can't tell your kids to respect others and then talk rudely to a customer service representative on the phone. You can't tell them that it's important to find and follow their passion and meanwhile work their entire childhood at a job that pays well but makes you miserable. You can't tell them that family is important if your actions don't show it.

You can't lecture your kids. You have to live up to the lessons you want them to learn.

January 24
When You Get Them to Listen . . .

E. H. Harriman was as rich as they come. A railroad baron. A captain of industry. Everything his children could possibly want or need, he gave them. Yet unlike some wealthy parents, he coupled this luxury with stern maxims and advice. He wanted his kids to do something with their lives, to make a difference in the world. He was fond of repeating, "Great wealth is an obligation and responsibility. Money must work for the country."

We all say things to our kids, just as our parents did to us. Little bits and bobs of wisdom that we picked up places. We hope they hear us. We hope it gets through.

And when it does? Oh, that is *the best*.

In 1901, when Harriman's daughter made her debut in society, she was, unlike her friends, appalled at the spectacle, at the parties people were throwing for themselves. It seemed so wasteful and self-indulgent. So she used her budget to found what would become the Junior League, a volunteerism nonprofit that exists to this day to help the less fortunate. She put her money to work not just for the country but for the world, and in doing so improved countless lives.

We have to remember that as parents we are always planting seeds. A comment here, a book we have them read there. A documentary we watch together, an example we set, a person we introduce them to. When we get them to listen? When they really hear us? Wonderful things can happen.

January 25
How to Deter Them

> We must be what we wish our children to be. They will form
> their characters from ours.
>
> —JOHN S. C. ABBOTT

There are things we don't want our kids to do. So we set up rules. We create punishments. We supervise them closely. And this works—to a degree—but it's also exhausting. Meanwhile, we neglect the most powerful deterrent and the most influential motivator: our own actions.

Plutarch tells us:

> Fathers ought above all . . . to make themselves a manifest example
> to their children, so that the latter, by looking at their fathers' lives
> as at a mirror, may be deterred from disgraceful deeds and words.
> For those who are themselves involved in the same errors as those
> for which they rebuke their erring sons, unwittingly accuse them-
> selves in their sons' names.

If you don't want them to do something, if you want to deter them from some negative influence or bad choice, let your actions be the guide. Let your life both spur them and deter them. In this way, you can be their inspiration in any moment.

January 26
Show Them What a Good Marriage Looks Like

Franklin Delano Roosevelt and Eleanor Roosevelt quite literally preserved a future for their children by fighting for world peace. And yet it's hard not to judge them for the fact that their five children would be married *an astounding nineteen times*!

One suspects that FDR bears the majority of the blame for this. He broke his wife's heart with his affairs. He could be imperious and condescending. He had been spoiled by his own doting mother. Nor was Eleanor blameless. She was *so busy.* She stuffed her resentments and her anger down. She often pretended everything was perfect when, of course, it wasn't. They were also distant cousins, which was more normal at the time . . . but still pretty weird!

How could their kids know what a good marriage was like? They had ringside seats to a complicated power marriage between two people who often put just about everything else ahead of their happiness (or duties) as spouses . . . and parents.

The point here is not to judge the Roosevelt marriage nor to insist that you must stay in your current one. It's to remind you: Your kids learn about everything important from you. Including relationships. So what are you teaching them with yours? What are they seeing that you might be blind to? You have to show them what a good marriage looks like. You have to embody what healthy connections and equal partnerships look like, because the example you set will be their first and the most indelible.

January 27
You Can Be a Parent Anywhere

When we think teacher, we think classroom. When we think leader, we think corner office or lectern or a general in front of their troops. But the truth is that a teacher can do their job anywhere and in many forms, just as a leader can.

As Plutarch said of Socrates:

> [He] did not set up desks for his students, sit in a teacher's chair, or reserve a prearranged time for lecturing and walking with his pupils. No, he practiced philosophy while joking around (when the chance arose) and drinking and serving on military campaigns and hanging around the marketplace with some of his students, and finally, even while under arrest and drinking the hemlock. He was the first to demonstrate that our lives are open to philosophy at all times and in every aspect, while experiencing every emotion, and in each and every activity.

As with teaching and leadership and philosophy, so too with parenting. You can be a parent anywhere. You can be a parent every minute of every day to anybody and everybody. You can be that parent in the same way that Socrates taught—by example, by getting down to their level, by being open, and by adapting to the situation at hand.

January 28
Let 'Em See You Work

> A parent who set an example of loving their work might help
> their kids more than an expensive house.
>
> —PAUL GRAHAM

Our instinct is to find that "work-life balance" that so many people have talked about. We aspire to succeed and achieve in each realm, but not if one comes at the expense of the other. We aim instead to silo work, to not let work intersect with our time with our kids.

The problem? Well, where are your kids supposed to learn the importance of a work ethic? How are they supposed to know what a hardworking dad looks like if they never actually get to see it? How are they supposed to learn what work looks like at all?

That is also your job. To be the example. There is an old Latin expression: *A bove maiori discit arare minor.* "The younger ox learns to plow from the elder." That's because the oxen would be harnessed together. Not only would the kid get to see their dad do what he did, but they'd be literally strapped into it together, *to learn on the job.*

Obviously good boundaries are important. Obviously you don't want your work life to overwhelm or interfere with your home life. But make sure that striving for this balance doesn't accidentally deprive your kids of an important example that will serve them throughout their lives.

TEACH BY EXAMPLE

January 29
Make Your Household First

A critic once advocated that Sparta become a democracy. Lycurgus, its great lawmaker, responded with the quip, "Make your own household a democracy first."

It's easy to have opinions about what other people do. It's less fun to hold yourself to your own standards. You don't like the ever-expanding national debt? Okay . . . but are your finances in great shape? You hate these ballplayers who sign contracts and then demand trades, abandoning the teams who made and paid them? But don't you have your eye on a new career opportunity? You don't like celebrities making a mockery of marriage . . . and how's your own these days? You think these politicians should grow a pair . . . but what truths are you speaking, and at what risk?

The point is: the place to apply your opinions about the way the world should work is first and foremost in the small world where you actually have some control. That is to say, at home. If you want to see a difference in the world, then model that change and make a difference at home. You've got plenty to work with, plenty to fix, plenty to improve. Start there.

Show your kids that change is possible. *Show* them why your opinions matter, and how they can make theirs matter. Let them witness the real impact that comes from practicing what one preaches. Help them benefit from a focus on the practical instead of the theoretical, the actual instead of the hypothetical.

Start *now*.

January 30
They Do Most of It

When the comedian Pete Holmes heard that Mitch Hurwitz, the creator of *Arrested Development*, had two daughters who were both in their twenties, he congratulated him. "You did it!" he said, acknowledging that his friend had made it through the gauntlet, successfully raising two daughters to adulthood.

But Hurwitz refused to take the compliment. "You know, he joked, they did most of it." Which is true! As we've said before, while being a parent is incredibly important, we're not nearly as important as we think we are.

We do our best to set a good example. They do most of the work.

As hard as our job is, they have it way harder. Don't you remember being ten? Or fifteen? Or twenty? You don't remember being a kid . . . probably because you were so busy literally developing a brain. So yes, it's amazing to see what they've become and what they've done.

Just remember that they get the credit (and you get the blame).

January 31
You Don't Stop Teaching Your Kids

Nell Painter was an accomplished adult. She was in her seventies. She was a world-class historian. Yet even then, her mother was teaching her.

How did she have the courage to leave a promising academic career at that age and go to art school? Well, her mother writing her own first book at age sixty-five probably had something to do with it.

"It took me years to sense the bravery, the sturdy determination her metamorphosis demanded, for she was tougher than I could see during her lifetime," she said. "I knew she delved deep to express herself with unadorned honesty. Hard for a woman. Doubly hard for a black woman. Triply hard for a black woman of a class and a generation." And yet her mother had done it. So when Nell reached her own golden years, she didn't find it strange to try something strange. She didn't mind looking odd or out of place. She didn't mind doing something hard. Her book *Old in Art School: A Memoir of Starting Over* is a testament to what her mother had taught her implicitly and explicitly.

We should take from this two things: We never stop teaching our kids. And though what we are doing right now may not be resonating with them, it can teach them something in the future.

Keep doing what needs to be done. Embody what you want your kids to be. Keep growing. Keep being the example they can follow. Keep teaching them, implicitly and explicitly.

FEBRUARY

LOVE UNCONDITIONALLY

(THE ONLY THING THEY REALLY WANT)

February 1
There Is No Substitute for Your Love

In his beautiful and vulnerable memoir, Bruce Springsteen writes that his father said fewer than a thousand words to him throughout his entire childhood. Maybe "you're not greeted with love and affection," he writes, because "you haven't earned it." So for decades, Bruce tried anything to earn his father's love.

In the 1980s, in his thirties, with a few Grammys to his name, Bruce began to struggle with depression. He wasn't exactly sure why. He'd accomplished more than he dreamed. As an artist, he was beloved by millions and was starting to be discussed in the same conversations as his idols—Elvis, Dean, Dylan. As a son, a man, a human being, things couldn't have been more different. He felt completely alone.

In that loneliness, Bruce picked up the strange habit of driving through his childhood neighborhood. After years of cruising old haunts, Bruce writes, "I eventually got to wondering, 'What the hell am I doing?'" He went to see a psychiatrist, who didn't need the background story to know that Bruce was sensing that something had gone wrong and now he was trying to fix it. "Well, you can't," the doctor said. You can't go back. No kid can turn conditional love into unconditional love, absence into presence.

Springsteen writes in the last verse of the song inspired by that trauma, "My Father's House," about how his father's house forever haunted him. It stood like a beacon calling him in the night, he sings:

> Calling and calling, so cold and alone
> Shining 'cross this dark highway where our sins lie unatoned

It's poignant, haunting, and heartbreaking. From the outside, it looked like Bruce Springsteen had everything; on the inside, he felt like he had nothing. It's evidence of our power as parents. No amount of money or celebrity or awards can substitute for your love. That's all they want.

February 2
You Can't Say These Words Enough

> One word frees us of all the weight and pain in life. That word
> is Love.
>
> — SOPHOCLES

Your kids shrug when you say it. It feels weird saying it in public—cliché, lame, vulnerable. You don't want to embarrass them. Or bother them. Or interrupt. Plus, *they know how you feel, right*? You've said it a thousand times before at home.

We have a million reasons not to say these words, but all of these reasons are wrong because it's impossible to say them enough:

I love you.

I'm proud of you.

It's you I like.

You are special.

You are enough.

You're the most important thing in the world to me.

At the end of your life, do you think, for one second, that you will kick yourself for saying any of those words too much? Or is it more likely that you'll wish you'd said those things more? Because it would absolutely kill you if you thought for one second that they might not know, that they might not feel in their hearts, how much you loved them, how proud you were of them, how nothing—not success, money, or lack of either—could change what they meant to you from the moment they were born.

Life is full of risks. This is one gamble you don't need to take. So say it. Tell them how you feel. Tell them that you love them. Say it again and again and again.

It's impossible to do it too much . . . but you might as well try.

February 3
Love without End. Amen.

Parents "don't just love their children every now and then." As the verse from the classic George Strait song goes,

> It's a love without end, amen.
> It's a love without end, amen.

Parental love is not something that is dispensed only when things are going easily with your kids. When they listen. When they conform to your expectations. Expressions of love are not just for when they succeed or when everything is going well in your life or in your job.

Not every now and then but always. Without end. Unconditionally. Even when they hit their siblings, when they lie about a test, when they don't want to eat their vegetables, when they want to quit something you paid a lot of money for, when they've acted in a way contrary to the values you've tried to instill in them.

Even if this kind of love isn't something you got as a kid. Even if it seems clouded when you're struggling or difficult to express when you're pissed off. Even when they take you for granted and make things so hard on you, you have to show them that you love them.

Now and then and every moment in between.

Love without end.

Amen.

February 4
Love Is About Service

Let us not love in word, neither in tongue; but in deed.

—JOHN 3:18

Being a parent is about getting them things. The cup of water they need before bed. The new clothes for school. The hug after they fall down . . . or fail.

Parenting is being there, literally. It's about being of service, literally. Driving them around. Tying their shoes. Coming over to do the dishes and laundry after they've come home from the hospital with their own newborn. Holding their hair back as they throw up from chemo treatments. It doesn't matter how old they are, or you are; that's what we're here for. That's what we do.

We ask them the question that Tom Hanks has described asking his own children: "'What do you need me to do?' You offer up that to them. 'I will do anything I can possibly do in order to keep you safe.' That's it. Offer that up and then just love them."

That is love. It's what your job is. You're here to serve.

February 5
Make Sure They Know That They Are Plenty

Despite becoming Senate majority leader before the age of fifty, being elected vice president and then president, and being the most formidable power broker in Democratic politics for decades, Lyndon Johnson carried a Texas-sized chip on his shoulder his entire life.

He grew up poor. His upbringing and his options landed him at Southwest Texas State Teachers College. A perfectly fine school but not the kind that a president attends—something he was convinced all of his learned and sophisticated Ivy League colleagues were thinking as they witnessed his ascendancy in American politics.

His insecurity began early. He never felt like he was good enough. From a young age, his mother placed unfair expectations on him and made him feel like he had to earn her love, that her pride in him was contingent on his succeeding. She made him feel terrible when he failed—like when he decided to stop playing the piano or dancing. "For days after I quit those lessons," he remembered, "she walked around the house pretending I was dead. And then I had to watch her being especially warm and nice to my father and sisters."

It's a sobering reminder to all parents: the feeling of deficiency is far worse than any potential deprivation. So make sure your kids know that they are enough, that they are plenty, that you have loved them from the moment they were born. And make sure *you* remember that there is nothing they have to do to earn this love. There's nothing they must accomplish to deserve tenderness and affection.

They are good enough. The talents, the interests, the goals they have, *are enough.*

February 6
It Takes Discipline

In the 1960s, the young poet Diane di Prima was at one of those legendary Beat parties that movies are made of. Everyone was there. There were drugs and ideas and romances. Jack Kerouac was there, holding court. And yet di Prima got up to leave and go home early.

Why? Because her babysitter was expecting her. All the other writers in the room judged her, silently laughed at her, believers in that line that the pram in the hall is the enemy of good art. Kerouac was not so silent about his disdain. "Unless you forget about your babysitter," he said to her in front of everyone, "you're never going to be a writer."

Di Prima, a good parent, left anyway. As Julie Phillips writes in her fascinating book about creatives and parenting, *The Baby on the Fire Escape*, "She believed she wouldn't have been a writer if she'd stayed. To write and come home on time, she argued, required 'the same discipline throughout': a practice of keeping her word."

So often important and talented people use their work and their talent as an excuse to neglect their obligations as parents. But di Prima was exactly right to see them both as a matter of discipline and commitment. The idea that anything (or anyone) is improved by neglecting one part of their life for another is nonsense. But the opposite is true—by keeping your word to yourself, to your children, you are strengthening an important muscle. By being disciplined and protective of your personal life, you are being protective and dedicated to your professional life.

Don't let anyone tell you differently. Don't let anyone judge you for that.

February 7
Wherever They Are, You Are Too

B uck Murphy was walking down the street in Whiteville, Tennessee, in the late 1950s when a white man yelled at him, "How's that jailbird son of yours doing?" It was a delicate subject in the segregated South—Buck's son Curtis had been arrested for taking part in the Nashville sit-ins, which would eventually galvanize the civil rights movement in America. "Where is he?" the man taunted. "Is he still in the Nashville jail?"

Now, there were many reasons for the Murphys to be concerned about their son's activism. Of course, they too believed segregation was an evil and they had suffered its many effects. But they also didn't want anything to happen to their boy. They feared reprisals at home. Maybe they even worried that Curtis was trying to change too much too quickly. But in that moment, challenged by a bully mocking his son, Buck demonstrated that thing that all children want from their parents—true support. Buck said firmly: "Wherever he is, I am too."

Your kids are going to make choices that scare you. People are going to doubt them. People are going to criticize them. Maybe you yourself doubt the wisdom of their choices. And?

Where they are, you must be too.

Love your kids. Root for them. Support them. Fight for them and fight with them. Be beside them and behind them. Wherever they are.

February 8
They Don't Have to Make You Proud

> Most people are proud, not of those things which arouse respect, but of those which are unnecessary.
>
> —LEO TOLSTOY

We say it casually. We mean well. "Make me proud out there, kiddo," we say as they trot out onto the soccer field. "Make your parents proud," we say as they head off to college. And when they do great stuff, we reward them by letting them know that the mission has been accomplished. They've made us proud.

We want this to motivate them. We use it, oftentimes unconsciously, to hold them accountable. But is this the way it should go? Doesn't it sort of imply that they owe us something? That our support is not unconditional or implicit? That if they don't score a goal or make the dean's list or land a summer internship, we are therefore *not* proud?

Our kids don't owe us anything. After all, they didn't ask to be here. It is we who are obligated to them, by virtue of our choice to bring them into this world.

February 9
Here's How to Tie Your Family Together

I t is my pleasure that my children are free," Abraham Lincoln once said, "happy and unrestrained by parental tyranny." Lincoln knew about parental tyranny. His father used force. He was controlling. He meant well, Abraham came to understand, but his father had few tools at his disposal, and the ones he did have didn't work. His kids were not fond of him, and they did their best to get away from him as soon as they could.

That's not what you want, is it? No, you want your kids to really listen, to buy in. You want them around, you want them to come to you. You want them to respect your rules and embody your values. You want them to do what they're supposed to do, the things that will make them successful.

So how do you get them to do those things?

Well, for most parents, the answer is to default to the easiest and most primal form of leadership: force. It's got a simple logic to it. You *make* them do it—*because I'm bigger than you, because I can take away the TV remote, because I said so.* And it seems like it works . . . for a while. Perhaps you remember how this worked from your own childhood. Eventually, the strategy falls apart over time. In the end, it turns out to be counterproductive.

Okay. Then listen to Lincoln. "Love is the chain whereby to bind a child to its parent."

February 10
When They Wander Back . . .

In one of the most famous parables in the Bible, Jesus tells of the Prodigal Son. "There was once a wealthy man who had two sons," Jesus says. "The younger one said to him, 'Father, give me my share of the estate now.'" The boy took his share, sold it, and fled with the money. He traveled, gambled, partied, drank, ate like a king, and within a week, he'd spent everything. He found work on a farm feeding pigs. He couldn't afford food, so he ate what the pigs ate. Finally, it occurred to him that back home, even his father's servants ate in abundance. So he set out for home, intent on confessing to his father, "I am no longer worthy to be called your son; treat me as one of your hired workers."

Before the boy could own up to what he had done, Jesus explains, his father called to his servants, "Hurry! Bring the best robe and put it on him. Put a ring on his finger and shoes on his feet. Then go and get the prize calf and kill it, and let us celebrate with a feast! For this son of mine was dead, but now he is alive; he was lost, but now he has been found."

Your kids may never demand their share of the estate, but they *will* stray. They will act out. They will try to establish their independence. They will get themselves into trouble. As parents, we have to accept that, and accept them all the same. We have to take them back. We have to give them what they need. And when they wander back, we have to make sure they're always met not with reproach or "I told you so" but with affection and understanding.

LOVE UNCONDITIONALLY

February 11
There's a Reason You're So Raw

> There really are places in the heart you don't even know exist
> until you love a child.
>
> —ANNE LAMOTT

In times that seem to bring out people's worst, parents feel something different. We're raw. We're vulnerable. We tear up when we hear about the loss of a loved one. We feel it in our gut when we think about families struggling to make ends meet. Those viral videos hit us differently. The stepparents gifted adoption papers, the military parent surprising their children with an unexpected visit home, families reunited at the border?

It's like instant waterworks . . .

What is that?

You're raw because having kids has opened you up. "I wasn't emotionally prepared for parenthood," the comedian and author Michael Ian Black writes, "after spending the thirty previous years in a cauterized emotional state." Parenthood forces you to engage the world in a more active way. It forces you to engage with yourself and your own emotions in an active way. Was it easier to go through the world closed off and cynical? Is there something tribal and reassuring about focusing on yourself and your problems and placing the blame for those things elsewhere, on those *other* people?

Of course. But that's less and less possible these days. This parenting thing has changed you. It's made you see that it's all connected, that *we're* all connected. It's made you better.

February 12
Love the Kid You Have

> You are a very special person. There is only one like you in
> the whole world.
>
> —MISTER ROGERS

The grade school teacher, bestselling author, and mom of two Jessica Lahey has talked to hundreds of thousands of kids about the things they want their parents to hear. "By far, the number one comment I get," she says, is some version of "'I am not my brother,' 'I am not my sister,' 'I am not my parents when they were my age,' 'I don't know who my parents think they are raising, but it's not me,' 'My parents think they know who I am, but it's all their expectations of me and they have no idea who I actually am.'"

Isn't that heartbreaking? If there were a list of things you never wanted your kids to think or feel, those responses—which Jessica says get emailed to her almost every day—are probably right at the top of the list. No kid should feel like their dad wants them to be someone else, to be something different. No kid should feel that they are a disappointment. They should know that they are special for who they are, that they make the world—and your life—better just by being in it.

Your kids need to be seen. They need to be heard. They need to be loved. They need to be *known*. For who they are, for what they choose to be. Not for who or what you want them to become.

That's all they really want from us. And they deserve to have it. So you better give it to them. Starting today and for the rest of their lives.

February 13
You Can Always Give Them This

A person becomes happy to the same extent to which he or she gives happiness to other people.

—JEREMY BENTHAM

You want to give them the world—or at least their own room and whatever material things they need. You want nothing more than to make them perfectly happy, but inevitably you'll come up short. That's the bad news. The good news is that there are some things you can always give them that, when others try to offer them to your kids, will never measure up to yours. These are things that are always possible to give, always within your reach: your attention, your understanding, and your love.

No matter what happens, no matter how rich or poor you are, no matter what mistakes you make or they make, no matter how powerful or powerless you are, you can always give them those things. In fact, you must always give them. Because, in the end, those are more important than all the other things you can and will do for them. Love and understanding, especially, are the only things that truly matter, because they last even beyond your death. Their impact is going to be one of the primary forces that shape the adult your child becomes.

And if you think about it, the only thing they'll truly (and rightfully) resent you for, all else being equal, is if you know these things are true and still you fail to provide them.

February 14
The Greatest Thing You Can Do

In *The Second Mountain*, David Brooks relates a conversation he had with an academic friend. "I don't really know of many happy marriages," the friend said. "I know a lot of marriages where parents love their kids."

In such a marriage, your son or daughter misses out on a powerful example. "One of the greatest things a father can do for his children," Howard W. Hunter once said, "is to love their mother." Our notion of what a family is has expanded since he made that remark. We have single families. We have divorced families. We have trans families. We have blended families and coparenting families. We have gay families and even poly families. To each their own.

But the truth of the sentiment doesn't change—in fact, it only expands. The best thing you can do for your kids is love the person who brought them into this world. The best thing you can do for your kids is love the person you are parenting them with. Even if you are no longer with that person, or if that person has deeply hurt or even betrayed you, you must love the person responsible for a good chunk of your kids' DNA or identity. You must love who they love—that's how they'll know that they are loved.

February 15
This Is What They Most Want

Eleanor Roosevelt had a rough childhood. Her mother was always difficult and judgmental, but she was still her mother, and Eleanor was devastated when she died at age twenty-nine . . . and then devastated again just months later when her father died. She was sent to live with her grandmother, a woman who, it quickly became clear, was the source of Eleanor's mother's emotional issues and judgmentalness.

It was a dreary, painful existence that didn't change until Eleanor was sent to school in London. There, at a special school for girls, she met her teacher Marie Souvestre, who finally saw in Eleanor not a plain, shy girl but someone special, with talent, with ambitions, with the ability to make a difference in the world. "Attention and admiration were the things throughout all my childhood that I most wanted," Eleanor later reflected, "because I was made to feel so conscious of the fact that nothing about me would attract attention or would bring me admiration!"

Don't we ourselves want attention and admiration? In our jobs? In our communities? In our marriages? Why wouldn't our kids want the same things in their young, fragile lives? And who could it possibly be more meaningful to come from than us?

It's hard to be a kid. They're overwhelmed. They doubt themselves. They wonder where they fit in, whether they matter. It's our job to help them with this. To let them know that they are loved, that they are special, that they are enough. To give them the attention and admiration they deserve.

February 16
Keep the Main Thing the Main Thing

> Most of what we say and do is not essential. If you can elim-
> inate it, you'll have more time, and more tranquility. Ask
> yourself at every moment, "Is this necessary?"
>
> —MARCUS AURELIUS

There's a wonderful little expression: *The main thing is to keep the main thing the main thing.*

Every family, every person, has a different main thing, of course. But if we could generalize, the main thing for us parents is to raise well-adjusted, self-reliant, decent, happy kids. The main thing is not college. The main thing is not making partner at our law firm. The main thing is not to have a clean house. The main thing is not to win some competition with other parents. The main thing is not grades, it is not following in your footsteps, it is not being captain of the football team or an expert cello player.

The main thing is for them to be healthy, to be prepared for life, to have good values, to have a good sense of who they are and what they want to spend their life doing. The main, main, main, *main* thing is to love them and for them to *feel loved.*

February 17
Let Them Wonder If You Know

As a young boxer trying to make it on his own for the first time, future heavyweight champion Floyd Patterson would find himself so hungry that he had no choice but to head over to his mother's house late at night.

"Don't tell Mom we're hungry," he told the friend who was with him. "I don't want her to know I haven't been able to manage on what I've been making." But no sooner had Floyd said hello than his mother was making him a snack.

"Don't bother, Mom," he said, playing it cool. "We had a big meal tonight at a restaurant and couldn't take another bite." *Just a snack*, his mother insisted, before serving an enormous meal. "I kept wondering if my mother knew that this wasn't a social call," Floyd would reflect years later in his memoirs, that "I wasn't eating just to be polite."

Of course she knew! A parent always does! But she didn't say a word. She just did what she needed to do, caring not only about her son's well-being but also for his feelings and his pride.

When our kids need help, our only job is to provide it. To *help*, not lecture. To be of service, never to humiliate. This is how you create the kind of relationship Floyd and his mother had—the kind where your kids know they can always come home for help at any time, day or night.

February 18
How to Convince Them

> The ardor of the young should be curbed slowly, lest by wishing to oppose them with sudden impediments we drive them to despair and perdition.
>
> —GIOVANNI BOCCACCIO

In 1941, Mary Churchill accepted the marriage proposal of a young man named Eric Duncannon. She was young and inexperienced. They barely knew each other. A war raged around them. Duncannon was almost certainly not the right fit for her. Naturally, her parents—the heads of a political dynasty in a time of rigid aristocratic marriages—were concerned.

But as Erik Larson details in his book *The Splendid and the Vile,* instead of condemning her daughter, Clementine Churchill simply asked her daughter if she was *certain* it was the right choice. She didn't disapprove outright, but she did let her daughter know she had some doubts. Then, understanding that no daughter wants to be told whom to marry by her parents, Clementine searched for someone her daughter trusted and respected whom she could ask to weigh in, independently and casually. She landed on Averell Harriman, one of Churchill's advisers, who was dating Mary's sister-in-law.

Harriman took the young, impulsive girl aside. "He said all the things I should have told myself," Mary later reflected. He told her that her whole life was before her. And that she "should not accept the first person who comes along. You have not met many people. To be stupid about one's life is a crime."

All this began to sink in with Mary, who then, after a few weeks, decided of her own volition to break off the engagement. It was her idea . . . but she came to later understand how lucky she was that her parents had helped her get there. "What would have happened had Mummie not intervened?" she wrote. "Thank God for Mummie's sense—understanding and love."

Our kids are going to do stuff we disagree with, but very rarely—especially as they get older—will we be able to convince them of this by force or fiat. We have to be understanding. We have to be patient . . . maybe even a little bit sneaky. We have to give them advice and the tools to make sense of that advice, because ultimately they are the ones who have to figure out the right decision for themselves. And we have to make sure they know that no matter what they decide, we love them.

February 19
Assume the Best

You have known your kids since they were little. You've seen them do the sweetest things in the entire world. You know who they are.

So here's a question: When they screw up, when they fail a test, when they crash their car, when they get in trouble, when they talk back to you, why do you assume the worst? Why do you treat them with anger and judgment? Why do you jump all over them with criticism or frustration or suspicion?

You know they are good and decent. You know they generally do their best. You know what they struggle with. You know their fears and vulnerabilities and weaknesses. You know what they've been through (deep down, you know one of the things they've been through is being raised by you!).

So why isn't that being reflected in your tone? In your assumptions? Where is the kindness? Where is the good faith? Why aren't you talking to them like someone who believes in them, who is a fan of them? Where is the patience? Where is the charity? Where is the demonstrable *unconditionalness* that you purport to have for them?

Mm-hm. That's right. Oh, and remember, all this could be said about your interactions with your spouse too.

February 20
These Are the Richest Kids

Everyone remembers the "rich kids" growing up. Even rich kids remember the other *richer* kids. We envied their ski trips, their huge houses, their equally big vacation houses, their electronics, their clothes.

And yet how many of those kids, when we look at them now, as adults, appear to have actually been quite poor?

At home they faced a poverty of attention. A deficit of happiness or stability. Maybe their parents fought all the time. Maybe they worked constantly. Maybe they played favorites and none were their kids.

As adults, we now realize that to be rich is not necessarily to be wealthy, especially as "wealth" comes in many forms. This is really good news. All of us have the ability to give our kids a rich life. We can measure wealth in the time and attention they get from us. By whether they feel safe and secure, whether their house feels like a home. Even if we only make $30,000 a year.

You can make your kid the richest kid in the whole school without spending a dollar.

February 21
Always Be Their Friend

The entrepreneur Ben Horowitz was coached for many years by the legendary Bill Campbell—the so-called Trillion Dollar Coach for his work with Larry Page, Steve Jobs, and Sheryl Sandberg. In a eulogy he wrote for Campbell, Horowitz told the story of one of the toughest things he had gone through as a dad and how Campbell helped him through it:

> My oldest child Jules concluded he was transgender and was going to change his gender by taking testosterone and having surgery. It's impossible to fully describe how one feels as a parent in a situation like that, but mostly all I felt was worry—worry that he wouldn't be accepted, worry that his health would fail, worry that the surgery would not go well, worry that he would be killed by some intolerant group. I was so filled with worry that I could barely function. . . . So, I decided to tell Bill. When I told him, I could see the tears well up in his eyes and he said, "That's going to be really hard." Then he immediately wanted to see Jules. And Bill made sure that he embraced Jules and let him know that he was not alone and would always have a friend in Bill. Bill *understood*.

This wonderful public moment about a private struggle, shared in honor of a personal mentor, speaks to the heart of what every child needs to hear from their parents, no matter what they're going through: *There are going to be things in your life that are very hard. But you're not alone. I'll always be your friend.*

February 22
Tell Them They Carry This Everywhere

In July 2008, the journalist David Carr saw his daughter Erin off to London for her first real job out of college. Erin had struggled in the previous years. She had the beginnings of a drinking problem. She didn't always date the best guys. But she never had to wonder if her father loved her deeply.

When Erin landed in London, a letter from her father was waiting in her email inbox. It's the kind of letter a great parent writes, the kind that in David's case—due to his tragic and unexpected death at age fifty-eight—would guide his daughter long after he was around. The letter opens:

> *Honey, we are so, so excited for you.*
> *Please understand that you carry with you not only our love and support, but our admiration and pride in your decision to bring your ambitions roaring into the world.*

Make sure your kids know that no matter what, they are loved, they are supported, they are accepted, they are enough. Make sure they know that no matter where they go, they carry your love and support and pride with them.

February 23
Teach Them Early Where Their Value Lies

> Young people must be taught from childhood that it is not
> right to wear gold on their bodies or to possess it, since they
> have their own personal gold intermixed into their soul, hint-
> ing . . . at the virtue that is part of human nature and received
> at birth.
>
> —PLUTARCH

Mister Rogers ended every one of his programs with a message directly to kids that became almost a proverb in its wisdom and timeless truth: "You've made this day a special day by just your being you," he would say. "There's no person in the whole world like you, and I like you just the way you are."

We must, as parents, teach our children where their value really lies. It's not in their accomplishments. It's not in what they earn or how they look. It's not to be found in anything external at all. Their value—to us, to the world—is inherent. It exists because *they* exist. Because there is no one on the planet with their same combination of DNA and experiences and cir-cumstances. That's what makes them special—what makes them rarer than the rarest jewels and more precious than the most precious metals.

February 24
All They Want

It's tough to know: What do your kids *really* need? What *must* a parent do? What's essential? What's optional? There's no easy answer, but in 2008 President Barack Obama came close to articulating one in a Father's Day speech about what our kids really need and want from us.

> Our kids are pretty smart. They understand that life won't always be perfect, that sometimes the road gets rough, that even great parents don't get everything right. But more than anything, they just want us to be a part of their lives. . . . In the end, that's what being a parent is all about—those precious moments with our children that fill us with pride and excitement for their future; the chances we have to set an example or offer a piece of advice; the opportunities to just be there and show them that we love them.

That's your job, above all others. To be a part of their life—*a positive part*. They need you to be there. To give advice. To be a good example. To understand them and to love them.

Everything else is extra.

February 25
Hit Them with One of These

Your kid is running upstairs and you stop them: "Hey, before you go . . ." You're watching TV and your daughter is walking into the other room: "Hey, I need to tell you something . . ." Your boys are wrestling in the backyard and the door opens and you come out: "Hey, guys . . ."

They think you're going to remind them about some piece of schoolwork. Or criticize what they're wearing. Or tell them to stop roughhousing.

No, you're going to hit them with those words we can't say often enough: *I love you.*

That it catches our kids by surprise when we tell them we love them? That we only want to put our feelings about them out there in the open, just so they know, and they're confused by it? That's our fault, not theirs. It says something about us, not them. And it's something we, not they, have to fix.

February 26
This Is What You'll Wish

J ohnny Gunther was the pride and joy of two loving parents—a brilliant young boy, fun and funny, headed for Harvard. And then, suddenly, there was a diagnosis, then a fifteen-month battle with a brain tumor, and ultimately a life that ended too soon.

At the end of *Death Be Not Proud*, the moving memoir by John Gunther about his son Johnny's short life, John's wife, Frances, reflects on the loss of her son. What is left, she asks, what does a person think and feel, looking back on the all-too-brief time they had with their child?

"I wish we had loved Johnny more."

That was it. That was what she kept coming back to. It's not that they didn't love him—no one can read the Gunthers' memoir and not be struck by what a wonderful family they were. It's that, when everything is stripped away, all Frances could think of were the opportunities she could have seized to appreciate him, and their time, more.

Let us hope that we never have to experience such a loss. No parent should ever have to bury a child. But still, let's try to think about the end of our own time here on Earth. What will we think then? When we are reflecting on our lives, what will we wish for? *We'll wish we had loved them more.* Even if we told them a thousand times in a thousand ways every single day, we'll think about how woefully short we came up in expressing just how much our kids mean to us.

So let us try, right now, while we still can, to love them more.

LOVE UNCONDITIONALLY

February 27
Give Them This . . . While You Can

Future love does not exist. Love is a present activity only.

—LEO TOLSTOY

The poet William Stafford had some beautiful, thoughtful insights about parenting. But his final insight was his best.

When Stafford fell dead of a heart attack at age seventy-nine, his wife and children found on his desk a piece of paper with a short phrase on it, perhaps the very last words he wrote in a fifty-year career. It was simply "And all my love . . ."

Now *love* was not a word that Stafford used much. It might not be one that you're comfortable using much either. But you should . . . while you can . . . while you're still here. And don't just *say* it. *Give* it.

Your kids, your family, your *loved* ones . . . they deserve that. All your love . . .

February 28
Love Is Not a Victory March

Life is warfare and a journey far from home.

—MARCUS AURELIUS

Leonard Cohen, who had two kids, said that love is not a victory march, it is a cold and a broken hallelujah.

The point is not to discourage you about being a parent. You already bought your ticket and now you're on the ride. It's just a reminder: if you go around expecting this to be an unending series of Hallmark moments, you're fooling yourself and setting yourself up for disappointment. If you're comparing how you're doing with what you see on television, you're being unfair to yourself.

This thing is hard. Really hard. There are dark moments. There are moments when you're convinced you have no idea what you're doing and you think you're the absolute worst. There are moments when you'll be *told* you are in fact the worst. But you have to keep going. You can't give up. You can't despair.

They're counting on you.

February 29
Take the Second Chances When You Get Them

You didn't exactly jump out of bed with joy when your daughter came rushing in at 5:00 a.m. to play. You didn't give your teenage son much of an opportunity to explain himself about his grades. You were distracted at dinner, checking your phone constantly.

There's no way around it. You screwed up. You weren't your best.

No way to change that. But the one thing about parenting is that it gives you second chances. It gives you a lot of leap days. Kids forget. They need you for something else. There are lots of tough conversations. Dinner happens every night.

While you cannot undo what has been done, you can choose to take these second chances as they come. You can will yourself to play, even though you're exhausted. You can stop yourself before getting upset this time, reminding yourself that you love the boy and that he's still figuring things out. You can put the phone in a drawer and actually be there for the family meal.

We don't get to do this forever. Tomorrow is never guaranteed. *Today* is a gift, a fluke (especially on a leap year). That's why each interaction we have with our kids matters, why we can't take it for granted. Still, we're not going to get it right every time. So when we're lucky enough to get another go? We better take advantage of it. We better try harder. We better show up.

MARCH

PUT YOUR FAMILY FIRST

(WORK, FAMILY, SCENE: PICK TWO)

March 1
You Can Pick Only Two

There isn't time enough, my friends— / Though dawn begins, yet midnight ends— / To find the time to have love, work, and friends.

—KENNETH KOCH

The prolific artist and father of two Austin Kleon was asked how he makes time for it all. "I don't," he said. "The artist's life is about trade-offs." And then he added a little rule that we should all keep with us always: *Work, family, scene. Pick two.*

You can party it up and hang on to a relationship, but you won't have much time left for work.

You can grind away at your craft, be the toast of the scene, but what will that leave for your family?

If you're as committed to the work as you are to a happy home, you will have no room for anything else.

It'd be wonderful if you could have the run of all these things all the time . . . but you can't. Being a parent is about making trade-offs, from the very second our kids enter this world: it's their needs versus our wants. At first, it can be a shock to the system. But once we know what to say no to, and we know why, we can say yes with comfort and confidence to the things that matter. To the things that last.

March 2
Everything but This Is Temporary

> When you are a narcissist mama takes the kids away from
> you . . . when you are a narcissist, things start to just go away.
>
> —SHAQUILLE O'NEAL

Charles de Gaulle helped save France. Then he ran it. Yet even at the height of his power, he tried to always remind himself, "The presidency is temporary, family is permanent." Accordingly, he put up boundaries between his personal and professional lives. He carved out private time. He refused to neglect the children who depended on him so much, particularly his mentally disabled daughter, Anne.

We can't ever let ourselves forget: we may be very important to the world, but to a small group of people to whom we are related, *we are the whole world.* Nothing matters more than family, and nothing is more permanent . . . until it isn't. You can lose family. You can break your family. You can drive your family away. And then it is their loss that becomes permanent.

By all means, pursue your success. Realize your ambition. Just make sure it's not coming at the expense of what actually matters.

March 3
You Are Not a Babysitter

The late ESPN broadcaster—and father of two girls—Stuart Scott, was once sitting in a restaurant with some friends and their respective children. It was one of those delightful, idyllic scenes. Everyone was having fun. The kids were behaving. The dads were present. Everyone was bonding. All was well.

Then a well-meaning mom walked by and, recognizing Scott, tried to pay him a compliment for "babysitting the kids." She did not realize how insulting this was to Scott—and in fact to all fathers. Because dads don't *babysit* their kids.

Babysitting is something somebody else does for your children on your behalf, usually for money. By definition, the babysitter is not the child's parent. These were Scott's kids. He couldn't babysit on his own behalf, even if he wanted to. It'd be like calling a homeowner a security guard every time you see them lock their front door.

Scott was doing his job. He was being a dad. No more, but certainly no less. As his friend would observe after Scott's tragic death from cancer, "We didn't see ourselves as an occasional parental figure who might take the kids off mom's hands for a couple hours."

See what you do as important. Because it is.

March 4
You Have to Make Adjustments

Queen Elizabeth II's father, King George VI, met with his prime minister, Winston Churchill, every Tuesday at 5:30 p.m. So you might think that when his daughter took over in 1952, she would have continued the tradition. Elizabeth was, after all, a traditionalist.

But she didn't. At that time, Queen Elizabeth had two young children, and every parent knows that 5:30 p.m. is dinnertime, knocking on bedtime. To avoid the painful question "Why isn't Mummy going to play with us tonight?" her biographer writes, Queen Elizabeth "moved the audience to 6:30, which allowed her to go to the nursery to join in their nightly bath and tuck them into bed before discussing matters of state with Winston Churchill."

The point is: whatever your children's ages, you have to be ready to make adjustments. Whatever your job is, it can and must be adjusted around what we all know is our most important job. If the queen can put off Winston Churchill for an hour, you can reschedule that conference call.

Family comes first. Before business . . . even the business of state.

March 5
When Is Their Time?

Ruth Bader Ginsburg explained her parenting strategy while she was in law school (at a time when women simply did not do such things) like this:

> Our nanny came in at 8 o'clock and left at 4 o'clock. I used the time in between classes to study, to read the next day's assignment, but 4 o'clock was Jane's time. We went to the park, played games, sang silly songs. When she went to sleep, I went back to the books. I had to make the most of the time I had. I couldn't waste time.

Of course you're busy. You have work. You have your spouse. You have your kids. You have all the obligations of adulthood. All these things are important. How do you fit it all in?

The truth is, if you're winging it every day, you *won't* get it all in. Something will fall by the wayside, and too often, it's the time with our kids that is the first to go. Because we can turn on the TV. Because we can strap them in the car seat and bring them along on errands. Because we can tell them, "Sorry, kiddo. I'm busy right now."

This is why it can be a good idea to have very specific, scheduled time. So you can be sure that they have *their* time. Nonnegotiable time. Just as you do with work or anything else that matters to you.

What does it say about us as parents if all we give them is the leftover time? Nothing good. *They* are the priority. Remember that the next time you put another new obligation on your calendar.

March 6
This Is What Putting Them First Looks Like

For his whole career, Archie Manning had been a company man for the New Orleans Saints. He was great but the team was terrible. For years they had lost. For years he had endured poor offensive lines, poor drafting, and never even coming close to playoff contention.

So you'd think when he was traded to the Houston Oilers and then to the Minnesota Vikings, it would have been a blessing. It could have breathed new life into his career. He still had years left in him, and now he had a real shot at being part of a winning team . . . finally! But instead, in 1984, he retired.

Why? His son Eli. As Manning explained in the book *My First Coach: Inspiring Stories of NFL Quarterbacks and Their Dads*:

> I sensed that my relationship wasn't quite the same with Eli that it had been with Cooper and Peyton at that age. . . . I was gone and I didn't like it at all. I remember that was one of the real joys for me when I retired: that I would be home, I would be around full-time for Eli.

That's what great parenting looks like, what true greatness—on and off the field—looks like. Would anyone back then have noticed two more seasons with the Vikings? Would anyone now have bothered to remember them? Maybe. Maybe not. You know who definitely noticed? You know who definitely remembers? Eli. And he benefited unquestionably and immeasurably from his father's choice. He has a happy family and two Super Bowl victories to show for it.

What could it look like if you put your family first? If you *really* put them ahead of everything else? You can't be sure exactly until you do it, but you can be certain that it will feel great.

March 7
How Are You Filling Their Bank?

> Each day of our lives we make deposits into the memory
> banks of our children.
>
> —CHARLES R. SWINDOLL

Think of your own childhood. What do you remember? Is it those big moments? You know, the planned ones. The ones on the calendar. Is it exclusively Christmas mornings? The annual spring break vacations? The Fourth of July barbecue?

Or are your memories much more mundane?

What we remember about growing up are the little moments. We remember sitting in the passenger seat next to Dad on a long drive. We remember going for pizza after soccer practice. We remember waking up from a nap and coming downstairs and watching a football game. We remember that little piece of advice. We remember thinking they were going to be mad at us for something and getting a hug instead.

Similarly, the wounds that we feel often come from other small moments. The feeling of being ignored. Getting yelled at for leaving our shoes in the living room. The time that Mom didn't stand up for us. The unspoken tension in the living room between our parents.

Today you'll be making plenty of these small deposits in their memory banks. How do you want that ledger to read?

March 8
Being Important Is Not an Excuse

> I've built an office behind our house. Someday my daughter will look at it and think . . . "That's where my dad worked to provide for us," and feel a little sentimental. What I never hope she thinks is, "That's the place my dad loved more than me."
>
> —DONALD MILLER

It would be wonderful if these quotes didn't exist, but they do. They come from the children of great men. From Albert Einstein's son. From Nelson Mandela's daughter. From kids whose dads were presidents or kings or rockstars or CEOs. They go something like this: "You were there for so many people as part of your job, but you were never there for me" or "You were the best in the world at everything you did . . . except for fatherhood."

It's heartbreaking. Obviously the world *needed* Nelson Mandela. It needed Eleanor Roosevelt. It needed Steve Jobs. It needed Albert Einstein. What they did was hard, and important. It required sacrifice. It came at the expense of their families—it had to.

But did it have to come at *such* a high cost?

There is no job, no career, no amount of responsibility that justifies being absent from the lives of your children. Being important, having a calling, achieving success, is great. But being important doesn't change what your most important job is: being a parent. Being there for *them*. Becoming world class at being *Mom* or *Dad*.

Because when your days in the spotlight are over, when your fame and import have receded, you will still be a parent and your kids will still need you for the things kids have always needed their parents for.

March 9
This Is the Only Success That Matters Now

> Anytime you feel guilty about not meeting some sort of
> insane, unachievable demand, ask yourself, "Does this help
> me improve my relationship with my children? And does this
> help my community?"
>
> —JESSICA GROSE

All of us, before we were parents, chased success in our own way. Some of us wanted it more than others. Some of us got it. Some of us didn't. Then we had kids. And what did that change? Well, it certainly took up more of our time and energy. It made financial security more important. It made us grow up. But mostly what it did was utterly and irrevocably change our definition of success. As Theodore Roosevelt explained:

> There are many kinds of success in life worth having. It is exceed-
> ingly interesting and attractive to be a successful businessman, or
> railway man, or farmer, or a successful lawyer or doctor; or a writer,
> or a President, or a ranchman, or the colonel of a fighting regiment,
> or to kill grizzly bears and lions. But for unflagging interest and
> enjoyment, a household of children, if things go reasonably well,
> certainly makes all other forms of success and achievement lose
> their importance by comparison.

We still want to be good at our jobs, of course. We want to win championships or land big clients. We want recognition and we want the thrill of the chase. But we know now—because we've felt it—how small these things seem compared to a quiet evening at home. A Sunday in the park. Breakfast full of laughter. Watching them on a stage or running from the sidewalk into your arms.

This is the only success that matters now.

March 10
Welcome To Unavoidable Reality

When the columnist and author David Brooks's son was born, a friend sent him an email that just said, "Welcome to the world of unavoidable reality."

Every dad knows what that means. It captures being a parent perfectly. The biggest change that comes from having a kid isn't financial—it's not the sleep deprivation, it's not even needing to take care of another person or the stress it puts on your relationships. It's that it rudely introduces you to the unavoidable reality that you are no longer the center of your own world—something you had been, despite what you thought, utterly ignorant of.

As an adult, you did what you wanted. Things operated on normal timelines. You made decisions and commitments and that was it. The world was logical and in your control. But now and for the rest of your life, reality is different. What time are you going to get to the party? When your daughter wakes up from her nap, that's when. They're sick with the flu? You're sick with the flu. They feel like having a tough morning or are reeling from teenage hormones? Looks like you are too! Unavoidable reality means that you're not in control. It means you're going to sit and play in the sandbox for the next ninety minutes because God knows you're not going to risk a tantrum. Unavoidable reality is weekends of soccer games and evenings of school plays and carpooling and school pickups. It means you can't just skip dinner or grab something on the go—life doesn't work that way anymore.

That's who you are now. That is the unavoidable reality. And guess what? It's wonderful. Get used to it.

March 11
It's About Being There ... a Lot

Don't you think maybe they are the same thing? Love and attention?

—GRETA GERWIG

How do you get through to your kids? How do you show them what's right? How can you make sure they know how much you care about them?

The answer is simple: you can be there. A lot. There is a joke that the word *love* is actually spelled T-I-M-E. It's true. Your kids won't have to wonder, they won't need to ask—you, or your partner, or other people—how you feel about them if you are constantly there to show them. *If you have prioritized your time with them over everything else.* Being there also alleviates the pressure to "find the words" in those trying moments, because you've been having an ongoing, regular conversation with your kids the whole time. *The words are there.*

But being a great parent is not just about those pivotal moments. It's not just providing for them or getting them into a great school so they can get ahead in life. It is mainly, and mostly, the day-to-day T-I-M-E. It's the modeling, each day, of what being a good person looks like. It's the showing, each time you see them, that you care, that they're important, that they are loved.

It's about being there. A lot.

March 12
They Must Come First

Queen Elizabeth II had just returned from a six-month trip abroad. Her kids had been aboard the royal yacht for days, eagerly awaiting her return. Did she have presents? Would she tell them wonderful stories? Would she smother them with kisses?

As she stepped aboard, Prince Charles, the future King, ran to her. Always a stickler for protocol, however, the queen politely greeted a group of dignitaries first. "No, not you, dear," she chided him, finishing her business before embracing her family.

Even some sixty-five years after the fact, even if you have an important job, even if you're an avid rule follower, even if you don't like Charles, it still breaks your heart. Especially when we know that she knew better, having moved her weekly meeting with the prime minister to be there for her babies at dinnertime.

But now, after that much time apart, those were her first words to her six-year-old son? What had changed? Couldn't she see the awful symbolism? Literally putting work before family? After having already put them on pause for six months?

Your kids must come first. Not just in the very first months or years but always. You must say to them, "Yes, you, dear," and never ever the opposite.

March 13
Don't Let Them Steal from Your Family

A few weeks before his tragic death, Kobe Bryant got a note from a reporter at ESPN. She was working on a story about a moment in Lakers history and she wanted to feature Kobe in it. It's one of those requests that public figures get all the time. It's part of their job—in fact, it's one of the things that attracted them to the job in the first place. To be in the news, to have people want to hear their opinion, to grow their brand. Kobe replied: "Can't right now. My girls are keeping me busy. Hit me up in a couple of weeks."

Do you have the discipline to send a message like that? How strong are you at putting your family first? How good are your defenses against the endless requests, opportunities, impositions, and obligations that come with your work in particular and with life in general? It's so easy to let people steal your time, to let them take you away from the thing that is keeping you busy: your kids, your family.

Kobe Bryant, tragically, will not get any more time with his kids, and they will not get any more time with him. Which is what makes that text he sent such a powerful reminder—a final feat of performance left there to inspire those of us continuing in the shadow of his death.

Put your family first. Put your kids first. Say that you're too busy. Politely decline. You have other priorities.

March 14
Do You Know Them?

It's a story so bad it has to be true. The 2nd Earl of Leicester was walking down the hallway of his enormous estate. A young nurse holding the hand of a child passed him in the corridor. "Whose child is that?" he asked her. Taken aback, it was all she could do to utter calmly, "Yours, my lord."

Needless to say, the earl died unhappy and mostly alone.

Now, thankfully, most of us are not this aloof. No one would accept or condone that kind of absentee parenting anymore—or even just the more benign aristocratic hands-off style the British were known for. But still, it begs the question: How well do you know your kids . . . *really*?

March 15
Their Needs Are So Modest

> Your kids are not keeping score on your career. . . . They just want a parent who's emotionally present and supportive of them.
>
> —BEN STILLER

David Letterman was the king of late night. His shows ran for thirty-three seasons, making him the longest-serving late-night talk show host in the history of American television. At its peak, he was making something like $30 million a year, watched by an audience of many millions every week.

In 2014, Letterman announced that he was hanging it up. On the day he made the decision, Letterman went to his young son (whom he'd had later in life) with the news. "I'm quitting. I'm retiring," he told Harry. "I won't be at work every day. My life is changing; our lives will change."

"Will I still be able to watch the Cartoon Network?" his son asked. "I think so. Let me check," Letterman replied. There he was, walking away from millions of dollars and one of the most coveted slots in all of television, and his son's main concern was whether *he* could still watch TV.

Kids will humble us like that. We think we're so important. We think our work is so important. In fact, that's what we tell ourselves—that we work those long hours to make the money to provide them a certain kind of life. In fact, our kids' needs are so humble. Mostly what they want is us. And beyond that? They're pretty content with snacks. The occasional video game. A sprinkler to play in. Some magnet you picked up at the airport on the way home from a business trip. A parent who doesn't yell at them all the time. They're pretty easily impressed. Their needs are small.

March 16
It's Not Possible without Struggle

At an event for female judges in the 1980s, during Sandra Day O'Connor's term as the first female Supreme Court justice, a law professor asked, "How do you take care of your family and have a career?" O'Connor answered: "Always put your family first."

It was an inspiring answer, but all the trailblazing women in the room understood it was not the full truth. As her biographer wrote, the women in the audience suspected that the real answer to the question was "By constant struggle," by painful choice, and by trade-offs. We can't be flip about it; putting your family first ahead of your ambition is essential; but it's also *tough*. If it were easy, every parent would do it.

Indeed, later in life, O'Connor would talk about how "desperately hard" it was to balance work and family. She would try to talk to her law clerks, male and female, about this struggle. She didn't dance around how hard would it be. She shared what she had learned. And most important, in being up front, she provided them, and now us, the relief of knowing: it's not possible without struggle.

March 17
You'll Never Regret Playing with Your Kids

Even if you've just put on your work clothes. Even if you're already late. Even if the pool is freezing. Even if they've been getting in trouble lately or been difficult to deal with. Even if you've got the weight of the world on your shoulders. You will never regret choosing to stop whatever it is you were doing, or were about to do, to play with your kids. You will never regret jumping in the water with them, picking up the video game controller with them, spending a few minutes with them, letting Saturday actually be a Saturday with family.

You will always be glad you took the time. Because none of us know how much of it we're going to get. There is no message more important to send than the one that says, "There is nothing more important to me than you." As busy as you are, as much as you're dealing with, there has never been a mind that was not improved or refreshed by temporarily entering the world of a child.

But of course, you will regret letting too many of these opportunities pass you by. In fact, you know that you already do . . . because you already have.

March 18
This Is the Real Dad Tax

One of the perks of parenting is the so-called Dad Tax—the bite of their ice cream, the pieces of their Halloween candy, the biggest pork chop on the serving dish. It's your house and you are bigger, so you get to exact the iron price from your kids anytime you want.

The basketball coach John Thompson, who grew up poor in Washington, DC, recalls that his father always ate whatever he and his siblings left on their plates. But as he got older, he realized that this was a different kind of Dad Tax—one his father was paying, not collecting. "Now I realize the man must have been hungry but sacrificed so we could have more than him," Thompson wrote in his memoirs. "Was I so selfish that I didn't realize the reason he chewed on that pork chop bone I left behind, why he sopped up the gravy on my plate? My father was providing. He didn't eat so we could eat."

Putting your family first isn't just a matter of your schedule. The author Simon Sinek famously wrote that "leaders eat last." So should dads, because the inherent, unquestionable responsibility that you assumed the minute you brought a child into the world was that they come first. They get the bulk of what's available. They don't get the biggest pork chop; they get as many pork chops as they need. They get to experience the fun and the sweetness of life. If there are any leftovers, even if it's just the scraps, then maybe you get a taste.

March 19
Don't Do This to Them

When she was a young girl, Angela Merkel's father was gone a lot. He had to travel to see his congregation. He had meetings and church business to attend to. Like all of us, he was busy. He had work responsibilities, spiritual responsibilities, adult responsibilities.

It took a toll on his family. "The worst was when he said he would be right back," Merkel later reflected, "but then it took hours for him to return." Often she would find herself waiting for hours in the street, expecting him home at any minute, always to be disappointed.

All of us do this in some form or another. "It'll just be a minute," we tell them as we run an errand. "Let me finish this quick phone call," we say, shushing them over and over again while they beg to play with us outside. "Dinner will be ready soon," we say, knowing it will be much longer than that. "I'll be home before it gets dark, I promise," we say, as if traffic could not delay us. Or, like Merkel's father, our trips and travels get extended and we miss things . . . or keep them up waiting.

While none of us fully control our time or our schedule, we do control how we communicate with our children—we control how we give our word and how we keep it. And it's essential that we take that seriously. Our kids shouldn't just be expected to deal with it. They should be communicated to and informed with respect. They deserve an explanation for the things that keep us away from them, that keep them away from the things that it is our adult responsibility to provide. It's a matter of duty, to be sure, but more important, it's a matter of trust.

March 20
They're Going to Ask You Only So Many Times

> Sometimes you will never know the value of a moment until it becomes a memory.
>
> —DR. SEUSS

They're going to ask you only so many times: to get in the pool with them, to sit next to them, to help with their homework, to talk about the problem they're having.

Not because you only get a certain number of summers and car rides and moments with your kids—though that is true. They're going to ask you only so many times because at some point they're going to get the message.

Dad is too busy; he isn't any fun anymore. Mom judges; she isn't actually a good person to ask.

That message.

So you can't defer the opportunity to answer till later. You can't afford to lose your temper because this is the nth time they've asked. You can't give anything less than your best, your most present, your most fun self. Because this ask—in this moment—is it.

It's your chance. You can't waste it. You can't send them the wrong message. You have to seize it. You have to show them who you are.

March 21
If You Want Your Children to Turn Out Well

Seneca called wealth a "preferred indifferent." It's not good or bad but nice to have. He was right. Money does make some things better. It's certainly better to have money than to not have it. But it's a mistake to think that money will magically create a wonderful childhood for your kids.

It's not true that money will guarantee your kids a good life. It's not true that it will prevent them from feeling pain or loss. It's not true that money is even high on their list of needs.

What kids actually want is *you*. What kids actually need is *you*. As Dear Abby quite brilliantly put it in a column back in the 1950s, "If you want your children to turn out well, spend twice as much time with them, and half as much money."

You can't pay someone to be there for your kids. You can't pay someone to do the job only you can do. Sure, money can make things easier; it can buy childcare and tutors. But it will never be as important as what you can provide by being hands on, by being a good example, by showing them you care for them and value them.

The proof of this? Just think about how many great people turned out just fine without much money at all.

March 22
They Are Your Work

> When you love, you wish to do things for. You wish to sacrifice for. You wish to serve.
>
> —ERNEST HEMINGWAY

All of us are busy. We have conflicting responsibilities and a lot to manage besides that. Still, we can't ever forget what our first, *real* job is. As the economist Bryan Caplan tells his children, all four of whom he now homeschools, "You are not an interruption of my work. You are my work."

Our job is to raise great kids. Or, more precisely, our job is to raise great *adults*. The time we spend with our kids—whether it's homeschooling or watching a TV show on the couch—is not a distraction from our work. It is the work. Really important work.

Who could really view their life as successful if they were famous but their kids were struggling? Who would be truly happy accepting a Nobel Prize knowing that they had failed as a parent? What good would a billion dollars be if all the money in the world can't convince your kids to come home for the holidays?

That's why kids can never "take away" from our careers or "hold us back." It's not possible for them to interrupt our work . . . because they are our work.

March 23
You Are the Exalted Creator

Whatever you have accomplished or hope to accomplish, there is something you will never be able to top. As the Catholic activist—and possible future saint—Dorothy Day wrote:

> If I had written the greatest book, composed the greatest symphony, painted the most beautiful painting or carved the most exquisite figure, I could not have felt the more exalted creator than I did when they placed my child in my arms. . . . No human creature could receive or contain so vast a flood of love and joy as I felt after the birth of my child. With this came the need to worship, to adore.

That feeling, the one you felt the first day you held your children. The feeling when they run into your arms and call you Daddy, or when they come into your room to ask for advice, or when you sit across the table from them and watch them eat. That feeling—the pride, the love, the connection—this is the feeling to carry with you.

You made that. You are the exalted creator of that. Parent in a way that proves it.

March 24
Give What You Didn't Get

NFL wide receiver Marqise Lee didn't play football in 2020. He could have played for Bill Belichick, but he didn't. Not because he was worn down or afraid of the grind—as an athlete and a football player, he was in the prime of his career.

No, he opted out of that season because, as it did for so many, COVID-19 disrupted everything. Sports, like business, involves travel and time at the office, away from family. But with COVID-19 protocols, with limited access to family and friends on the road, that NFL season was different. It would have been too much time away for Lee, more than he was willing to bear. As he told ESPN:

> People who know my background and where I came from, and things like that, I didn't really have my pops in my life. I never really had a real father figure besides coaches as I got older. This is my opportunity to be there for my daughter. I was hoping she could be there watching this season, but clearly she wasn't going to be able to do that. I felt like it was important to just spend this year with her, and get back to it next year. Football is going to be there at the end of the day.

Lee was putting his family first. He was doing something his father didn't do for him. He was drawing a line. He was deciding not to waste the most precious thing we have with our children: time. Each of us must decide the same.

March 25
Why Didn't You Make Time for Me?

Not to be always ducking my responsibilities to the people
around me because of "pressing business."

—MARCUS AURELIUS

hope you are quite well," a young Winston Churchill wrote to his always-
busy father from his boarding school in 1886. "You never came to see me
on Sunday when you were in Brighton." It was not the only time he would
write such a thing to his father. "I cannot think why you did not come see
me, while you were in Brighton, I was very disappointed but I suppose you
were too busy."

As Josh Ireland observes in the fascinating book *Churchill and Son*, it's
not just the disappointment of the boy that registers all these years later
but also his sad attempts to rationalize his father's selfishness.

We will not be perfect as parents. We will make mistakes. But we must
do our best to avoid inspiring that painful question: *Why didn't you make
time for me?* Because there is no good answer for it. And the rationalizing
answer *they* come up with has the potential to mess with their minds and
redouble the damage of our absence.

Your kids don't care that you're president. They don't care that this is
the busy sales season. They don't care that your own parents were sick.
They don't care that you were fighting over custody. They just care that you
weren't there.

Time is not given. It is made. We have to make time. That's our job. It's
our biggest priority.

March 26
Here's What You Mean to Them

Sean Lennon, the only son of John Lennon and Yoko Ono, had to grow up without a father. Tragically, John Lennon was assassinated outside his New York City apartment building when Sean was just five years old. Still, it was those few years that Sean got to spend with his father that shaped him into the man he became.

In an interview with Marc Maron, Sean explained that on an almost daily basis, someone will come up to him and say something to the effect of "You have *no idea* what your dad meant to me" or "You *can't understand* how important your dad's music is to me."

It's a strange claim, Sean explained, because of course he understands. John Lennon and his music are *even more* important in Sean's life. Because John Lennon was Sean's father. Because he has been holding on to that relationship every minute since his father was taken from him. Because John's music is the only way he gets to talk to his son anymore.

Each parent should take to heart what that means: even the greatest musician of all time is more important as a parent to his children than he is as an artist to the world. It doesn't matter how great our work is, how wealthy it makes us, or what it ends up meaning to billions of people—nothing will eclipse the impact we have on our kids.

March 27
It's Okay to Be Ambitious

You have things you want to do in this life. Maybe you want to write a book or you're in the middle of starting a company. Maybe you're trying to win a championship or run for president. But you want to be a great parent too, obviously, which necessarily makes your other goals more difficult to achieve.

Is this a moral quandary? A Sophie's choice? Is it possible to yearn for personal achievement and desire to be a great parent and expect to accomplish both? Or does one, as the stories of Justice Ginsburg's and Justice O'Connor's early careers might remind us, require sacrifice from the other?

For most of history, it's been women who have felt the tension of these conflicting desires the most and have been forced to choose one over the other. Fathers, on the other hand, have been encouraged—expected even— to look outside the home for fulfillment and recognition, because for men professional success *was* good parenting.

As society has evolved, however, every parent has had to manage the tension of serving two masters, even prime ministers and billionaires.

In her autobiography, Margaret Thatcher, the first woman to be UK prime minister, quotes Irene Ward, a pioneering British politician: "While the home must always be the centre of one's life, it should not be the boundary of one's ambition."

You're allowed to think bigger. It's okay to have a career and want to be great at it. It's okay to strive to change the world. Because in these things, as long as you share them and open them up to a wider view, you are teaching your kids about you and about the world. You are teaching them about hard work, about doing what's right, about fulfilling one's potential, about being of use to others.

March 28
It's a Family Affair

Taylor Branch's incredible series on Martin Luther King Jr. and the civil rights movement spans three volumes. It's almost three thousand pages with hundreds of footnotes. It won awards like the Pulitzer Prize for Nonfiction and the National Book Critics Circle Award.

Undoubtedly, Branch is quite pleased with this masterwork of historical scholarship, which he spent untold hours researching, writing, editing, and talking about. But there is a note tucked away in the acknowledgments of the final volume that truly captures both the experience and the family effort such an achievement required. Branch writes,

> Our son, Franklin, who was born weeks before my first trip to the Lorraine Motel, finished college in time to help me with my final research.

Your kids are with you on this journey, whatever it is. It can be so easy to see your career as something that is *you*-centric. It's not. It's a family affair. The same is true of the ambitions of every member of your household. And the more you can be involved with each other on these personal journeys, the better. It makes the accomplishments sweeter, the work more complete . . . and the sacrifices less painful. Because all of them have been done together.

March 29
Here's How to Spend More Time with Them

Every parent wishes they could have more time with their kids. We envy the parents who don't seem to have this problem, who don't work the same hours we do, who have the flexibility we dream about to spend more time with their kids.

If only we could be so lucky . . .

The comedian Aziz Ansari tells a joke about a conversation he had with the musician Frank Ocean. Marveling at the autonomy Ocean seems to have in his career, Aziz asks how he gets away with making music only when he wants, touring only when he wants, doing only the kinds of things he wants.

It's not that hard, Ocean tells him; *you just have to be comfortable making less money.*

If we're being honest, how much of the time we spend away from our kids for work is actually related to putting food on the table? How much of it is truly rooted in need? In the basics of a healthy, sustainable life? Probably not nearly as much as we tell ourselves (or them).

We work for other reasons—often good reasons—but not because we *have* to. We could have more flexibility if we wanted. We could choose a different job. We could choose to put family over career advancement, over six- or seven-figure salaries, over keeping up with the Joneses.

Let us stop acting as if the freedom—and opportunity—we crave isn't within our grasp. We *can* spend more time with our kids. We *can* be there more than we are. We just have to be comfortable making less money.

March 30
An Important Rule

The economist Russ Roberts lives his life by a number of rules and rituals. He keeps Shabbat, for instance, and he commits to regularly tithing his income. He has another rule, as a father, that we should all observe as parents:

If your child offers you a hand to hold, take it.

Life and relationships are an endless dance of reaching out and pulling away. You reach out to your kids, they pull away—they're busy, they're in front of their friends, they're mad at you. You try to help them and they don't want it. You want what's best for them but they don't understand.

We can't control that. What we can control is that whenever they do reach out—whenever they offer us a hand to hold—we take that opportunity and grab it. When they want to lie in our bed with us, we can let them. When they call on the phone, we can answer—even if we're in a meeting. When they ask to talk about something, we can listen, *whatever* it's about. We can hold them tight every chance we have.

We can't demand that those things happen, but we can make a rule that when they do, we take it for as long as it's being given.

March 31
This Must Be the Top Priority

What does it actually look like to put family first? It looks like Ricky Rubio letting it be known publicly that his professional basketball career would be over before anyone expected. The NBA star said,

> When my son starts school, the NBA will not be worth it. I will have to go back [to Spain]. I don't want to make him dizzy moving around when he's six years old, at the age of starting to make friends. It was discussed with my wife and we have it very clear. There will come a time when basketball will not be the priority.

Will he follow through on this? Is our career inherently at odds with being a good parent? That's for him and for each of us to decide. Still, at some point our kids must come first. We must do what's best for them. We must sacrifice for them. We must give them the life they deserve—a life with us in it.

Your career is important. But family is forever. It must be the top priority.

APRIL

MASTER YOUR EMOTIONS

(LESSONS IN PATIENCE AND SELF-CONTROL)

April 1
Always Grab the Right Handle

Every event has two handles—one by which it can be carried,
and one by which it can't. If your brother does you wrong,
don't grab it by his wronging, because this is the handle in-
capable of lifting it. Instead, use the other—that he is your
brother, that you were raised together, and then you will have
hold of the handle that carries.

—EPICTETUS

Each day, possibly hundreds of times per day, you're presented with
situations you have to deal with. A kid who lied to you about doing
their homework. A wife who snapped at you. A car that's got to be taken in
for an oil change. A boss with their head up their ass. Grandparents whom
your kids love but who drive you nuts. A family you've got to get to the
airport two hours before takeoff.

How will you react? Will you get angry, pull away, argue, hold a grudge?
Or take a deep breath, have some empathy, apologize, let go a little bit, and
not be such a control freak?

Every day, with every situation, there is a choice. Which handle will we
grab? Which handle will we show our kids how to grab? The easy one? Or
the right one?

April 2
Your Job Is to Make Fast Transitions

The leadership coach Randall Stutman, who has worked with nearly every major hedge fund and CEO on Wall Street, talks about what it means to be a leader at home:

> Your job as a leader is to make really fast transitions. You play many different roles in many different places—your job is not to carry the last conversation. . . . If that means you need to settle yourself and sit out in your car for a couple of minutes before you walk in the house so you can now be Dad, then that's what you need to do. But your job is not to walk into that house and carry with you anything that came from before.

You can't let a bad day or a bad person prevent you from being a good parent. You can't bring your garbage from the office into your home. You must keep a clean house—free of the detritus of adult responsibility that your kids couldn't possibly understand. You must leave that stuff outside, and you must do it quickly, in the space between leaving work and walking into your home.

April 3
Again, Which Will It Be?

Anger always outlasts hurt. Best to take the opposite course.
Would anyone think it normal to return a kick to a mule or
a bite to a dog?

—SENECA

Arthur Ashe's time with his daughter was cut tragically short. At the end of his memoir, as he lay dying, knowing how little time he had left, he wrote some advice to her that touched on something we spoke about on January 5.

"We are being watched by our ancestors, as I am watching you," he told her. "We possess more than they ever dreamed of having, so we must never let them down."

We are watched by our ancestors, yes, but we are also, as Bruce Springsteen put it, haunted by their ghosts. Which will you be for your child?

Are you the kind of example they need? Have you left the kind of legacy that will protect them? That will guide them? That will inspire them to be decent and disciplined, great and good, as Arthur did for his young daughter? Or will you haunt them with your mistakes, with the pain you inflicted on them, with the things left unsaid or unresolved?

April 4
You're Too Old to Act Out

> Being silly is still allowed, not excluded by adulthood. What's
> excluded by adulthood is thoughtlessness, so be thoughtful
> and silly.
>
> —HANK GREEN

We have all sorts of rules of thumb for when various behaviors are age appropriate: the age they should stop having accidents; the age they should stop throwing a tantrum just because they're tired; the age it stops being okay for other people to have to pick up after them.

Then, when our kids mess up, we say: *Aren't you a little old to act this way? Grow up!*

Unfortunately, we apply this standard to ourselves far less often. Whether it's as serious as an affair or as silly as getting hangry because we neglected to eat, we seem to forget that we should be policing ourselves first. Our kids are at least still *kids*, even when they're acting a bit beneath their age. You're an adult. What excuse do you have?

Remind yourself today and every day that you are getting older, that it's time to grow out of these silly habits you've lazily allowed yourself to fall into. Remind yourself that you're too old to act out, to stoop this low, to not be responsible for yourself. And remember, your kids are always watching, so act like the adult that they believe you are.

April 5
Don't Forget How Small They Are

The world would be a terrible place without children, who
bring with them innocence, and the hope of man's further
perfection.

—JOHN RUSKIN

There's a wrenching scene in the haunting novel *The Sweet Hereafter*. A widowed husband is folding up the clothes of his late wife. He's struck, holding her things, by just how physically small she was. This tiny person he loved and misses, she took up so much space in his heart, occupied so much of his waking thoughts, that he came to see her as much bigger than she really was.

This is true for our kids too. They take up so much space in our lives. They have such big presences. *They are so loud.* So we can easily forget that they are tiny, tiny people. They barely have control of themselves. They are dwarfed by us physically, by our experiences, by our confidence in the way things will go.

We have to be careful. Whether they are teenagers or toddlers, we can't forget how small they are. When they fall asleep in the car and you carry them to bed, take a second to notice their size. As you pack up their stuff to take them to college, take a look at just how *little* stuff they have—because their life is still so new.

The smaller you realize your kids are, the kinder you will be. The more protective and patient you will be. The more you will appreciate how hard they are trying to figure things out—themselves, their relationships, the world.

They are so tiny. Don't forget it.

April 6
Are You Using This Power?

*Between stimulus and response there is a space. In that space
is our power to choose our response.*

—VIKTOR FRANKL

In her book *Bringing Up Bébé*, the author Pamela Druckerman talks about "le pause"—the pause—as the secret to French parenting. Druckerman describes it in the context of sleep training, but le pause can actually be a great strategy for parents in all facets of their kids' lives.

When your son trips and falls, do you need to rush over? Or can you *pause* and let him figure out how hurt he is first, whether he wants or needs to cry? When your daughter comes over and tries to tell you something, do you have to complete her sentences? Or can you *pause* and let her struggle to find the words and work through what she is trying to say? When your teenager announces that they are quitting the basketball team, do you have to start arguing right away? Or can you *pause* and listen to their reasons and what they want to do instead? When your kid is home from college and scratches the car while borrowing it for the weekend, what if you don't get upset? Can you *pause* and consider that it was almost certainly not intentional?

As parents, we have to choose our responses wisely, not reflexively. We have to suspend judgment, listen, and think things over. We have to practice le pause so that our kids never have to stop and think about whether they will come to us with their problems, their questions, their hopes, and their dreams.

MASTER YOUR EMOTIONS

April 7
You Have to Move On

Let the dead Past bury its dead!

—HENRY WADSWORTH LONGFELLOW

Remember that time you really needed your dad and he wasn't there? Because he had his own emotional issues. Because he worked too much. Because he was an alcoholic. Remember how your mother's overweening affection made you feel smothered or small? Remember how her strictness kept you from enjoying the things that children should get to enjoy? Remember her jealousy or her pettiness or her mood swings? Remember how their self-absorption seemed to make everything—including the things you really needed help with—about them?

Of course you remember. How could you not? These were defining experiences. They hurt so much. And now you're angry. As you should be. They had a job they were supposed to do. And they didn't do it—not well, anyway. You, the innocent child, suffered for this. You carry the wounds of their failure.

But here's the thing: *you have to move on.* As justified as your anger is—as ongoing as these behaviors may still be with your parents—you have to get beyond this. Because now you have children of your own. And they deserve a parent who is all there. Not one who is clinging to the past. Not one who is putting his or her baggage on their shoulders.

It will not be easy moving on. No one said it will be. You'll have to process it. You'll have to go to therapy. Or read books. Or find a support group. You'll have to sit alone with your thoughts. You'll have to forgive—or cut people out of your life. As they say: your problems might not be your fault, but they are your responsibility.

It's your responsibility to *move on.* Your kids need you to. You need to.

April 8
To Have a More Peaceful Home, Have Fewer of These

These things are not asking to be judged by you. Leave them alone.

—MARCUS AURELIUS

At the core of most of the conflict between parents and children—and so often spouses—is one thing: judgment. We have opinions and they have opinions, and these opinions are the source of disagreement. If we, as parents, would like to have a better relationship with our children, there is one simple thing we can do: we can have fewer opinions.

Do you really need to have an opinion on what kind of food is served at your daughter's wedding (even if you are paying for it)? Do you need to have an opinion on the way they do their hair? Their friends are *their* friends—what does it matter what you think of them or their parents? So what if they like music that sounds weird to you? So what if they want to raise their own kids a different way?

Few things in life are better off with your judgment hovering over them . . . your family most of all.

MASTER YOUR EMOTIONS

April 9
Leave It at the Door

All day at work you experience stress. You witness other people's stupidity. You are the victim of their moods and emotions. Your phone pings constantly with alarming news of the world, the pangs and envies that drive social media.

What are you to do? Much in the way that politics are supposed to stop at the water's edge, so must the stresses of the world stop at the threshold of your front door. You can't bring that crap home with you. You definitely can't have it running on CNN in the background while you eat dinner as a family.

As Randall Stutman said, you need to make that fast transition from frustrated professional to fully present parent so that your home remains a safe place that you are the protector of. Not a protector in the sense of a warrior but closer to the role of a bouncer: *No, sorry, you're not on the guest list.* You have to be Teflon. Your boss's temper can't be allowed to stick to you. The contagion of panic or divisiveness shouldn't be tracked into the living room on the bottom of your shoes. You must keep a clean house. You must turn these things away.

When you arrive home, you must be ready to be present. Ready to have fun. Ready to be the parent they need . . . not the one that's left over after the ravages of the day.

April 10
Embrace This Mindset

In Tibet, Buddhist monks make beautiful mandalas out of sand. They spend hours, even days, crafting these complex, geometric designs . . . only to wipe them clean and start over as soon as they're finished.

Isn't that a way we might see all the work we do as parents?

You clean, then the house is dirty. You do the dishes, then five minutes later the sink is full again. Literally before you've even finished helping your kids put their toys away, the toys are splayed out across the floor. Those new clothes you just bought them? Now they're filthy and frayed.

This can drive you nuts if you let it. It can piss you off. Or you can learn to love it. You can learn to see it all like the mandala—an unending, ephemeral process that we begin again and again and again. You can learn to see it not as work we're doing but as art. *Finish?* To be finished would mean the end of this—the end of their childhood, the end of our lives together.

No, we like that it's a little bit like Groundhog Day. We love that it means a chance to wake up and do this with them again.

To do it beautifully. To do it well. To do it together.

April 11
Don't Be Mad at Good People

Speak when you are angry and you will make the best speech
you will ever regret.

—AMBROSE BIERCE

When you lose your temper, whom does it inevitably seem to be with? Your family. It's strange. We'll stomach some pretty rude behavior from strangers on the street, but God forbid your son leaves his shoes out! You were professional while asking your assistant (for the thousandth time) to do something, but you'll get short with your spouse because they couldn't hear you over the noise in the other room.

It feels like a paradox, but really this is a problem of proximity. Precisely because they're closest to you, you have more opportunities to get upset with them than with anyone else. It's a sad, twisted state of affairs. The people who are all bad but far away are rarely targets for our rage. But the people who are mostly good—who on the whole have helped and loved us many times more than they've hurt us—they're the ones who get the brunt of it?

"Let's not be angry at good people," Seneca writes in "On Anger." Today, when you find yourself getting upset at someone you love, remind yourself that their positive traits far outweigh whatever is bothering you in the moment. Remind yourself that yelling doesn't make them hear you better. Remind yourself that they probably know they messed up and probably feel bad enough already. Remind yourself how small they are. Remind yourself how *good* they are.

The fact that we *can* get mad at someone, because they love us enough to put up with it or because they're kids and they just have to live with it (and us), is not an excuse. We should try not to get upset with anyone, but if we are going to get mad, let's make sure the object of our frustration is a target of offense, not of opportunity.

April 12
What Kind of Energy Are You Bringing?

The ubiquity of the word *energy* these days is probably a sign of how pervasive pseudoscience and charlatans have become in our culture. We are inundated with energy healers and energy crystals. You can hire consultants to analyze your company's energy. You can take a sound bath to remove negative energy or have an aura reader interpret the energy you put out into the world. The amount of sage that has been burned in apartments after breakups rivals the amount of sage that has been used in restaurant dishes.

Yet for all that nonsense, energy is a real thing in parenting. Just as Cesar Millan talks about projecting the right energy to your dog, so too can your kids pick up on the energy emanating from you. Bad day at work? They can feel it. Hate where you live? They can feel it. Pissed off at your spouse? They can tell, even if you argue only when they're asleep.

Why are your kids running around like crazy, acting like monsters today? Well, maybe you ought to check what kind of energy you're generating. Why is your son hitting his little brother? Maybe because you're a ball of tension and frustration, and it's contagious. Why is your daughter being such a terror? Maybe that resentment your wife is holding onto has something to do with it. Maybe your daughter just couldn't stand how things were at breakfast this morning—how awkward and weird it was.

When you see behavior and attitude problems, adjust your energy. Look in the mirror first. If you want a happy home, a home with kindness and love and peace, then bring that energy with you. Project it consciously and deliberately—show that things are good with you, and they will be better with everyone else.

April 13
This Is Their Language

The primary language of children is behavior. Not words. If you want to know what they're thinking or how they're feeling, watch what they do, not what they say.

When we say that "actions speak louder than words," this is what we mean. The younger your kids are, the more likely they are to speak entirely with actions *instead* of words. This is for one simple, undeniable reason: they don't have the words yet. But even if they did, kids don't understand their feelings—the physical ones or the emotional ones—enough to know how to put words to them. Quite often they don't even know they're having feelings.

Watch an eighteen-month-old with an earache—there are no words, there is only discomfort and pawing at the side of their head or waking up in the middle of the night screaming. Watch an eight-year-old with anxiety—there are no words, there are only stomachaches and panic and wet beds. A teenager who has been hurt by someone may in turn hurt others.

This is why we need to "listen" to our kids in more ways than just the obvious, literal way. We have to watch them. We have to be patient. We have to understand that a screaming tantrum about the iPad is almost certainly about something else. We have to understand that lethargy and sliding grades are statements; they are symptoms. It's your child speaking to you through behavior.

Will you hear them? Will you be able to talk to them about it, not just with your words but with your own actions?

April 14
It's the Hardest Thing

Chesty Puller fought in the banana wars. He fought in guerrilla wars. He took islands in the Pacific during World War II. He fought in Korea. So you'd think that he would have been able to handle just about anything life threw at him. But like you, he was a parent, and he found that it was just about the hardest thing a person can ever do.

When he was just home from Korea, where he had landed at Inchon and fought in the brutal cold at close quarters, Chesty and his wife had to take their daughter to get her tonsils out. Chesty, who had always been a sweetheart underneath, carried the girl to the operating room. Talking to her softly, he tried to lay her down on the bed and let the nurse prepare her for surgery. But his daughter, scared and overwhelmed, refused to let go. She cried and screamed and clung to him until they were eventually able to separate and sedate her. "She will never forgive me, Virginia," he said to his wife when he returned to the waiting room. "This is worse than Peleliu."

He was only half exaggerating. This thing called parenthood demands more of us than just about anything else in life. It challenges us emotionally, physically, mentally. It tugs on every one of our heartstrings. You can toughen yourself up for war, you can coolly bet millions of dollars at work, but there's nothing you can do about the gaping soft spot your kids have access to. Nothing can get you quite like they do . . . because nothing matters to you quite like they do.

This is the hardest thing you'll ever do. Know it. Accept it. Be grateful for it.

April 15
Have You Seen Their Perspective?

Have my parents forgotten that they were young once? Apparently, they have.

—ANNE FRANK

We think they're making excuses. We think they're making stuff up. We just want them to go back and sleep in their bed. Or listen to their coach. Or get their work done. It's fine, we tell them. Just give it a try. Wear your jacket; it's not that uncomfortable. Do your homework; it's not that difficult.

Do you remember reading *To Kill a Mockingbird*? Where Atticus talks about climbing into somebody's skin and walking around in it? Well, have you actually done that? Not with someone you pity or someone you wish to be, but with someone you aspire to lead and teach and nourish? Someone like your own child?

Your kid wakes up and comes into your room at night? Try sleeping in their bed. Maybe it really is scary in there. Watch soccer practice. Maybe the coach really is a jerk. How do you think that jacket feels to a kid? Maybe it really is way too hot in there. Did you like doing your homework when you were their age?

See their perspective. Crawl inside it, walk around in it. Then take a step back and parent accordingly.

April 16
This Solves Most Problems

Any experienced parent can tell you about the magical panacea called *food.*

Why is your kid screaming? Why are they terrorizing their sibling? Why can't they focus during homeschooling? Why can't they fall asleep? Why is your teenager so moody?

The answer is simple. They are hungry. They're hangry. *And they don't know it.*

Moms have long carried snacks in their purses for a reason. Because it will solve most problems. Soothe most frayed nerves. Calm down most difficult situations.

Somebody always forgets to eat. So feed them. Ask them if they're hungry. Remind them that they're hungry. Keep a tight meal schedule. Watch what happens.

Oh, also, when you're grouchy and frustrated and anxious and short with your spouse and your kids—you might be hangry yourself. In 2014, researchers from Ohio State University found that most fights between couples are because someone is hungry. So, like taking a walk or taking five deep breaths, grabbing something to eat will probably solve most of your adult problems too.

April 17
Do You Know What You Look Like Angry?

It has often been useful for angry people to look in a mirror.
The great transformation in themselves has disturbed them.

—SENECA

A nger might *feel* deserved or appropriate, but it almost always *looks* awful.

The next time you are out, try watching for other parents who are getting angry at something their kids are doing. Observe the crowd at your son or daughter's next soccer game. Track that family traveling on vacation at the airport. Pay attention to the group at the big family table across from you at the pizza place.

It's as close to a look in the mirror as you're likely to get.

How do you think you look when you tell your child way too loudly, "*Sit down. I told you already, sit down!*" when they bounce around with too much energy? How do you think you look as you grab their arm in frustration and jerk them closer to you in line? Do you think you sound good when threatening to take away some basic privilege of theirs—like a tyrant—because they're not behaving exactly as you like? Or when you shout at them to hurry up at the airport? You think you don't look like a monster when, after the argument escalates beyond your ability to manage with words, you slap them across the face?

You look *terrible*. You look as awful and shameful as the people looked when you saw them do the same thing in public, to their kids, as you tried to avert your gaze. No one looks good angry. Worse still, that image can etch itself into our kids' brains for a long time.

April 18
This Is the Enemy

> Do not be afraid to get rid of things which distract your attention.
>
> —LEO TOLSTOY

You're distracted because this weird work email just came in. You're in a bad mood because of something you saw. You're feeling off because of something somebody said to you. And what happens? Well, your kids get the brunt of it. Or they get only 50 percent of you at dinner, because you're home but not really *home*.

Preoccupation is the enemy of good parenting. And the worst part? Kids can sense it. They are simultaneously sponges and mirrors, and unflattering ones at that. When they act out, make a mess, bite their brother, dye their hair pink—that's what is happening. They sense your energy and are responding to it.

The sad truth is that most of what we're preoccupied with doesn't even matter. We give the jerk at the office free space in our head. We *choose* to go on Twitter and doomscroll. We don't need to check our email as much as we do. Worrying about money never solves our money problems.

We have to push all that stuff away. So we can be present. So we can be patient. So we can be *parents*.

April 19
Don't Waste These Opportunities

Yes, it was annoying—those hours delayed at the airport on the way to your vacation. Yes, it was disappointing when your daughter came home with a terrible report card. Yes, it was scary when you came home with that diagnosis from your doctor. Yes, it was exhausting that you spent another sleepless night with your toddler.

But the question, or rather the opportunity, is: Did it bring you closer together?

It doesn't have to, of course. You can get angry. You can be annoyed. You can be overwhelmed and distracted. Or . . . or you can relish the moment—even if they're crying, even if you're disappointed, even if *you're* crying. You can feel *love* and *gratefulness* and *happiness* instead.

Because this is a chance to talk. This is a chance to see them from a different angle. This is a chance to ask questions. This is a chance to spend time together. A crisis, as politicians like to say, is a terrible thing to waste. It's a chance to do things you couldn't do before. Things that wouldn't be possible in ordinary circumstances.

It's always a chance to get closer. To love more. To understand better.

April 20
It's Not Fair

> Old people are always very impatient with young ones. Fathers always expect their sons to have their virtues without their faults.
>
> —WINSTON CHURCHILL

We expect so much of our kids. We push them. We prod them. We tell them what to do. We punish them—however lightly—when they fall short.

What we lose track of is how impossible our expectations often are for these little humans who lack the decades of life experience we're absentmindedly taking for granted.

There is no blueprint. To assume there is or, worse, to imagine there is and then hold your kids to those expectations is wildly unfair. Can we have expectations for our kids? Yes. Can we try to make sure they don't fall into the same traps or develop the same vices as us? It would be criminal if we didn't.

But we have to remember that they are like us . . . for better *and* for worse. They've lived their whole lives in the same house as us. They've learned from our examples—even the bad ones . . . *especially* the bad ones in many cases. They're not going to be perfect. They're going to have our weaknesses . . . perhaps some of their own too. And to punish them with our unrealistic expectations, even unintentionally, quite literally for the sins of the father, is profoundly unfair.

Our job is to love them and to be patient with them, not to demand the impossible from them.

April 21

Don't Ever, Ever Do This

[Cato the Elder] used to say that a man who beats his wife or child is laying sacrilegious hands on the most sacred thing in the world.

—PLUTARCH

Thankfully, we're at a place in history where most people don't need to hear this anymore, but unfortunately, some people still do. Maybe they're reading this book. Maybe they're not. But it's worth laying it down again; it's worth a reminder of the precious treasure you've been entrusted with.

To raise your hand, open or closed, to your spouse or your children is unacceptable.

It doesn't matter how angry you are. It doesn't matter who started it. It doesn't matter how many times you told your son. It doesn't matter that your parents used to do it. It doesn't matter that some cultures still accept it.

For two thousand years, we've known deep down that it's wrong. You are here to protect and to serve and to love them. To violate that obligation because you can't control yourself in the moment, because you're mad? This is to violate a sacred oath. And once done, it can never be undone.

You cannot do it. *Ever.*

April 22
Is It Good When They're Bad?

In a *New York Times* piece, Melinda Wenner Moyer (author of the fantastic *How to Raise Kids Who Aren't Assholes*) asks you to consider perhaps the most counterintuitive idea in all of parenting: that maybe, just maybe, it's not such a big deal when your kids misbehave. Perhaps, she proposes, this is actually a sign of how loved and safe they feel. She writes:

> Think of it this way: When kids are always respectful, complacent and obedient with adults, it is often because they are afraid of those adults. It's not a coincidence that people who boast about how well behaved their children are may also be those who throw around phrases like, "Spare the rod, spoil the child."

This is not to say that chaos is a good thing, that no rules should be enforced. It's a reminder that before you write yourself off as a terrible parent because your kid challenged you or because they had a meltdown, consider *what it means that they feel comfortable doing that in front of you.*

It might actually be that they do listen to you—especially when you tell them that you're there for them, that you love them unconditionally, that you want them to think for themselves. It's possible they actually respect you quite deeply. But even more than that, it could be that they trust you more than anyone in the world.

April 23
Don't Thrust Them Away

Of course, kids can be annoying. Painfully so.

Kids scream in your ears and ruin your clothes with their food- and dirt-covered hands. Kids can cut off your air supply as they crawl onto your back for a piggyback ride.

Yet you have to absorb all of this. Even though it hurts. Even though you love that shirt. Even though you can't breathe. You can't thrust them away.

Yes, of course, you have to explain to them what's appropriate and what isn't. You have to protect your own physical well-being. But the point is, they have no idea yet how their actions affect other people. Even teenagers don't fully comprehend the concept of consequences, of cause and effect. (Why do you think they drive like crazy, eat like crap, and talk all kinds of trash?) What they do comprehend is you getting upset, you pulling away.

Kids can feel your energy changing, even if they can't put words to what it is they are sensing or how it makes them feel. And what's most difficult about all this is that it very well might be this painful, confusing feeling— as provoked and instinctual as it is—that sticks with them forever. So work on getting control of yourself. Work on toughening yourself up a bit.

You can gently unwrap their arms from your throat. You can get a new shirt. You can turn the game around and chase them instead. You can make what was annoying become fun. You can talk to them calmly, correct them, and then gently turn the pain into a moment of profound connection. That's entirely up to you.

April 24
What If Someone Else Treated Your Kids This Way?

If you hired a babysitter or a nanny and caught them staring at their phone instead of watching your kids, you'd be livid. If you walked into a room and discovered a teacher or a grandparent or *anyone* yelling at your kids, you'd be difficult to stop. If you heard someone make a snide remark or tease them or bully them, you'd put an immediate end to it.

And yet . . . you do some of these things all the time! You feel your frustration rising as they refuse to listen and *bam*, you grab their arm and yell, "STOP IT NOW!" right into their little faces. You're ignoring the soccer game. You tune out their incessant attempts to get your attention. Worse, your attention is elsewhere while they're playing in the pool . . . and for what? For an email? For a text? To scroll Twitter? You think you're funny and you like to joke around . . . but if you saw someone else doing it, you know what you'd call it? You'd call it *bullying*.

We'd never let anyone else get away with what we rationalize or excuse of our own behavior. That's not to say you're abusive or a bad parent—not at all. It's just a reminder: Your job isn't just to protect your kids from other people. It's to protect them from your own bad habits, your own temper, your own flaws too. It's to demand of yourself what you'd expect from *anyone* to whom you'd entrust your children's safety. That is to say: you have to demand *the best* of yourself.

No excuses. No double standards. Watch yourself as you'd watch a nanny cam. Trust but verify, just as you would a new school or day care. Ask yourself: Would I let anyone else get away with what I'm doing right now?

MASTER YOUR EMOTIONS

April 25
Delay, Delay, Delay

An angry man opens his mouth and shuts his eyes.

—CATO THE ELDER

Seneca said that "delay is the greatest remedy for anger." That's the truth.

Delay is the best way to let your mind clear, to make sure that anger doesn't drive you to do something you regret. Anger is an exaggerator. It magnifies the worst in every situation. Anger is an exacerbator too. It takes a bad situation and *makes* it worse with the overreaction it produces in us.

Delay will help you make sure that doesn't happen, that anger doesn't win. The next time you're angry, take five deep breaths and see if you can get yourself that wound up again. It's next to impossible.

Now, no one is saying you can't respond at all. You probably will have to address whatever has made your blood boil. You will have to say something. Your kids do need to learn that lying is not acceptable, talking back to their mother will not be tolerated, leaving the stove on could burn the house down. But wait a minute. Take a walk. Put a reminder down to bring it up tomorrow. Deal with it when you get home from work. Let cooler heads prevail.

Make it a teachable moment. Teach them that it's possible to control how you react.

April 26
The Moments of Leniency Matter

To err is human; to forgive, divine.

—ALEXANDER POPE

In Georgia in the mid-1930s, when he was but ten years old, Jimmy Carter was fishing with his father. As they caught fish, his father attached their growing haul to a trotline that he hooked onto Jimmy's belt loop, a point of great pride for the boy.

But then, several hours later, Jimmy looked down and realized that the line had broken or become unclipped without him noticing. Frantically, desperately, he dove into the water, searching, hoping, terrified his father would be upset. "What's wrong?" his father asked. "I've lost the fish, Daddy." "All of them?" his father replied. "Yes, sir, yes, sir" was all Jimmy could say through his tears.

"Daddy was rarely patient with foolishness or mistakes," Carter would reflect eighty years later. But then, after a long pause, his father smiled and said, "Let them go, Hot. There are a lot more fish in the river. We'll get them tomorrow." All those years later, it was this moment of patience and kindness and forgiveness that Carter remembered. The fish no longer mattered; in fact, they never did matter. What mattered was that his father knew what Jimmy needed in that moment.

What about you? Do you understand the power of leniency and tolerance? Can you let things go? Can you control your temper and frustrations? Do you know when it's time to push and when it's time to pull them in close to you?

April 27
You're the Voice in Their Heads

The power broker in your life is the voice that no one hears.
How well you revisit the tone and content of your private
voice is what determines the quality of your life.

—DR. JIM LOEHR

You're just trying to get them to behave, to listen to you, to stop hitting their sister, to take school seriously, to do *whatever.* So you speak firmly, even harshly. You're tired, you've had this conversation a thousand times, you're not as kind as you could be. Maybe you try to make a joke out of it, to soften the delivery of your honest opinion about what they're doing—except the joke hits a soft spot and cuts too close to the bone.

You know what you're doing, *really*, in these moments? You're cementing a very specific voice in their head.

Everything we say, every interaction we have with our kids, is shaping them. How we speak to them informs how they will speak to themselves. If you want proof of this, think about all the complexes and scripts you picked up from your parents—maybe things you're working on in therapy right now, decades later.

So while you can, before it's too late . . . catch yourself. Think about how you can be an ancestor instead of a ghost. Make this interaction a kind one, a patient one, a friendly one. Speak to them the way you'd want them to speak to themselves. Because it's not a matter of *if* they will internalize the things they heard growing up; it's a matter of *what* they will internalize. Put a *good* voice in their head so they might remember the good stuff.

April 28
Do You Really Care?

> A key point to bear in mind. . . . You're better off not giving
> the small things more time than they deserve.
>
> —MARCUS AURELIUS

It seems like it's really important to you. That the door not be slammed. That the chores be done a certain way. That everything be put away immediately. That feet go on the ground, not the furniture.

But the truth is, you don't actually care about the things themselves. *You don't.* If you had to choose between your kids having fond memories and you having clean walls, you'd choose your kids having fun. If you had to choose between slightly lower grades and better self-worth, you'd choose their self-worth. If you had to choose between just about anything and your kids' safety, happiness, and self-image, you'd never choose that other *stuff.*

Yet here you are, arguing about it again. Choosing to die on some stupid hill. Choosing to protect a piece of Sheetrock that—*admit it*—you don't actually care about. What you really care about—what these rules actually represent—is obedience and control. What you're really worried about, hence the fixation, is the deep-seated anxiety that you might be screwing them up.

Relax! Let this stuff go. Seriously, just let it go. You won't regret it.

April 29
How Long Can You Go?

Kind people are never involved in arguments, and those who like to argue are never kind.

—LAO TZU

At the end of it, you'll wish you'd fought less with your kids. You'll wish you'd made less of an issue of so many things. Nobody looks back on their lives or their kids' lives and thinks: *I'm so glad we got in all those arguments. I'm glad I was so hard on them. I'm glad they finally learned all the rules.*

You know this. Okay, so today, how long can you go?

How long can you go without chiding your kids about this or that? Without making remarks about your teenager's choices? Without reminding your young one to stop dragging their feet, leaning on the table, leaving their things lying about?

See if you can make the majority of your interactions uncritical. That doesn't mean you have to be disingenuously positive about them, only that you try to stop bothering them about so much piddly crap. None of that stuff matters now—as much as you might try to convince them, and yourself, otherwise—and it definitely won't matter years from now when you're all reflecting on your lives together.

So dial back the criticism. Remember: you don't need to have an opinion about everything. If you can keep some of that stuff in your back pocket, you'll both be happier for it.

April 30
Who Gets Your Patience?

The father of the former chancellor of Germany Angela Merkel was a pastor in East Germany. He was beloved by his flock. He forged a deep bond with them over many years. But at home, things were a little different. At home, he was stern and impatient. "What really made me angry as a child was his way of showing so much understanding for everyone else," his daughter would reflect, "but if we children did something wrong, his reaction was completely different."

Clearly he was *capable* of being understanding and kind—he did it all day every day as part of his job. But maybe that was the problem: he'd used up all his patience at work and had none left for his family when he got home. Or maybe he held himself to a different standard professionally than personally, because it wasn't in public. Or maybe he made the mistake that many of us do, forgetting that our children are little people with the same problems as everyone else, just of a different size. And because of that, we sometimes fail to treat them with the appropriate level of dignity, respect, and compassion.

You don't yell at a colleague just because they left a door open. You don't punish one of your players for wanting more of your attention and counsel. And yet children all over the world, throughout all time, can speak to relationships where that was the exact kind of treatment they received from parents who were at the end of their ropes and had run out of patience.

Be kind to your family. Make sure they get the same patience and understanding as everyone else. Actually, scratch that. Make sure they get *more*. Because long after you've left this job or stopped coaching that team, they will still be your kids.

MAY

CHARACTER IS FATE

(LESSONS IN RIGHT AND WRONG)

May 1
This Predicts Everything

Character is fate.

—HERACLITUS

Who a person is determines what will happen and what they can do. It's true in sports. It's true in politics. It's true in business. No matter how talented a person is, how great the incentives, how great the system around them—in the end, character is everything. It can't be hidden. It can't be compensated for.

It comes out.

Your job as a parent, as you seek to create a better world for your kids and raise them to be good in that world, is to value character. To teach it to them. To model it for them. To reward it when you see it in them. Yes, you want them to be smart. Yes, you want them to be ambitious. Yes, you want them to be creative and hardworking. But these traits are worthless if not yoked behind good character.

We're seeing the costs of ignoring that fact in every facet of life right now. We need to fix it. And the fix starts at home.

May 2
Your Character Builds Theirs

The image of the black Escalade crashed into the tree was everywhere. Then women began to come forward—first one, then another, then still more. Eventually, he admitted it. Tiger Woods confessed to extramarital infidelity . . . with more than 120 women.

It was news to almost everyone. But those who knew him were less surprised. And those who knew him *well* weren't surprised at all. Tiger Woods's biographers Jeff Benedict and Armen Keteyian note the "well-worn clichés": "Like father like son . . . The apple doesn't fall far from the tree." For years, when Earl Woods took his son Tiger to golf tournaments around the country, he didn't make "any effort to camouflage his vices." Women came and went from hotel rooms. He'd stop at convenience stores and come out with paper bags holding forty-ounce bottles of liquor. He'd ask waitresses to join him for a cigarette.

The gambling, the waitresses, the infidelity—it wasn't out of character for Tiger. *It was his character*, or rather, it was character traits *taught* by his father. Built from the blueprint drawn from his father's, Earl's, example. The apple didn't fall far from the tree, because the tree made the apple.

CHARACTER IS FATE

May 3
Nourish This Wonderful Trait

The primary and most important influence on Queen Victoria was not her mother but her beloved governess Baroness Lehzen, who later became her adviser and friend.

It was from Louise Lehzen that Victoria got the backbone that made her one of England's great queens—one who ruled for some sixty-three years, more than forty of them by herself. As Lehzen said with trademark modesty:

> I have, to be sure, not created, but nourished in the Princess, one quality which is to test, consider, and to stand firmly by that which the Princess finds right and good.

You have a lot of responsibilities as a parent, but none of them trump this one. Yes, you want your kids to be smart. You want them to be helpful and healthy. You want them to do well in school. But none of that will be possible without having nourished the ability that Lehzen helped Victoria cultivate.

So do it. Every day.

May 4
Teach Them These Four Virtues

> If, at some point in your life, you should come across anything better than justice, truth, self-control, courage—it must be an extraordinary thing indeed.
>
> —MARCUS AURELIUS

Aristotle worshipped them. The Christians and Stoics too. In the West, we call them the "cardinal virtues"—from the Latin word *cardo*, which means "hinge." These are the virtues upon which the good life hinges. These are the virtues that every parent is obligated to teach their children:

Courage: To stand up. To charge ahead. To not be afraid or timid in life.

Moderation: To know balance. To be in control of oneself. To avoid excess or extremes.

Justice: To do the right thing. To care for others. To do your duty.

Wisdom: To learn. To study. To keep an open mind.

Those are the four essential tenets for living.

As a parent, you must worship these virtues . . . and raise kids who do the same. You have to model these virtues and teach them—by example and by instruction—how they can too. Their life—and the future—hinges on it.

May 5
Everything You Do Is Teaching Them

Preach the Gospel at all times. Use words if necessary.

—FRANCIS OF ASSISI

As a young man, the champion boxer and civil rights activist Floyd Patterson was all trouble. He stole. He skipped school. He got into fights. He once, tragically, took a picture of himself and scratched out the eyes looking back at him—because he didn't like himself. So finally the authorities sent him away.

It could have been another sad chapter in a sad life. Instead, Patterson was lucky enough to be sent away to a boys' commune in upstate New York. There, under the guidance of a kind and unconventional psychologist, Dr. Papanek, Patterson's world was changed. For the first time, he was seen. He was more than "reformed," in the language of the American prison system; he was loved. As Dr. Papanek explained his philosophy:

> Punishment teaches the child only how to punish. Scolding teaches him how to scold. By showing him that we understand, we teach him to understand. By helping him, we teach him to help. He learns cooperation by cooperating.

Most likely, your children have not found themselves in such serious trouble. Hopefully they are not as far gone as most of the people around Floyd felt he was. Regardless, the lesson is the same: In everything we do with, to, and around our kids, we are teaching them. Even when we mean well, even when they are screwing up, just as Dr. Papanek explained, we are teaching . . . often the very opposite of what we'd like to show them.

May 6
Teach Them to Sweep the Sheds

The New Zealand All Blacks are the most successful rugby franchise of all time. They have a legacy that rivals the great teams in nearly every other sport, from the San Antonio Spurs to the New England Patriots to the U.S. women's national soccer team. How have they done this?

By being tough, of course. By being extremely talented, obviously. But there is a lesser-known and counterintuitive element to their success as well: they clean up after themselves. In his book *Legacy*, James Kerr portrays the team tidying up the locker room after a game:

> Sweeping the sheds.
> Doing it properly.
> So no one else has to.
> Because no one looks after the All Blacks.
> The All Blacks look after themselves.

If you want your kids to clean up after themselves, you have to teach them why it matters. If you want them to look after themselves, you have to teach them to find pride and satisfaction in that. If you want them to sweep the sheds, you have to teach them that it isn't just a chore. It's a statement of priority. A statement of character and commitment and self-sufficiency—an illustration of who you are.

How we do anything is how we do everything is the lesson parents have to pass along to their kids. Leaving a mess isn't just a mess—it shows that *you're a mess.*

CHARACTER IS FATE

May 7
Don't Give Them an Ego

You love your kids more than anything. You think they're God's gift (which they are, to you!). You want them to know how you feel about them, and you feel bad when they feel bad about themselves. These are all perfectly healthy and laudable feelings.

At the same time, we have to make sure we're not puffing up their ego with our endless praise. We have to manage our natural bias toward their virtues and limit our blindness to their vices. As Seneca wrote, this requires speaking honestly—with kindness—and holding them accountable for their actions. Even if that pains us. He explains:

> Flattery must be kept well out of the way of children. Let a child hear the truth, and sometimes fear it: let him always reverence it. Let him rise in the presence of his elders. Let him obtain nothing by flying into a passion: let him be given when he is quiet what was refused him when he cried for it. Let him behold, but not make use of his father's wealth: let him be reproved for what he does wrong.

Seneca knew this balance was not easy—it isn't for any parent. But if our goal is to raise well-adjusted, self-aware kids, we'll have to work for it. Even if our instinct is to rush over and tell them they're the greatest, most specialest little kiddos there ever were.

May 8
Punishment Should Make Them Better

> To punish others is like putting more wood in the fire. Every crime already has punishment in itself, and it is more cruel and more just than the punishment created by people.
>
> —LEO TOLSTOY

Randall Stutman is asked a lot about parenting by the CEOs and executives with whom he works as a leadership coach. We already know his admonition about making fast transitions between work and home, but he has another piece of advice for high-powered leaders who also want to be great parents:

Punishment should make them better.

It's pretty fitting advice coming from a coach too. Think about it: A basketball coach who is disappointed in someone's effort makes them do sprints or push-ups. It's not fun *and* it makes the kid stronger. A football player who didn't make their GPA has to go to extra study sessions. An athlete who gets in trouble off the court might have to do community service or write an apology letter. These are more than simple deterrents. They're punishments that make the transgressors better both as players and as people.

When you get upset, when you catch your kid doing something they're not supposed to do, make sure that you don't punish them from a place of heightened emotion—whether that's anger or fear or shame. Take a minute. Come up with a punishment that makes them better. Something that they wouldn't *choose* to do but that is good for them. Vocab drills. Memorizing state capitals. Volunteering somewhere. Picking up trash. Painting the house.

They won't like it, but one day they may actually thank you for it.

May 9
Too Busy to Be Bad

Harry Truman was once asked if he ever got in trouble as a kid. "Very, very seldom," he said. "I was too busy. I told you I'd read all three thousand books in the library by the time I was fourteen years old." Were there any troublemakers in your neighborhood or at school? "We had boys who were terrible," he said. "But I was too busy reading books to be bad."

The September chapter of this book is filled with the benefits of raising a reader, but Truman gives us a great one to add here in May: readers very, very seldom get into trouble. They're too busy. They already live in a world of high stakes—that of history, of great novels, of epic stories—why do they need to go around creating drama and problems in the real world?

Of course, kids get in trouble for a lot of reasons, but "not having anything better to do" is one you can solve for right now. Introduce them to the world of books. Challenge them, incentivize them to read. Let them fall in love with those worlds and live there as much as they want.

It'll cause a lot less trouble for the both of you.

May 10
Remember What Success Looks Like

The Bible puts forth a pretty good definition of an actual successful life: "An elder must be blameless, faithful to his wife, a man whose children are trustworthy and are not open to the charge of being wild and disobedient."

We can strip the gender out of this and it's still true. Our job is to:

- live an honorable life
- treat our spouse well (and respect our marriage)
- teach our children to be honest and reliable
- refrain from spoiling them

If you can be successful or famous or respected at your chosen craft above all that? Fantastic. Just remember: no amount of worldly gains will matter—especially at the end of your life—if you have failed at being a parent to those with whom you would most love to share those gains.

May 11
Are You the Good Guys?

That's what the boy asks his father in Cormac McCarthy's *The Road*: "Are we still the good guys?"

It's the boy's sweetness, his insistence on doing the right and kind thing, despite the darkness of the world, that keeps the father from spiraling into despair or cruelty.

Are you the good guys? Or have you curdled along with your political party? Have you been corrupted by your industry? Have you grown callous and indifferent with all the responsibilities and stresses of life? Are you too busy worrying about your mortgage and your golf game to care about other people? Are you too far down the road to change? To question and reflect? To see things from a new perspective?

The good news is that you have a boy like that in your own life. Your kids are a wonderful source of innocence and purity. They see things with fresh eyes. They are not yet jaded. They are also a kind of warrant. Why should you change? Why should you be one of the good guys? *For them.*

Give them hope. Give them a model. Be one of the good guys.

May 12
What Matters More Than Results

The actress Tracee Ellis Ross has a famous, successful mother in the multiple Grammy Award winner and Motown legend Diana Ross. You might think that someone that successful would care a lot about success. The driven parent drives their children—to get good grades, to win games, to be the strongest, prettiest, or most popular, to follow in their footsteps. Their high standards extend right down through the college their kids go to or the profession they pursue.

But Tracee got lucky. Her mom did it right. Most parents would ask their kids, "How are your grades?" "Did you win?" "Are you number one in your class?" But after school, Diana Ross would ask, "Did you do your best? How do you feel about it, Tracee?" Tracee—who, amid some fits and starts, went on to become a very accomplished actress—would explain that her mother's emphasis taught her an essential perspective shift: "how to navigate a life through how it feels to you, as opposed to how it looks to everyone else."

What matters more than your kids' grades in school is the priorities they pick up and the values they absorb. So that's the question: Are you teaching them that test scores matter or that *learning* counts? Are you teaching them that success is winning arbitrary competitions or that it is becoming the best version of themselves?

Results don't matter—not the obvious ones, anyway. What counts is the person your kids are shaping themselves into and the things you do along the way to help them.

May 13
Ask Them This Question Every Day

> Wherever there is a human being there is an opportunity for kindness.
>
> —SENECA

We're always asking our kids questions: *How was school? How did baseball practice go? Did you stay out of trouble? What did your teacher say about your math grade? Did you have fun with your friends?*

We ask these questions because we want to have something to talk about. We ask these questions because we're concerned. We ask these questions because the answers matter to us. Our kids realize this. They are smart enough to understand that these questions are a reflection of their parent's values, of how the world measures a person and determines what success looks like.

Which is why it's important that we go out of our way to ask questions that reinforce what is actually important in life. That we don't just consider it insignificant small talk. The way Diana Ross asked Tracee Ellis Ross about her day is a great example.

But here's another. Instead of asking your kids if they behaved well or performed well or even if they had fun, be sure to check in with them *about whether they did something kind.* Ask them, every day: *What good turn did you do today? What was something you did for someone else? Who did you help?*

Think of the message this sends. Think of how it makes them think about their own day—to review their own actions through the lens of empathy, how their actions affect others. Think of the priorities it sets through your monitoring—that their parents are on top of not how many answers they got right but how many *right things* they did. Think about how much better the world would be if everyone thought this way, if everyone was raised this way.

May 14
Compete on This

Compete with yourself and root for everybody else.

—CANDICE MILLARD

We all find ourselves in competition with other parents. Maybe we see how our car compares with everyone else's at school drop-off, or we dress up really fancy for that school fundraiser, hoping to turn heads. Very quickly, that kind of competition can transfer to our kids: we want to make sure they have the same gadgets as their peers; we look at what colleges they can get into compared with their friends, and we start to push them to be valedictorian or captain of the baseball team or president of the student council.

This is not just a superficial competition but a stupid and possibly destructive one (as those Varsity Blues parents serving prison sentences should remind us), not just because it's one we'll inevitably lose—there will always be someone richer, someone hotter, someone whose kids are more naturally gifted—but because it can rub off on our kids in the worst way.

If you're going to compete with anyone, we should tell our kids, compete with yourself, to be the best version of yourself. Compete over things *you actually control.* And make no mistake, we should take that advice ourselves.

Compete with yourself to be more present, to be kinder, to have more fun with your kids . . . to beat what you got from your own parents. Focus on the stuff that's up to you, that can be an example for your kids as they grow into the people you want them to become.

May 15
Teach Them Empathy

One of the wonderful benefits of reading fiction, studies show, is that it helps cultivate empathy. By reading and experiencing the interior lives of the characters on the page, we are reminded that not everyone thinks and acts like we do. We are reminded that not everyone has been as lucky as we've been.

It also happens that fiction can teach us this empathy by way of specific advice and admonition. Perhaps you remember this opening line from *The Great Gatsby*:

> In my younger and more vulnerable years my father gave me some advice that I've been turning over in my mind ever since.
> "Whenever you feel like criticizing anyone," he told me, "just remember that all the people in this world haven't had the advantages that you've had."

We need our kids to understand this. That's why they have to read *Gatsby* and every other great novel. It's also something we have to explicitly remind them—the way Nick Carraway's father did in the book. Most important, it's something we have to model ourselves.

May 16
What We Do Ripples Through

> It is from numberless diverse acts of courage . . . that human history is thus shaped. Each time a man stands up for an ideal, or acts to improve the lot of others, or strikes out against injustice, he sends forth a tiny ripple of hope, and crossing each other from a million different centers of energy and daring those ripples build a current which can sweep down the mightiest walls of oppression and resistance.
>
> —ROBERT F. KENNEDY

In the beautiful children's book *Each Kindness*, Jacqueline Woodson tells the story of a young girl named Chloe who, in the casual way that kids often do, treats a classmate cruelly. She is moved to change one day when her teacher demonstrates the way that water ripples when a stone is dropped in it.

So it goes with kindness, the teacher explains. When we do something nice for someone, it ripples through their lives and into the world, radiating goodness outward. Chloe is inspired by this . . . but it's too late. The girl she was cruel to has moved away. Now when she throws a rock into the pond near her house, all she can think of are the lost opportunities she had to improve someone's life, to make their day brighter.

This is something we must teach our kids—moreover, we must *demonstrate* to our kids. By treating them well, by showing them compassion and empathy and unconditional love, we help not only them but everyone they encounter. We can take heart knowing that this kindness, big and small, will ripple through their lives long after they've moved out, they've grown up, and we're long gone.

May 17
Teach Them to Give It Their All

Rudyard Kipling's beautiful poem "If," which was written as advice for Kipling's son, is about toughness and virtue, honor and duty. But there is one line that doesn't get as much attention, maybe because it's a bit confusing:

> If you can fill the unforgiving minute
> With sixty seconds' worth of distance run

Kipling is talking about the importance of giving your all to something, physical or otherwise. There is an expression in sports about "playing through the whistle." In boxing and martial arts, you punch through the opponent until you hear the bell. In baseball, you swing through the ball. In running, they talk about running through the finish line. It's about completing the action. Giving 100 percent. *Playing the right way.*

This is an important lesson to teach our kids. We don't stop at the finish line. We give our all to something. We concentrate on a single task until it's done or until the clock runs out. We fill that unforgiving minute.

It's the proper way to play . . . and to live.

May 18
Teach Them to Do the Right Thing

Just that you do the right thing. The rest doesn't matter.

—MARCUS AURELIUS

In the beautiful and hilarious novel *A Man Called Ove*, a young Ove is working at the same rail yard as his father. He is cleaning a car with another worker, Tom, when they find a briefcase left by a passenger. Instinctively, Tom goes to steal it. Ove is surprised. A few seconds later, he finds and picks up a wallet left by a different passenger.

Just then, Ove's father walks in. He asks Ove what he wants to do with the wallet. Ove suggests that they return it to the lost and found, where it is quickly claimed by the woman who lost it. "Not many people have ever handed in this much money," the woman says. Well, Ove's father replies, "many people don't have any decency either." Later that evening, Ove asks his father why he didn't tell management about the briefcase that Tom had stolen. His father shakes his head and replies, "We're not the sort of people who tell tales about what others do."

In both instances, Ove's father is showing his boy what decency looks like. Decency is about what *you do*. It's not a standard you hold others to. Decency is what *you do* with money you find. It's how you raise *your* kids. It's not something you wield; it's not something you gossip about. It's something you embody and embrace.

May 19
Teach Them to Be Bigger

A ten-year-old Jim Lawson was walking down the street when, as he passed a car, a small child looked at him and called him the N-word. Stunned by the hate and the meanness of it, Lawson reached into the car and slapped the boy in the face.

When his mother found out about this, she was understandably worried. In the then-segregated and racist South, the actions of a young black boy could so easily lead to something terrible and tragic at the hands of awful and unaccountable adults. But more than that, she wanted her son not to be defined or changed by the hate of the world around him.

"What good did that do, Jimmy?" his mother asked him. "We all love you, Jimmy, and God loves you," she explained, "and we all believe in you and how good and intelligent you are. We have a good life and you are going to have a good life. With all that love, what harm does that stupid insult do? It's nothing, Jimmy, it's empty. Just ignorant words from an ignorant child who is gone from your life the moment it was said."

This was a life-changing exchange. It put Jim Lawson onto his world-changing path of nonviolence. (He would organize the first sit-ins in Nashville in the 1960s.) It helped him realize that he was above the horrible things that other people said and did, that what mattered was *what he said and did*. What mattered was responding with kindness and love. What mattered was knowing that he was good and that he was loved and nothing anyone else thought could change that.

Lawson's parents gave him the gift of teaching him that he was bigger than the small people who lived around him. That *he* could be the bigger person and *do* bigger things. Now, here today, can you do the same for your children?

May 20
Don't Just Assume It Will Work Out

In *Meditations*, Marcus Aurelius takes a moment to remind himself of the "malice, cunning and hypocrisy that power produces," and the "peculiar ruthlessness often shown by people from 'good families.'"

Even though you're well educated, and you've done well for your family, and you're not some monster, there are no guarantees that you will pass these laudable traits down to your kids. Life is full of temptations. Bad habits and bad influences are easy to fall prey to. Look at Marcus Aurelius's own children. Marcus and his wife were calm and wise . . . and still, something went wrong with his son and heir Commodus, who was deranged and a terror for the empire—exactly as bad as Commodus in the movie *Gladiator*. Or worse.

The point of this is: just because you're successful, just because you can pay to send your kids to the right schools, just because you showed up more than your own parents, doesn't mean you're out of the woods. This is a hard job we've committed to. The stakes are high. The margin for error is low. Kids don't just "turn out" as good people. They are *made* that way—molded, guided by ancestors, taught by example, and buoyed by a constancy of parental presence.

You must provide all of this. You cannot slack. You cannot assume it will handle itself. They need you.

May 21
"And What Did You Do?"

In the 1920s, long before he was a poet, before he was a conscientious objector, before he had kids of his own, William Stafford was just a kid living in an era when bullying and racism and all sorts of cruelty existed out in the open.

One day, young William came home and reported to his parents that two young black kids were being taunted at school. His parents had one question for him: "And what did you do, Billy?"

Notice that the elder Staffords didn't dismiss what was happening as *not their kid*. Nor did they rush to the phone to call his teachers. They did not yell. They did not make assumptions. They used the incident as an opportunity to emphasize a core life teaching: We are responsible for each other. We cannot sit on the sidelines while bad things happen in front of us.

One can imagine they were hoping to hear an answer that revealed their son had absorbed the lessons they'd been trying to teach in their home his whole life. Like any good parent, their question was a test to see if he understood how virtue and duty and kindness and human decency must be practiced to be perfected. And one can only imagine how they felt when they heard his reply . . .

"I went and stood by them."

May 22
Teach Them These Three Duties

Life is vexing, especially when you're little. As children, we constantly find ourselves in situations for which we have no experience, for which we have not been prepared, for which there does not seem to be a clear or obvious answer. Some of these are big situations, like being bullied or breaking an arm; some are small, like being nervous to go to your first sleepover or being jealous of something you wanted that your best friend got instead. Sometimes it's a blessing; sometimes it's the curse of misfortune.

How are they supposed to respond? Well, it's your job to show them. Because as disparate and vexing and unique as every moment of life can be, each of us has a set of duties that we can find guidance from in any and all situations.

You can teach your kids that whatever they're facing, they can respond with:

- hard work
- honesty
- helping others as best they can

It's not always going to lead to success, of course, but it will always lead to something they can be proud of. It will always serve them well. Whether it's a sudden reversal or a sudden bounty, whether they're at fault or an innocent bystander, what life demands—what we as their parents expect of them—is work, honesty, and compassion.

May 23
It's Better to Be Kind Than Clever

There is a story about Jeff Bezos, the founder of Amazon, from when he was a young boy. He was with his grandparents, both of whom were smokers. Bezos had recently heard an antismoking PSA on the radio that explained how many minutes each cigarette takes off a person's life span. And so, sitting there in the back seat, like a typical precocious kid, he put his math skills to work with this new knowledge and proudly explained to his grandmother as she puffed away, "You've lost nine years of your life, Grandma!"

The typical response to this kind of innocent cheekiness is to pat the child on the head and tell them how smart they are. Bezos's grandmother didn't do that. Instead, she quite understandably burst into tears. It was after this exchange that Bezos's grandfather took his grandson aside and taught him a lesson that he says has stuck with him for the rest of his life. "Jeff," his grandfather said, "one day you'll understand that it's harder to be kind than clever."

Cleverness comes easily when you want attention. It takes work to be a nice person and patience to reap its rewards. It requires extra effort to stop and think about how what you say and do affects other people. But a truly successful person—a truly great kid—is the result of parents who take the time to equip them with this skill. Parents who reward them for their kindness and compassion, not just their intelligence or their grades or their clever tongue. Because these self-obsessed traits, if not balanced with empathy and with kindness, can become a wicked and lonely combination.

May 24
Remember This About Most People

> No intelligent man believes that anybody ever willingly errs
> or willingly does base or evil deeds.
>
> —SOCRATES

There are a lot of selfish people out there. Cruel people. Stupid people. Even evil people. Sometimes they're all one person. Your kids are going to meet some of these people. Are they ready? Perhaps a better question is, are you ready? To protect them from the worst of that sort, of course, but also to make sure that your cynicism about the world—about *people*—does not affect your children too early.

There's a great children's book called *Most People* that reminds us: Most people are good. Most people are trying as hard as they can. Most people will help you if they can. Most people want the same things, the book says. Most people are happy . . . and even the people who aren't, its author reminds us, would rather be happy if they could.

With our life experience, we might struggle to believe that is true. Regardless, we can't pass on the psychic burden of our own experiences and frustrations with the people from our past. This is the difficult tension we have to resolve as parents. We have to prepare our children for a world that is not all sunshine and kittens. We also have to get them to understand that the darkness in the world is not complete. In fact, it's distinctly the minority.

We want our kids to carry the fire, to keep the brightness alive. We want them to seek it out in other people. And we want them to be like most people: Good. Kind. Happy. Helpful.

It's we who will chart that path.

May 25
Are You Teaching Them Values?

> Any system of education which does not inculcate moral values simply furnishes the intellectual equipment whereby men and women can better satisfy their pride, greed and lust.
>
> —HYMAN RICKOVER

It's true, we want them to go to great schools. We want them to learn as much as possible. This is why we monitor their grades. This is why parents are concerned about changes in curriculum, why they save and invest in order to pay for college.

But are we really focused on the right things? This isn't just to make the tried-and-true point that education must give our kids actual job skills they can use out in the world. It's also to question whether our kids are being taught how to be good people—at home, in the classroom, and out in the world.

Plenty of children go to expensive private schools or make it to the Ivy League. Yet they end up being corrupt politicians or soulless businesspeople who devastate industries. Plenty of children learn how to succeed but are deprived of the skills and the decency necessary to manage this success ethically and responsibly.

The purpose of education is not to make your kids more selfish, more greedy, more convinced of their own ideas or superiority. No, it's to make them better citizens, better human beings, and hopefully, someday, better parents themselves.

May 26
Epithets for Your Kid

One of the most interesting passages in Marcus Aurelius's *Meditations* is this one:

> Epithets for yourself: Upright. Modest. Straightforward. Sane. Cooperative. Try not to exchange for others.

These were essentially the words Marcus wanted to live by—his principles expressed in the fewest syllables possible. What if, as a parent, you sat down—ideally with your coparent—and fleshed out what those words mean for each of your children too? As in, what kind of kid are you trying to raise? What are the watchwords that you are attempting to move them toward with the choices you make as parents?

Some obvious ones: *Kind. Loyal. Moral. Honest.*

And maybe some more specific ones to help them succeed in the world: *Creative. Bilingual. Hardworking. Lifelong learner.*

Maybe to some parents it's important for their kids to be athletic. For others, that they be readers. For others still, that their kids live a life of service. There is a lot of room here for choice and, thankfully, most of the answers you come up with will be right. The important thing is not so much which epithets you choose but that you have chosen at all.

For, if you don't know what you're aiming for, how can you expect to hit a target? How do you know you're not accidentally teaching them to exchange one epithet for another? The truth is you can't. So get writing.

May 27
The Main Thing We Have to Teach Them

M ichael Schur's fun book of moral philosophy, *How to Be Perfect*, ends with a meditation on what is one of the toughest jobs for even the wisest and best of us: how to pass the important lessons of life on to our kids. This passage captures perfectly what those lessons are:

> You are people on earth. You are not alone here, and that means you owe the other people on earth certain things. What you owe them, more or less, is to live by rules they wouldn't reject as unfair (assuming they're decent, reasonable people).

He has a great little exercise for his kids to remember too. As you go through life and are thinking about doing something, he says, ask if your brother or sister would think it was a good idea. Then keep going, and ask if a friend would think it was a good idea, or a teacher, even a kid you don't like but think is smart. Explaining Kant's categorical imperative to a five-year-old, ask, "Would it be okay if everyone did this? What would the world be like if every single person were allowed to do whatever I'm about to do?"

The way to raise decent and kind human beings is to teach them how their actions affect other people, what their obligations to other people are. You don't have to be a philosopher to pull that off . . . just a good and decent person yourself.

May 28
It's Usually Not an Accident

Florence Nightingale was an incredible woman. She revolutionized nursing. She saved thousands of lives. This came as a surprise to the high society of Victorian England, because women weren't supposed to do career type things, let alone something as hands-on as work in a hospital.

But anyone who looked at Florence's family tree should not have been surprised. She wasn't just some saint who came from nowhere. Her great-grandfather was a philanthropist who supported the American Revolution, even donating large chunks of his holdings in Savannah to the cause. His son—Florence's grandfather—was a member of the British House of Commons and a leading abolitionist in the UK. The fact that his daughter, Fanny (Florence's mother), didn't seem to care much about the less fortunate was the exception, not the rule, in their family.

It wasn't an accident that Florence Nightingale was inclined to charity and selflessness. She learned it in the fashion that all great traditions are created—from the choices made by family. She was inspired by her ancestors.

We can't choose the family tree from which we spring. But as parents we can choose *who* in our family tree we look to for guidance. We can, like Florence Nightingale, pick which family members to be inspired by, whose example to follow. As parents, we can choose which branches of the family to tell our kids about, which stories we want to highlight and which lessons we want to fill their heads with.

Raising great, selfless, courageous kids is not an accident. They aren't *sui generis* or *ex nihilo*. They come from a tradition. They come *from us*.

May 29
Always Think About How Other People Are Doing

Perhaps you're familiar with the scene in the Bible where Moses—aided by God—parts the Red Sea. It was a miracle of epic proportions that allowed the Israelites to race through and escape the Egyptians who were chasing them. Less known about the miracle is what happened next. When Moses released the sea, the Egyptians were trapped. The water crashed around them and thousands perished.

Naturally, the Israelites broke out in song and celebration. As the angels went to join them, God rebuked them, according to the Talmud. "How dare you sing for joy," it was written, "when My creatures are dying."

Whether any of these events actually occurred is beside the point—it doesn't change the lesson. It is easy in the midst of victory and success to think of how wonderful this is for you. It's also easy to forget whom you defeated and what your victory has cost them. It's not unlikely that they've lost more than you've gained.

We must be careful to be good sports in this life, to be empathetic and caring enough to realize that things are not always as great for other people as they are for us. "Rejoice not when thine enemy falleth, and let not thine heart be glad when he stumbleth," the Bible says in Proverbs 24:17.

It's these kinds of ancient and timeless lessons that we must pass along to our children. You can still enjoy what you have, and you should still want to win in life. But don't be so clueless as to think that other people are not suffering; don't be so self-absorbed as to not care. And don't raise children who are indifferent to either.

May 30
You Make Debts Your Children Must Pay

Nobody wrote more beautifully about the history of conquest and adventure than Theodore Roosevelt. Nobody wrote more poetically about war and glory and empire than Rudyard Kipling.

In the end, though, these things left them grieving the sons they loved so much. Roosevelt lost his son Quentin, shot down over France. Kipling lost his son Jack in the trenches in 1915, so destroyed by "shot and shell" that they never identified the body. Roosevelt was broken by the loss of his eldest boy and followed him soon to the grave. Kipling, who had written "If" to his son when he was just twelve years old, would write one of his last poems in grief:

> "Have you news of my boy Jack?"
> *Not this tide.*
> "When d'you think that he'll come back?"
> *Not with this wind blowing, and this tide.*

These were tragic, devastating events that no parent should ever have to experience. But it's also indisputable that these two great men were not blameless in their occurrence—not only because of the pressure and impossible expectations they put on their children but because they were part of a generation that had encouraged, celebrated, and glibly supported the policies that led to the carnage that claimed their sons.

It's a cautionary tale for *all* parents. Our generation, just like all past generations, makes decisions in the present that have consequences borne primarily by future generations. Our children and grandchildren will live in the world created by your choices . . . and you yourself may live long enough for it to break your heart.

May 31
A Theory About Life

In the 1930s, languishing in college and struggling to live up to the expectations of his illustrious family, a young Walker Percy wrote a letter to his uncle and adopted father, Will Percy. He probably expected to receive a lecture about his grades in reply. Or to be admonished for letting the family down. Or perhaps to be sent money for a tutor.

But the reply surprised him. Because there wasn't any of that. Instead, Will waved off those concerns, telling Walker:

> My whole theory about life is that glory and accomplishment are of far less importance than the creation of character and the individual good life.

Isn't that wonderful? Isn't that exactly what every stressed, self-critical, confused kid needs to hear about life? *Who you are is more important than what you do. I'd rather you be good than successful. Character is more important than cash.*

It can be easy to lose sight of this. We all know how competitive the world is, and we see the potential our kids have. We don't want them to make the same mistakes we did. But ultimately, those things will take care of themselves if we raise them right.

The ancients knew that character was fate, and we need to remember that with our own kids. The good life, a life lived well, full of doing good, will be a successful life—and a more important one too.

JUNE

DON'T NEGLECT YOURSELF

(LESSONS IN SELF-CARE)

June 1
It's Okay to Ask for Help

> Don't be ashamed to need help. Like a soldier storming a wall, you have a mission to accomplish. And if you've been wounded and you need a comrade to pull you up? So what?
>
> —MARCUS AURELIUS

If your kid was struggling, you'd want them to tell you, right? If they didn't understand something in class, you'd want them to ask the teacher. If your neighbor needed something, you wouldn't mind if they mentioned it. If your spouse was overwhelmed and needed a hand, you'd expect them to come to you.

Okay. But what about you? *Are you okay?* More important, are you asking for help where you need it when you are not okay?

Remember, we have to model the behavior we want our kids to learn. So if you refuse to ask for directions when you're obviously lost, what does that tell them? If you refuse to admit you don't know something, and you make up an answer to a question instead of looking it up with them, what does that show them about learning and problem-solving? Why would they be okay being vulnerable with a doctor or a therapist, with Mom and Dad, if they have been regularly shown that this is something to be ashamed of?

But this is about more than even that. *You can't be a good parent if you're hurting and not getting help. You can't be a good parent all by yourself.* None of us are islands or invincible or omniscient. To do our best, we have to be able to learn, to rely on others, to admit mistakes, to ask for help. Show them that it's okay to ask for help. Be better, for them, by asking for the help you know that you need.

June 2
The Most Important Decision You Make

The most important decision you make is to be in a good mood.

—VOLTAIRE

When you're in a bad mood, you know what your kids are thinking? *They think it has something to do with them.* They don't understand all the responsibility you're shouldering. They don't know about the co-worker whose stupidity you had to put up with all day or your boss's short temper and unrealistic expectations. They can't see the stress all this stuff puts you under. These are all complex emotional issues that are hard for a young kid to understand, especially when the issues are outside their own lived experience.

Our moods and choices and the examples we set are affecting our kids always, changing how they see the world and how they see themselves. How we are managing all this stuff makes them feel better or worse, worthwhile or worthless, safe or vulnerable. And in the process, we are creating a pattern for them that becomes hard not to follow—for better or for worse.

Your kids are either suffering or benefiting from your moods and emotions. Behave accordingly.

June 3
Transcend This Bitter Math

When you get married, you give away fifty percent of your life," the novelist Susan Straight was warned by her mother. "What about the other half?" a young Susan asked hopefully. "When you have a baby, you give away the other half," her mother replied matter-of-factly.

Yikes.

Yes, marriage and relationships are hard. And in the past, they have been particularly and oppressively cruel to women. For all time, having kids has forced parents to make changes. They deprive us of sleep and money and freedoms we used to take for granted. But does that mean we have to lose ourselves, lose all our freedoms? Absolutely not.

We can transcend the bitter math. By working on ourselves and our relationships. By asking for help. By refusing to give up on dreams, even as we get older. By focusing on all the things that marriage and kids *give* us too, all the experiences we've gained and the opportunities created.

To quit on ourselves is to quit on our kids—it's teaching them a terrible lesson.

June 4
Protect Your Wealth

The greatest of follies is to sacrifice health for any other kind
of happiness.

—ARTHUR SCHOPENHAUER

Of course, our job is to provide for our kids. To work hard. To spend
wisely. To save judiciously. To put away some money, if not for their
future, then to have the financial wherewithal to make sure their needs are
met and our family is protected in case of emergency. But all that work on
our financial health will take us only so far if we don't pay similar attention
to our mental health.

Wealth comes in forms other than money. Charlamagne tha God, a
bestselling author and host of the radio show *The Breakfast Club*, has
helped popularize the concept of *mental wealth*. Meaning: your sanity,
your well-being, your happiness. It's really hard to be a good parent, to
truly *provide*, when you're stretched way too thin, when you're depressed,
when you haven't cultivated the friendships and resources critical to main-
taining good mental health.

Just as you seek to protect your financial wealth, make sure you are
protecting your mental wealth. Don't feel bad spending money on a therapist. Or a book. Or even deciding to pass on that overtime opportunity
because you're just too tired. Your sanity, your clarity, your well-being—
these things are essential. It's not selfish to take care of them. It's selfless.
Because your job is to be the best parent you can be. And that is going to
require a full store of mental wealth.

June 5
You Have to Take Care of Yourself Too

When I first began to write , , , I needed to use the time before they said, Mama—and that was always around five in the morning.

—TONI MORRISON

One thing far too many parents have in common is that they are always putting off taking care of themselves. *I'll start going to the gym once they're out of this sleep regression. I'll start eating better once they're less picky about food. My wife and I will get our relationship back on track once the kids move out.*

This may come from a good place, but the results are good for no one. *You have to take care of yourself.* Now! You think your terrible eating habits aren't contributing to your temper? Of course you're grouchy—you feel like a disgusting piece of crap! You think you're doing your kids a favor by shortening your life span? You think you're modeling what a good person looks like when you're struggling to get up the stairs or pick up a bag of groceries? You think you're making them feel safe and loved by letting your relationship bleed out on the dining room table?

You have to take care of yourself. For them. For you. Because you'll be a better parent if you're healthy, happy, and wise. Don't put this off. It's not selfish. It's essential.

June 6
It Takes a Team

It's impossible to do this all, isn't it? We have all the tasks, responsibilities, and aspirations we've always had—eating and sleeping and working and paying our taxes and taking out the trash and following our dreams—but now we have little people to care for on top of all that. Little helpless people with infinite needs. How can we do it all?

Ursula Le Guin was a full-time writer. She was prolific, publishing twenty-three novels, thirteen children's books, twelve volumes of short stories, eleven volumes of poetry, five essay collections, and four works of translation. Additionally, she worked as an editor and taught college undergraduate classes.

Oh . . . she was also the mother of three and the wife of a history professor, Charles Le Guin.

How did she do it all? How did he do it all? They didn't.

"One person cannot do two full-time jobs," Le Guin once explained. "Writing is a full-time job and so is children. But two people can do three full-time jobs. . . . That's why I'm so strong on partnership. It can be a great thing."

Parenting is so hard to do alone; so hard. For too long, too many mothers had to do it alone, were forced to sacrificed alone. But, of course, we are stronger when we, our children's parents, parent together. We go farther, together. It's one of the only ways to make the math work—not just for the benefit of the children, but for the parents as well.

DON'T NEGLECT YOURSELF

June 7
You Need to Take This Time

Certainly, someone always needed him for something. His wife, one of his thirteen kids, a courtier, the pressing business of state. But for a few minutes to an hour every day—sometimes in the morning, sometimes in the evening—Marcus Aurelius was unreachable. The twentieth-century American philosopher Brand Blanshard marvels at what Marcus accomplished there in the "midnight dimness," alone with his journal and his thoughts. It didn't matter where he was or what was happening; Marcus stole the time to sit and think and write.

Do you do that? Do you take this time?

James Clear, author of the wonderful bestseller *Atomic Habits*, said that since becoming a father, he has carved out "two sacred hours" in the morning to do his writing. Sometimes he gets more, but never less. Those two hours determine whether he has a good day or a wasted day, whether he is productive and making progress . . . or slacking.

A few minutes or a few hours—in the morning, at night, or in the middle of the day—this idea of sacred time is important. You have to carve it out. You have to stick to the schedule like clockwork, protect it as you would a doctor's appointment or a big meeting. Of course, this isn't the only time you'll need. It's just the minimum. So make sure you give it to—or take it for—yourself.

You'll marvel at what you can accomplish in those few sacred minutes that you've kept all to yourself.

June 8
This Is When You Are Happiest

Before his tragic death, Anthony Bourdain gave an interview where he explained that he was "never happier than when I'm standing in the backyard being, like, TV dad." His life had been so exotic and glamorous before fatherhood, filled with travel and fame and money and, of course, delicious food. It had also been filled with struggle—addiction, depression, loss. But there was something so normal, he said, about just having a normal family, standing in the backyard, wearing an apron, flipping burgers. "When I find myself doing that," he said, "I am, like, ridiculously stupid happy."

It would not be long before Bourdain was found very far from that idyllic backyard, on another trip to film another show. That depression, that addiction, they came with him and ultimately took him very finally away from the thing he loved the most—his family. It's a sobering reminder to all of us. First, to enjoy the present while we have it. Second, to remember how little we actually need in order to be happy, how wonderful the ordinary moments can be. Third, to understand how quickly it can all be taken away.

If you're struggling with addiction, if you're in that dark hole of depression, please just know that as difficult as it is to fight, to break free and climb out, the simple joys and tenderness and compassion you will find in victory with those you love will come with equal ease and ridiculously stupid happiness.

June 9
They Need Structure (and So Do You)

> If a person puts even one measure of effort into following
> ritual and the standards of righteousness, he will get back
> twice as much.
>
> —XUNZI

If you talk to a sleep expert about sleep training your infant, they'll tell you: kids need structure and routine. If you talk to an educational expert about helping your kid do better in school, they'll tell you: structure and routine. If you talk to a behavioral expert about helping your kid behave, they'll tell you: structure and routine. Hell, if you talk to a dog trainer, they'll tell you the same thing about your pet: structure and routine (and exercise).

Pretty much whatever the problem or whatever the issue, structure and routine are the solution. Which makes sense. The world is scary. So much of it is new and overwhelming. But if you give them structure and routine, they can relax because they have less to figure out, less to worry about. Instead, they can explore. They can get comfortable and accept things. They can feel safe.

But what about you? What about Mom and Dad? Do *you* maintain structure and routine for yourself? You put them to bed at the same time each night, but do you wing it after that? You plan their dinners in advance . . . but what about your lunch at work? You give them quiet play-time in the afternoon and downtime on the weekends. But do you create that kind of regular time for yourself? Structure and routine are essential no matter who or how old you are. They're important for kids and they're important for parents.

And guess what—when you keep a routine for yourself . . . it's easier to keep them on one.

June 10
You Are Capable of Change

Ted Williams was a great baseball player, but for a long time, he was a really selfish and ruthless person. He had a horrible, abusive childhood and struggled to find the ability to love or care about anyone.

But Williams's story has enough hope in it to inspire even the most hard-boiled and reluctant of fathers. Because, over time, Ted Williams started to change. As a friend would say about him:

> What's incredible as an observer was to watch him fall in love with his kids. . . . It was everything against his grain to succumb to this outside influence of children. Love had control over him. He felt vulnerable. A vulnerability he had never had in his life.

This softness started to show itself in little hints, in the oddest and yet most personal of places. It was entries in Williams's fishing journal, where for the first time he began to write about the kids he had long ignored. It was the signed poster his daughter found under piles of memorabilia after her father's death that just said, "To my beautiful daughter. I love you. Dad."

You have that kind of vulnerability now. Those same powerful forces are gnawing at you too, hopefully, and making progress on that tough exoskeleton you developed to protect yourself from the world. You can let this parenthood thing change you. You can let this make you better. You can even begin—no matter how far you are down the road, as Williams was—to make up for mistakes you might have made early in your parenting days. It's never too late.

June 11
Make Sure You Make Time for Crazy

Douglas MacArthur was a man of routine—most military men are. So it shouldn't surprise us that, when his son, Arthur, was born, he built a family life around routine. But unlike far too many parents who make routine a form of control, MacArthur's morning routine began with a moment of joy. As William Manchester details in his book *American Caesar*, it was a kind of scheduled crazy fun:

> At about 7:30 A.M. the door of the General's bedroom would open and the boy would trudge in clutching his favorite toy. . . . Mac-Arthur would instantly bound out of bed and snap to attention. Then the General marched around the room in quickstep while his son counted cadence: "Boom! Boom! Boomity boom!" After they had passed the bed several times, the child would cover his eyes with his hands while MacArthur produced the day's present: a piece of candy, perhaps, or a crayon, or a coloring book. The ritual would end in the bathroom, where MacArthur would shave while Arthur watched and both sang duets.

No one is too important or too busy to have some crazy time at home. No one is above getting pummeled by their kid in bed. No father should hesitate before singing at the top of his lungs while he shaves. These moments are the best moments. If they're rare, you're doing it wrong.

They should be regular, they should be routine.

June 12
We Are All Complicated

Naturally, we want to be perfect for our kids, in no small part because for the first several years of their lives, to them we can do no wrong, and we want to prove them right. But since we know we're not perfect, inevitably we feel guilty or inadequate when we let them down—even if they're unaware of it at the time. This feeling of insufficiency can be so powerful that we are prone to hiding it or lying about it or, worse, acting like hypocrites.

You might think it was devastating for the comedian Pete Davidson, who lost his father on September 11, to learn that his father was far from perfect. His parents' marriage had not been great (which is why they were separated and divorced not long before that tragic day). His father had done drugs and gotten into trouble more than once in his adult life. As Pete grew older and discovered more and more about his heroic father, who died saving people in the collapse of the Twin Towers, he wasn't disappointed, he was heartened.

These failings and foibles humanized his father in a way that the stories his friends and family told the then seven-year-old Pete about his dad never could. "It made me realize that he had his own issues," Pete explained to Judd Apatow in *Sicker in the Head*. "He had problems just like everybody else. But it also made me realize that even with all that, his morals were still intact, and none of that prevented him from being a hero."

No one is perfect, least of all you. We are all complicated. We are all works in progress (emphasis, though, on *progress*). You don't need to hide it. You don't need to feel guilty. It won't prevent you from being great at this most important job . . . nor from being a hero if the moment calls for it.

June 13
Try Not to Give Them Anything Extra

We all have issues. We know that. Our goal as parents is to not pass them on. To stop the cycle of dysfunction. To not let the demons we wrestle with find softer targets in our children.

But even more than that, we can't let our demons invite new ones to the party. As best we can, we must not inflict more damage or create more issues. This Philip Larkin poem expresses this tendency so perfectly:

> They fuck you up, your mum and dad.
> They may not mean to, but they do.

Worse, he says, is that they give us not just their own faults but some extra ones too.

The Buddhists speak of *samsara*, the way that suffering transfers from generation to generation. Why is that? Why is it that suffering rarely ever fully discharges from a generation, leaving the next one free to flourish unhindered? It's because we don't do the work. It's because sometimes we are not even aware of our own suffering. And when we are, and we still don't do the work, it's often because we tell ourselves we're helpless.

Look, we are going to screw up. It's inevitable. We are imperfect people. It's impossible that we'll raise perfect kids. Still, that doesn't mean we're helpless against the demons knocking at our door. We can work on ourselves. We can go to therapy so maybe they won't have to. We can try to be healthy so they'll grow up thinking that's normal. We can try to move on from our own anger and frustration and pain so that, at the very least, they do not inherit our burdens.

June 14
Keep Your Head Up and Take Another Swing

And now that you don't have to be perfect, you can be good.

—JOHN STEINBECK

No person has a perfect track record. Certainly no parent does. We all mess up. We all fall short. We make mistakes. We lose our temper and our patience. We handle certain situations in ways we wish we hadn't.

Is there anything worse than that feeling? Knowing that you screwed up? That you might have hurt them?

Shane Parrish, creator of the wildly popular *Farnam Street* blog, explained:

> I remember calling my late mom one night, exhausted and feeling overwhelmed. I had lost my cool on the kids. She gave me a piece of advice that stuck with me, "If you don't learn to let go of your mistakes today, they'll compound tomorrow. Get some sleep and start again tomorrow." I still remember that when I have bad parenting days. Tomorrow I've got to get up and start all over.

You can't go back and undo what you did yesterday. You can't erase from their memories that time you lost your cool or that time you said those regrettable things. But what you can do is make this just one memory among many greater, more positive ones. What you can do is show them that this one moment isn't who you are. You can strive to get better.

Keep your head up. Step up. Try again tomorrow.

DON'T NEGLECT YOURSELF

June 15
This Is the Secret

When you look at successful people with kids, it can be easy to marvel at all they've accomplished: How do they do it? How do they get it all done?

Fortunately, there is an answer, and it's definitely not magic: They have help. They have nannies and tutors and house managers. They have chiefs of staff. They have personal assistants. They have personal trainers. That's how they get it all done. If you could afford it, you'd be just as efficient and seemingly carefree as them.

Now, the point of explaining this is not to make you jealous or to point out the inequities of our society. In fact, it's the opposite: it's to nudge you into following in their footsteps. Of course, hiring a full-time staff is beyond most of our capabilities, but surely there are things you are doing that you don't have to do, that you could afford to pay someone to do for you. And yet you continue to do them . . . Why? Because your dad changed the oil in his car? Because your mom always served home-cooked meals? Because you feel guilty outsourcing this or that?

C'mon. Forget the gender roles. Forget "the way things used to be." The way things used to be almost invariably involved parents spending *way less time with their kids than we do now.*

Take a minute today and calculate what an hour of your time is worth. Think about how much more present you could be for your kids if there were less on your plate. You don't have to outsource everything, hire help for everything, but you don't have to *do everything yourself either.*

Get help.

June 16
Do as You Say

I t was on an ordinary day that Jimmy Carter's father pulled his son aside for a conversation. "Jimmy," he said (and he never called his son Jimmy), "I need to talk to you about something important." "Yes, sir, Daddy," Jimmy replied. "There is something I want you to promise me," his father continued. "I don't want you to smoke a cigarette until you are twenty-one years old."

This was the late 1930s, when something like 40 percent of the population smoked and cigarettes could still be marketed to children with advertisements that made claims like "More doctors smoke Camels than any other cigarette!" Carter's dad himself was hopelessly hooked too. "I won't," Jimmy promised. And then his father sweetened the deal: "When the time comes, I'll give you a gold watch."

When he was twenty-one years old, then in the Naval Academy, young Jimmy Carter finally tried smoking. By then, it was too late. He'd missed his window and he hated it. He never smoked another. Tragically, Carter's mother and three of his siblings followed in his father's footsteps. Each one of them died of pancreatic cancer. Carter, as of this writing, is still alive at age ninety-eight.

When it comes to the important things with lifelong implications, you have to make them promise, as Carter's father did. But you also have to learn from his failure and lead by example. The costs of not doing it could be everything.

June 17
Find Your People

Keep company only with people who uplift you, whose presence calls forth your best.

—EPICTETUS

Michael Chabon was worried about his son, as all fathers worry. His son seemed lonely, seemed uninterested in the things his peers liked. Then one day, they found themselves at some type of fashion industry event as part of Chabon's work. And his son was fascinated.

These creative and artistic people were so unlike the parents of his friends or the kids at his school. He came alive with a kind of infectious excitement that was reciprocated kindly by the other attendees. After the event, Chabon looked at his son, who seemed suddenly possessed of a confidence and purpose he didn't have before. "You were with your people," Chabon said to him. "You found them." His son nodded. With both pride and understanding, all Chabon could say was, "That's good. You're early."

We need to help our kids find "their people," but nothing would benefit us more than doing the same. The ancient proverb is: "If you dwell with a lame man, you will learn how to limp." We become like the people we spend the most time with. The random people you went to school with or met through work or your kid's friend's parents? Don't settle!

Find *your* people. Lean on their support. Let them make you better.

June 18
All That Matters Is This

Flea, one of the greatest musicians of all time, was a longtime dabbler in drugs and alcohol. Unlike his Red Hot Chili Peppers bandmates, Flea never got fully strung out. Drugs never blew up his life or turned him into a zombie. He knew it wasn't healthy, but he told himself he was managing the habit successfully—never taking drugs around his kids or blowing opportunities because of them. So why did he suddenly get sober?

He explained it in an interview with the comedian and podcaster Marc Maron:

> I remember having a talk with someone once . . . about being a dad, and my daughter was about four years old or something. And I would get high when I was away from her or whatever, and say, "Oh, I don't do it when I'm around her." And they said, like, "All that matters as a parent is to be present for your kid and be communicative. And you have to be communicating with them when you're not around them." You have to be—it's like being in a state where you're always there for them. Like your spirit is always available whenever they need you. And that really resonated with me. And I love my kids so much and I was just like, "That's it, I gotta be there."

Presence, *being there*, is the key to parenting. And what are drugs and addiction and unaddressed issues in our lives but *means of not being there*. Which is why we have to sober up and deal with our demons, because even if they don't feel like they are actively manifesting themselves at home, they are. They are taking us away from our kids. They are putting us in a position to not be there for them when they need us (and they *will* need us).

That kind of self-inflicted disconnection is unacceptable.

June 19
You Must Find the Stillness

All profound things, and emotions of things are preceded and attended by Silence. . . . Silence is the general consecration of the universe.

—HERMAN MELVILLE

This change we've made, this decision to become a parent—it has uprooted everything. It's like we were hit, suddenly, by a cross-fire hurricane. The house is a mess. The schedule is grueling. There is never enough sleep, never enough time in the day.

Even the cool, quiet dark is pierced by the shriek of a man who has stepped on a pile of LEGOs . . . and the shriek is coming from your mouth. Yet to be good at our jobs, to be good at this fatherhood thing, we must endeavor to find stillness. Because we need time to reflect, to focus, to find the calm that will restore and reboot us.

Where will we find it? It won't be in those measly two weeks of vacation or by cutting and running and fleeing. No, we must find the stillness *within* the chaos. It might not feel like these moments of quiet can exist with all the crying babies or arguing teenagers, but they can.

If we just look within. We can find stillness, if we take advantage of the early morning before the house is awake or those precious minutes after the kids are in bed. But we really have to drink those moments in to get the most from them. We can't defer these chances in favor of our phones or Netflix. We must take time with a journal. We must enjoy that cute but preposterously slow walk from school to the car or from the car back into the house. Soak up the quiet. Store these moments in your soul so you can have them always.

Find the stillness. So much depends on it.

June 20
Access the Child in You

The darkness of World War II raged around him. He was an old man with a million important concerns. He had power and success. He had seen it all. But in 1944, when Winston Churchill came across a young soldier at 10 Downing Street assembling a toy train for Churchill's grandson, he was transfixed.

As Erik Larson describes it in his fascinating book *The Splendid and the Vile*, the soldier stopped to salute the prime minister. Churchill waved it away and simply stood watching. After the soldier had finished, Churchill asked him to see if it worked, and together they watched the train go around the track. "I see you have two engines," he said. "Put the other one on the track as well." The soldier did as he was instructed, and then Churchill—leader of the British empire, the man who had stared down Hitler and pulled his country back from the brink—got down on his hands and knees with a grin and said, "Now, let's have a crash!"

One of the wonderful things about having kids (and grandkids) is that they allow us to access that childlike part of ourselves that never fully goes away. They give us an excuse to get down on the floor and crash two trains together. To build something cool with LEGOs. To dress up for Halloween. To be silly at a tea party. To listen to the music of our youth, to watch the movies we loved.

It's more than a fun excuse—it's an important part of life. Don't forget to access that joy and fun . . . and maybe, you know, invite your kids to join you in it.

DON'T NEGLECT YOURSELF

June 21
It's Good That You Worry About This

> One great thing about having kids is that they force you into
> an active practice of love whether you are ready for it or not.
>
> —MICHAEL IAN BLACK

The question hits you in a soft place. It hits you when you least expect it . . . and yet it's there constantly. *Am I a good parent? Am I screwing this up?*

Your own parents will try to reassure you. "Every parent thinks this," they'll say. Except that's not true. There are, in fact, two types of parents who never think that. There are parents who are so convinced that they're the center of the universe that they never question themselves, never wonder what they're doing wrong. Then there are the parents who don't even care enough to ask. Although they are very different, in the end, these two types are the same: they're not good parents.

But you? The type who is always checking in and wondering, *Am I doing enough?* Who actually *cares* about whether you're doing a good job? You are—by definition—a good parent, because you are thinking about your kids first, not yourself. It's proof that you care, that you have self-awareness, that you're always trying to improve. That you would stop to evaluate your own performance, that it would bother you to give anything less than the full measure of your devotion, is all the evidence you need to reach a positive conclusion.

So if you feel that negative thought—that doubt—come up today, be reassured. It means you're putting them first. It means you're doing a good job.

June 22
Just Go to Bed

Sleep is the interest we have to pay on the capital which is called in at death. The higher the interest rate and the more regularly it is paid, the further the date of redemption is postponed.

—ARTHUR SCHOPENHAUER

You know your kids are a mess when they don't sleep. That's why you follow the bedtime ritual religiously. You know that kids get into trouble at night, if left to their own devices. That's why your teenager has a curfew that you enforce with an iron fist.

And yet here you are, up late again, mindlessly watching TV. Here you are, tired in the morning—again—because you were up late on your phone. You could have gone to bed, you knew you should have gone to bed, but you didn't.

Who suffers? Your kids do. Because you're grouchy. Because you don't have energy. Because you're behind. Because maybe they even sense that you're a hypocrite!

If you want to be a better parent, start going to bed earlier. Give yourself a bedtime that you honor and respect and enforce. Value sleep. Take care of yourself. Everyone will benefit.

June 23
This Has Made You Invincible

Parenting, like exercise, is a process of growth through pain, through struggle against resistance. It would be wonderful if raising kids were easy, if it demanded little of you, but that's just not how it works.

We've been sleep-deprived. We've worried. We've been bitten and kicked. We've been judged. We've been leaned on and then taken for granted, kept up late by infants and then by missed curfews. We've been blamed and bothered and bludgeoned by and for their wants and needs. It is a gauntlet in a crucible through a minefield with no trophy at the end. And yet here we are. By necessity we have become capable of things we never could have conceived of for ourselves before.

It was Leonardo da Vinci who said that patience was bitter but its fruit was sweet. This holds true for many of the virtues that parenting has demanded we embody. We've been patient, we've been resilient, we've been brave, we've been selfless, self-effacing, steadfast, and silent . . . none of which were particularly fun at the time.

But the result was that we grew stronger for it. Our families survived and thrived because of it. They are where they are right now because of how far we've come as parents. There is no trophy on the other side of the parenting minefield, but there is a happy, healthy, bonded family. And that prize is the sweetest of them all.

June 24
Just Pick Yourself Back Up

Maybe lately you haven't been as good a parent as you would like to be. You were on your phone too much. You let your short temper get the best of you. You prioritized work over family. You got too wrapped up in your expectations, you were too harsh, you refused to see things their way.

Well? That's all in the past. It happened. It shouldn't have, but it did. And there's nothing you can do now to undo it. The question is, now what? We have the power, at any moment, to get back on track. We can choose, always, to return to the standard we want to live up to as parents.

It's like with a diet. You can slip a little, then a little more, then the next thing you know, you've eaten a whole sleeve of Oreos. Okay. It happened. But tomorrow hasn't yet. You have a choice. Will you do better? Will you do what you know is right? Will you follow the plan you set out for yourself before the Oreo debacle?

No parent has time to indulge in pity parties. Nor can any parent justify a continued slide. We screw up. We fall short. We're not what we want to be—what we promised ourselves we'd be, what we owe to our kids. And? We can choose right now to get back on track. We can choose right now to do better.

June 25
You Would Tell Them This. So Tell Yourself Too.

But I couldn't speak my dream without a caveat. "I don't know," I said, "by the time I finish school I'll be fifty." He smiled at me. "You're going to be fifty anyhow," he said.

—DR. EDITH EGER

It's hard to imagine any situation that you would describe to your kid as hopeless. "Sorry, it's too late, you're a failure" is something no parent would ever say. If they were falling behind their peers in math, you'd tell them that it was just a matter of work and time. If they were trying to write themselves off as a baseball player, you'd tell them about how many athletes were late bloomers, that they are still *so* young, that next year they can come back stronger and better, that they can turn things around. Even if they had a cancer diagnosis with terrible odds, you'd be encouraging them to fight, to never give up, to prove the doubters wrong.

You wouldn't just be saying this. You'd *mean* it. Because it's true. Nothing is fixed in this life that you haven't fixed yourself. Nothing is permanent. Especially when the person, deep down, is good and decent and full of potential.

Okay. So why are you whispering the exact opposite of this to yourself? Telling yourself that you've just got to accept that your dreams are done. Telling yourself, *I used to be in good shape—but that's in the past.*

No! It's never too late. You still have so much time in front of you. So much ability, so much potential to fulfill. You decide the rest of the story. It's up to you. But this is the important part: the story you decide for yourself is also going to determine what kind of stories your kids believe. Your story is the compass and the map on the journey that will lead them to realism, optimism, skepticism, cynicism, or fatalism.

Which will it be?

June 26
You Have to Face Your Flaws

Each of us picked things up in childhood. We all have issues. We have baggage. We have flaws. The decision to have kids means we have to face those flaws. As Jessica Lahey, the wonderful author of *The Gift of Failure* (a great book for parents and teachers), said when asked about what she's learned being a mother:

> Having to face the flaws I thought I could keep secret and buried from the world because I wanted to be better for this new person . . . The flaws in me I've been so good at hiding through excelling academically or being charismatic start to poke through because it matters to someone other than me. For me, those flaws are defensiveness around my potential flaws (go figure), my tendency to disconnect and be distracted from whatever is happening right in front of me in favor of whatever is next, and notably, substance abuse. If I'd never had children, I probably could have kept that stuff buried, but parenthood demanded that I deal with it . . . in order to model a healthy, loving, productive humanity to my kids.

If you want to be a great parent, you're going to have to deal with your crap. You can't carry baggage—it's too dangerous with a kid around. You risk dropping it on them. There can be no more hiding, no more deferring. The bill is due and you have to pay it: in therapy, in conversations with your spouse, in the pages of your journal. You have to face your flaws. Because there are little people who did not choose to be stuck in the same house with you and should not have to be trapped with a monster or a brick wall for a parent.

June 27
Don't Get Sick

> If you want to find something mean on the internet, you're
> going to find it.
>
> —JUDD APATOW

There's a great term floating out there in the culture that describes what happens when we spend too much time on our phone. Whether it's an adult doomscrolling or a kid going down a YouTube unboxing rabbit hole, when you spend too much time staring at a device, you get *screensick*.

You know, that insane reaction your kids have when you suddenly turn off the TV. Their catatonic state when they're locked into some video game, when the walls could be falling down around them and they wouldn't even blink. The fantasy world your teenager comes to mistake for reality after too many hours on the computer in their room. And you? You know the symptoms: You're grouchy and hate humanity after seeing too much of its underbelly on social media. You can't pay attention to anything but your email. The phantom vibrations of the phone haunt you like a ghost.

The good news is it seems like a pretty easy illness to cure. A phone-free day can cure it. Going outside for a couple hours can refocus your mind and reset your spirit. The bad news is, the people who made your phone and everything that goes on it know there's an easy fix too. Which is why they've spent so much time and energy and money engineering ways to keep you connected to it, addicted to it, beholden to it. You have to fight that.

You can't let the technology use you; you always have to be the one using the technology. It's the only way to have a healthy relationship with your phone and to avoid the screensickness that infects us.

June 28
Delight in Attending to Your Improvement

It's a sad sight when you see a dad who has clearly stopped trying. He puts on weight. He checks out of his marriage. Maybe he starts drinking more. He resigns himself to the fact that he hates his job. He accepts whatever grades his kids bring home from school. He makes their behavior somebody else's problem.

We see that dad and we think, *I never want to be that guy.*

Good. Okay. But what steps are you taking to make sure you don't? In the start-up world, they say that if your company isn't growing, it's dying. In a way, it's sort of true for people too. If you're not actively developing yourself, what's happening? You're atrophying. You're getting worse. Entropy is winning.

Epictetus liked to quote Socrates, who said that he delighted in attending to his own improvement day to day. Brilliant. It's the perfect thing for you to think about. How are you improving yourself day to day? Are you working out? Are you reading? Are you setting goals for yourself? Are you clocking in at home as well as at the office?

Your kids will be better served by a parent who's getting better. More important, they will be inspired by your example. Show them that you're trying—that we can never stop trying—and they'll follow you in their own way.

June 29
It's Not Over for You

Susan Straight was helping her mother move when she found an old painting thrown in the trash can. Sensing that this wasn't something that her mother had bought, she asked her about it. "I took a painting class at the YMCA," Straight recalled her mother explaining. "Then I found a book—teach yourself to paint." Straight recalls: "My mother was an artist. She made beautiful sketches of our garden and our house in Switzerland."

Surprised and moved, they began to talk about the painting. Was this a secret hobby that Susan hadn't known about? Did her mother have a creative side she never shared? Were there other paintings? Sadly, no. "Just after I finished this," her mom stated matter-of-factly, "I had you, and then I never painted anything again. My life was over."

Ouch.

Yet there is a part of us that understands this sentiment, right? A part of us that felt, when our house was suddenly flooded with babies and diapers and our routines were disrupted by carpools and soccer practices, like life was over. Or at least the fun, free, *good* life. No more time for hobbies. No energy for self-exploration, let alone self-actualization.

Certainly, we have been taxed and burdened in a way we never expected. But we can't throw in the towel. We can't use being a parent as an excuse. On the contrary, because our kids are watching us, we have to keep pushing ourselves. We have to transcend the bitter math. We have to keep growing. We can't give up on ourselves or our interests.

Our lives are not over. Not even close. In a way they're just beginning. Beginning anew.

June 30
Here's How You Can Help Other Parents

There is the professional you and the parental you. It makes sense that we try to keep these things pretty distinct and separate. We even have a name for this distinction. We call it "boundaries" or "work-life balance." And it's good that we try to leave our work at the office when we head home.

But one way we can help other parents—or prospective parents—is by making sure that we don't leave our kids at home . . . figuratively, anyway. By talking about our kids, by putting pictures of them up on our walls, by being honest and up front about trying to balance our careers and family, we are all helping each other.

For too long, parents have had to struggle in silence. They've been overwhelmed or burned out. They've wrestled with priorities. They've worried, they've hurt, they've wondered *what the hell they were going to do*. They've done all this alone even as the person in the office next to them was going through the same hell, even as the boss was wondering the exact same thing about their kids.

We can all help each other if we end this charade. We can help the parents we work with by creating an environment that's open and safe, that allows us to stop pretending that we aren't all trying to work two jobs at the same time, and to work them well.

DON'T NEGLECT YOURSELF

JULY

HELP THEM BECOME WHO THEY ARE

(LESSONS IN NURTURING AND DISCOVERY)

July 1
Is It Nature or Nurture?

Plutarch tells the story of how Lycurgus reformed Spartan society from rebellious, rowdy, and soft to self-disciplined, temperate, and courageous. He bred two dogs from the same litter, then raised one in the home and one out in the hunting fields. When they were fully acclimated, Lycurgus brought both dogs to a public assembly. He set down the house dog's food then the hunting dog's. Before he released the dogs, he let loose a hare. The house dog went to his food. The hunting dog went after the hare.

"You see, fellow citizens," Lycurgus said, "these dogs belong to the same stock, but by virtue of the discipline to which they have been subjected, they have turned out utterly different from each other, and you also see that training is more effective than nature for good."

After his demonstration proved that nurture trumped nature, Lycurgus said, "So also in our case, fellow citizens, noble birth, so admired of the multitude, and our being descended from Heracles does not bestow any advantage, unless we do the sort of things for which he was manifestly the most glorious and most noble of all mankind, and unless we practice and learn what is good our whole life long."

And so it goes with your own family. If we want great kids, then we have to do the work. We have to nurture the traits we want them to have, correct the ones we don't.

July 2
Help Them Become Who They Are

> A lot of parents will do anything for their kids, except let
> them be themselves.
>
> —BANKSY

In his autobiography, Bruce Springsteen takes us back to when he was seven years old and he watched the controversial rock star Elvis Presley's appearance on *The Ed Sullivan Show*:

> I sat there transfixed in front of the television set, my mind on fire. I had the same two arms, two legs, two eyes; I looked hideous but I'd figure that part out. . . . So what was missing? THE GUITAR! The next day I convinced my mom to take me to Diehl's Music on South Street in Freehold. There, with no money to spend, we rented a guitar.

Our job as parents is not to mold our children into our successors or into superstars. It's to help them be what they are meant to become. We expose them to things, we let them find what interests them, and then we support those interests. We shouldn't pressure; we shouldn't criticize. We should believe in them, cheer for them, be proud of them . . . and be ready to catch them if they fall or fail on the path to becoming who they are meant to be.

July 3
You Have to Help Them Discover This

Almost every talented and successful person can remember their introduction to whatever it was that became *their thing*. In *Mastery*, Robert Greene explores countless examples of this beautiful process by which some of the world's most notable experts discovered their "life's task." He talks about Martha Graham's first time watching a dance performance, for example, and he tells the story of the compass that Albert Einstein's father gave him as a present when he was five years old:

> Instantly, the boy was transfixed by the needle, which changed direction as the compass moved about. The idea that there was some kind of magnetic force that operated on this needle, invisible to the eyes, touched him to the core.

At the core of most of these stories are a few key ingredients: Luck. Openness. Curiosity. And, of course, often a parent who actively exposed their kid to different things.

It's your child's job to figure out what they want to do in life. No parent can or should make their child master anything. But it is your job, especially when they're young, to open their eyes, to introduce serendipity into the equation, to expose them to all the possibilities that life has to offer.

Show them what's out there. Help them discover.

July 4
Don't Tie Down Your Eagle

When a young Florence Nightingale began making moves toward volunteering in hospitals, her aristocratic parents were horrified. It had been difficult enough raising a precocious child. Now she wanted to debase herself with work below her station? They were embarrassed. What would their friends think? How would it look? Like a lot of parents with determined, independent children, they felt rejected. They thought her choices rebuked theirs.

"We are ducks who have hatched a wild swan," her mother once lamented. But a biographer responded perfectly: "It was not a swan they had hatched: in the famous phrase of Lytton Strachey's essays—*it was an eagle.*"

You can't hold your children back. You can't resent that they're different. You can't hold them back with antiquated notions about gender or class. Their choices say nothing about your choices. They are their own people. They deserve their own lives. They deserve your support and encouragement in whatever direction that takes you or them.

That's what we're here for. We can't forget it.

July 5
Ask If They'd Like to Learn

A rthur Ashe became a brilliant tennis player and an ardent civil rights activist because of a question. He was seven years old and sitting in a park in Richmond, Virginia, watching an accomplished black tennis player named Ron Charity practice. Ashe's father was a park supervisor and often left his son to entertain himself while he worked. After about an hour, Ron Charity took a break and walked over to the boy. "Would you like to learn how to play?" he said kindly. With that simple, generous question, Ashe and the game of tennis were changed forever.

"As casually as that," Ashe reflected, "my life was transformed." How many lives have been changed in similar ways? Because an adult took the time to notice the interest of a child, had the patience to introduce them to something, was willing to teach them a skill or a trade?

Of course, we cannot rely solely on the kindness of strangers. It's our job as parents to take the time to do this for our kids. We have to cultivate that flicker of curiosity into full-blown love affairs, we have to channel their energy into productive pursuits. We have to teach them stuff.

Especially the things they're too afraid to ask about, or don't even know to ask about. Often, that is where the magic resides.

July 6
You Have to Do This. We Need It.

> I think that the major obligation of parents and educators is
> to give children an understanding of the divine beginning
> that exists within them.
>
> —WILLIAM ELLERY CHANNING

Cormac McCarthy talks about "carrying the fire" in his haunting novel *The Road*, which he wrote for his son. Alanis Morissette put her own spin on it in her beautiful song "Ablaze," which she wrote for her two children.

"To my girl, all your innocence and fire," she sings, "my mission is to keep the light in your eyes ablaze." And to her son, whom she calls a precious gentle warrior, with all his wild energy, she sings the same thing.

Our job is to keep our kids the way they were born, which as *The Road* was written to show us, means *fundamentally good*. Innocent. Pure.

We have to help them carry the fire. We have to keep that light in their eyes ablaze. No matter how dark the world gets. In fact, we have to do it now, more than ever, *because* the world is dark. That's our job. That's our warrant.

If we fail . . . God help us.

July 7
Your Kids Will Be Whatever You Make Them

The Holocaust survivor-turned-psychologist-and-author Dr. Edith Eger had a son who was born with athetoid cerebral palsy. One day, on a visit to the doctor's office, Dr. Eger expressed some of her fears and worries to the specialist. It was there that she got some advice that is worth sharing with *every* parent, whether your family ever has to face that kind of adversity or not.

"You son will be whatever you make of him," the doctor explained. "John's going to do everything everyone else does, but it's going to take him longer to get there. You can push him too hard, and that will backfire, but it will also be a mistake not to push him hard enough. You need to push him to the level of his potential."

Your kids will be whatever you make them. No one is saying that things won't be hard. No one is saying that any of this is fair—dyslexia or disabilities, being a refugee or losing your job, being a genius or being short. What matters is how we push them (and ourselves). What matters is the kindness and the love and the patience that accompany that pushing.

We can't do everything for them, but we can believe in them and help them believe in themselves. We can help them reach the level of their potential. We can make them be what they are capable of.

July 8
But Which Parts of Them Will You Nurture?

What the circumstances of your upbringing were make a significant difference in how well you do in the world.

—MALCOLM GLADWELL

Here's an interesting idea, perhaps not totally supported by science but true enough to jibe with experience: We contain within us, at birth or by an early age, all the virtues and vices we will have in our lives. All our strengths and weaknesses are there, more or less, from the beginning. The question for a father, then, and for educators and mentors, is: Which of those strengths and virtues will you nourish? Which vices will you allow to fester?

In her beautiful novel *Memoirs of Hadrian*, Marguerite Yourcenar has Hadrian pour his heart out to young Marcus Aurelius, his adopted grandson. He explains, "I was at 20 much what I am today, but not consistently so. Not everything in me was bad, but it could have been: the good or the better parts also lent strength to the worse."

We all have good traits and bad traits. What matters, then, what your job is as a parent, is to help your kids nurture their good parts and give them the strength to challenge their bad parts. We need to help them become who they *can* be. We need to help them be consistent—consistently the best version of themselves.

July 9
Don't Let Them Wish to Not Be Who They Are

One of the more vulnerable moments of Pete Buttigieg's pioneering campaign for president (as a front-running, openly gay man) came in South Carolina when he talked about how he struggled with his identity, with his sexuality:

> When I was younger, I would have done anything to not be gay. When I began to halfway realize what it meant that I felt the way I did about people . . . it launched in me something I can only describe as a kind of war. And if that war had been settled on the terms I would have wished for . . . I would not be standing here. If you had offered me a pill to make me straight, I would have swallowed it before you had time to give me a sip of water. It's a hard thing to think about now. It's hard to face the truth that there were times in my life when, if you had shown me exactly what it was inside me that made me gay, I would have cut it out with a knife.

No parent ever wants to hear that their kid would like to cut a part of themselves out, that their son or their daughter is at war with themselves. Of course, much of the shame and doubt that Pete felt had nothing to do with his parents and everything to do with the time and culture he was growing up in, but nevertheless.

It's your job to make sure your kids know that there isn't a part of them that you'd want them to change if they could. It's your job to show them that you love the *whole* them. Through your words, your actions, and your choices, you must teach and prove to them that they make the world better just by being in it and by being themselves.

July 10
Work with Them to Find Their Lane

As we bring up our children, we have to remember that we are caretakers of the future. By improving their education, we improve the future of mankind, the future of this world.

—IMMANUEL KANT

John Adams's father wanted nothing but for his son to go to college. John Adams wanted to do anything but go to school. He often skipped class to go fishing or hunting or to fly his kite. He didn't like his teachers. He didn't think he was learning anything useful. He had no interest in furthering his education.

So when he declared that he wanted to be a farmer, his father took him down to the salt marsh to cut thatch and wade through muck, showing him what that work would actually be like. The next day, John went back to school, though soon enough he was struggling again. "I don't like my schoolmaster," he told his father. "He is so negligent and cross that I can never learn anything under him." The next day, Adams's father enrolled him in the private school down the road. There, under a schoolmaster named Joseph Marsh, Adams made a dramatic turn. He was studying. He was reading. And in less than a year, the fifteen-year-old was pronounced "fitted for college." The following fall, he was enrolled at Harvard.

Our job as parents is to put our kids in environments in which they can thrive and blossom. Our job is to work with them to find their lane. That environment may not be the first school we drop them into. It might take several tries and a fair amount of experimentation. It will definitely take patience. That doesn't matter.

What matters is that we help them realize who they are meant to be.

HELP THEM BECOME WHO THEY ARE

July 11
Let Them Decide

If I had one wish for my children, it would be that each of you would dare to do the things . . . that have meaning for you as individuals . . . but not worrying if you don't please everyone.

—LILLIAN CARTER

When Will Ferrell was in middle school, he qualified for the gifted and talented after-school enrichment program, so his mom signed him up. When Will found out, he told her there was a conflict—he had signed himself up for square dancing. He could only do one or the other.

To a parent, there is an obvious choice. It's not even a discussion. We know which one will teach more, which one will be better for career prospects, which one is "cooler." But our kids, they don't know anything about decision-making. They don't know about mental models. They don't know about long-term consequences or second-order thinking. They don't know about weighing pros and cons. They don't know what's best for them. They know only what they like, what excites them, what they want *right now.*

But as actress and fellow SNL cast member Ana Gasteyer tells the story, Will's mom put all that aside. She looked at her son and said, "It's up to you. You decide." Will chose square dancing. "And that, to me," Gasteyer said, "sums up why Will is the amazing Will Ferrell." It explained, in her mind, how Will Ferrell became one of the greatest comedic actors of all time. His parents had encouraged and *allowed* him to. They didn't intrude with their "real-world" priorities—they let him follow his heart.

When your kids feel a pull toward something creative or fulfilling, the worst thing you can do as a parent is prevent them from going in that direction. Your job, it's worth repeating whenever there's a chance, is to encourage them to be who they are, to follow their natural inclinations, to decide what *they* want to do after school.

July 12
Don't Judge Them Too Harshly . . . or Quickly

In the spring of 1921, a young ballplayer named Louis Gehrig had a tryout for the great John McGraw at the Polo Grounds. McGraw was the manager of the New York Giants and one of the greatest evaluators of talent in the history of the game.

It was a good tryout. Gehrig hit a few deep shots. He was lively and quick. He was already showing off his almost inhumanly large lower body, which was key to power at the plate. But then Gehrig headed to first base . . . where he promptly let an easy ball go through his feet. According to biographers, the tryout ended almost immediately. McGraw had seen all he needed to see.

We might call this moment McGraw's Folly. In an instant, he sized up and judged this kid—and make no mistake, Gehrig was a kid. He was painfully shy, sheltered, inexperienced . . . and McGraw's inability or unwillingness to factor that into his evaluation meant he would miss out on the career of one of the game's greatest talents and human beings.

Gehrig would go on to play first base for the Yankees, hit hundreds of home runs, win six World Series and hold the record for the longest streak of consecutive starts for over fifty years. Maybe he would have been worth a little more patience? A slightly more open mind?

It's essential that we learn from these misses when it comes to talent. People are ciphers, even our own kids. We are not nearly as good at evaluating ability and predicting the future as we think we are. So we have to be forgiving. We can't jump to conclusions. We have to give kids the benefit of the doubt. We have to root for them, not write them off.

July 13
Teach Them to Choose

If your choices are beautiful, so too will you be.

—EPICTETUS

It makes sense that parents make most of the decisions for their kids. Parents know more. Kids basically know nothing. About life. About what the weather is going to be tomorrow. About how the world works.

The problem with this is that you're depriving your kids of a very important skill: the ability to make decisions. Is it any wonder that so many teenagers are utterly overwhelmed when it comes to choosing where to go to college? Or what to major in? For most of them, it's the first real decision they've made in their whole lives.

That's why, as a parent, you have to actively work to not choose everything for them. Ask them whether they want to go to the park or play catch in the yard. Ask them what movie they want to see. What should we cook for dinner? Do you want to take a shower tonight or a bath? Would you rather try out for the baseball or the basketball team? If you don't like mowing the lawn, what's another chore you'd like to do to contribute around the house? Shorts or pants today? Go pick out something to wear.

Teach them how to choose. Empower them. Make sure they know how to decide, and to be okay with their decision even if they decide wrong. It doesn't matter that you know more. What matters is that you let them learn.

A life is the sum and substance of a person's decisions. Prepare them to make good decisions so they can make the best possible life for themselves.

July 14
You Must Adjust Accordingly

The scientist Jennifer Doudna's father was an English professor. It wasn't until he had a young daughter that he realized that almost all the books he assigned to his students were written by men. Having a daughter made him realize how acutely unfair this was, how this deprived his students of valuable perspectives and inspiration. So, as Walter Isaacson writes in his fascinating biography of Jennifer Doudna and the work that won her a Nobel Prize, her father quietly "added Doris Lessing, Anne Tyler, and Joan Didion to his syllabus." He started bringing books home to his daughter that might inspire her too.

Like a good father (and human being), he adjusted. Not out of political correctness but out of real empathy. And what was the effect? Did he lose his spine or his manhood? Did censorship win? No, his choice made the world better! His students were better and his ability to connect with his daughter was better. Then decades later, *the world* became better as a result of this adjustment (you can thank Doudna and by extension her father for your family's COVID-19 mRNA vaccine).

Don't be frozen in time. Don't close your mind. Be open . . . and adjust.

July 15
Always Keep Their Interests in Mind

You should remember that in every person lives the same spirit which lives in us.

—ARTHUR SCHOPENHAUER

There will always be a gulf between parents and their children, at least when it comes to taste. That is as it should be. Your tastes are informed by years of experience and theirs by the yet unjaded joy of discovery. Why would you like what they like? You know more!

And still, it remains an imperative—if you want to connect with them and shape and encourage them—that you always keep their interests in mind, because your job is to figure out what they like and help them continue to explore it.

Oh, they liked this movie? Here's another they might enjoy. Oh, they like this book? Here's the author's entire catalog for their birthday. Oh, they like dinosaurs? Here come the weekend trips to museums; here come the photos of you in front of the Brachiosaurus in the United terminal at O'Hare; here comes a dinosaur video you can watch together.

When their interests become your interests, they become opportunities to connect and explore and to share. Let them be the driver; you just provide the fuel.

July 16
Original Is Better Than Smart

The "C" students run the world.

—HARRY TRUMAN

We think we want smart kids. That's why we monitor their grades, why we hire tutors, why we help them study for the SATs. It's even how we find ourselves praising them: *You are so smart!*

But is this really setting them up for success in life? The essayist, entrepreneur, and venture capitalist Paul Graham warns parents against fighting the last war—trying to get their kids into good colleges to then get good jobs available to smart people. Einstein wasn't special because he was *smart*, Graham writes, but because he had *original ideas.*

Think of the people we admire most; they share that feature. It wasn't that they were smart—it was that they had a different way of looking at the world. They were unique, and with this uniqueness (which was often coupled with intelligence) they did great things. So as you try to mold your child—well, maybe stop trying to mold them and just help guide them as they grow.

Encourage them to be their original, unique selves. Encourage them to explore, to find new things. The world is full of smart people . . . and most of them are insufferably boring and unimpressive. What we need are fresh thinkers and creative people. What we need are originals.

July 17
Your Job Is to Show Them What's Possible

That the children of successful parents turn out spoiled and lazy is a cliché that has proven itself true across time more often than any of those parents would like to admit. But there is also no shortage of examples that subvert this preconception. There are numerous professional athletes with kids who make it into the pros. Both John Quincy Adams and George W. Bush followed their fathers to the White House. There are plenty of writers and artists whose children went on to be successful in the arts.

How does this work? Obviously there was no shortage of natural talent. Nepotism too. These kids were gifted and then were given big advantages. But there is another force at play too, one that every parent should think about. Could it be that the biggest privilege afforded to these kids was seeing their parent passionately and practically pursue a career that most people have trouble even imagining? That the real gift they got was seeing that following your dreams *was actually possible*? And that it wasn't magic, it was just a lot of hard work?

Too many parents spend time either consciously or subtly telling their kids to think small, to be realistic, to consider the odds. But living in the same house as a professional athlete or a head of state or an award-winning author sends a powerful message: *It can be done!* It just takes work, dedication, and, of course, confidence.

That's your real job, whatever you do for a living. To show them what's possible. To push them to go for it, whatever "it" is.

July 18
Don't Give Them This

The biggest impediment to happiness in life is something that many of us picked up very early in our lives: shame.

Shame is guilt's evil twin. Where guilt is feeling bad about things you've done; shame is feeling bad about *who you are*—for things about yourself that you don't control. Having normal, biological urges. Being uncoordinated. Having unique artistic tastes. Struggling with social cues. Having a limited palate or an extremely adventurous one. There is almost no limit to the things about ourselves that we are capable of feeling shame over.

What's so tragic about shame, though, is that it does not come naturally. Watch an innocent child play intently with their food or pretend completely to be a princess or a dragon, and there isn't a whisper of shame to be heard. Because they have not been made to feel ashamed about these things yet.

Shame is inherited. It is passed along, often by parents, on the back of cutting remarks, unnecessary judgments, and thoughtless choices. It's up to you to not let them inherit shame.

It's up to you to let them be their own people, to let them be comfortable in their own skin—pretending to be dragons, flailing to music you don't like, trying things you'd never try yourself, it doesn't matter . . . as long as it matters to them.

Embrace your children, so they might embrace the things that make them unique and wholly themselves. There is no shame in that.

HELP THEM BECOME WHO THEY ARE

July 19
Encourage Them to Be the Best

There are the parents who just want their kids to have fun. And there are the parents who push their kids to be winners. The one side believes competition doesn't matter; the other side believes competition is the only thing that matters. Like so many two-sided debates, there's a third option that both sides miss, which is actually far superior to either, though much more nuanced.

The great John Wooden—one of the winningest coaches in college basketball history—said it was what he learned from his father:

> Dad's message about basketball—and life—was this: "Johnny, don't try to be better than somebody else, but never cease trying to be the best you can be. You have control over that. The other you don't." It was simple advice: work hard, very hard, at those things I can control and don't lose sleep over the rest of it.

As you put your kid out there in soccer or on the debate team, as you talk to them about their class rank or their mile time, make sure that you are letting them know that how they compare with other people is far less important than how they measure up against *their own potential*. Somebody who gives their best effort at everything they do is going to go much further in life (and have a happier one) than somebody who is obsessed with coming in first place or who never earnestly tries for fear that they will lose.

So tell your kid to be the best *they can be*. Tell them to measure themselves against their own potential and their own progress. Not only does that usually lead to winning, but it is also what winners do.

July 20
Help Them Go Find It

Ayoung Kwame Onwuachi was cooking with his mother in their apartment in the Bronx, when suddenly the apartment was overwhelmed by a strange smell. As he would write in his memoir, the "thick fragrant smell of curry came on so strong both of us stopped what we were doing and looked up." But it wasn't actually the smell that he remembered. It was what his mother did next.

"Let's go find it!" she said to him with palpable excitement, and then together they raced down the hallways of each floor of their building, trying to locate the source. As soon as the doors opened to the third floor, they knew they were close. Without so much as a hesitation, his mother knocked on the door that had so beckoned her. "My name is Jewel," she said confidently. "This is my son, Kwame. We live on the sixth floor. We couldn't help but smell what you were cooking."

The woman was stunned. Fear registered across her face. Were they about to complain? To say something offensive? No, that wasn't his mother's style. "It smells wonderful," she said. "I don't know how to say this, but we'd like to try it!"

How did Kwame go on to start his own catering company, graduate from the Culinary Institute, work at Per Se, and start one of the most talked-about restaurants in America, before his twenty-fourth birthday? It can all be traced back to this surreal exchange. His mother showed him in that moment so many wonderful traits: Curiosity. Confidence. Assertiveness. Figure-out-able-ness. Passion. Neighborliness.

These are all things we can and must teach our children in our own way. But it can start by following our nose.

July 21
Stop Trying to Change Them

> My wife and I, our whole job is to provide, to protect, to love,
> to facilitate. . . . It's to find out who our children are, find out
> their likes and their dislikes, and try to help them through
> life, to find themselves. It's not about us.
>
> —DWYANE WADE

We should always try to learn from parents who have had it harder than us, who have really been through the wringer.

Brandon Boulware is the son of a minister. He's a lawyer, an avowed Christian man, a husband, and the father of four children. In 2021, he gave deeply moving testimony to the Missouri House of Representatives about his struggles with his transgender daughter. He told the lawmakers that he'd long tried—out of fear and love and a desire to protect—to keep his child from wearing girls' clothes and playing on girls' teams. Then one day, she asked him if she could go play with the neighbors. It's time for dinner, he said. *But if I go out in boy clothes, can I play with them?* came the reply. Then it hit him: he'd accidentally taught his child that not being who she is was a way to be rewarded.

What Boulware so beautifully communicates in his brief testimony is a lesson for all parents. "Let them have their childhoods," he pleads. "Let them be who they are."

Maybe you're artistic and your kid is not. Maybe you're athletic and your kid is not. Maybe you're not religious and your teenager is. Maybe you're liberal and your kid is not. Whatever it is, let them be who they are. Let them experiment. Let them discover themselves—let them discover their truths. Let them have their childhoods.

You might not like the results of these explorations. They might challenge your most deeply held assumptions. But guess what? That's a *you* problem.

July 22
They Don't Know What They Want

Nobody knows anything.

—WILLIAM GOLDMAN

As a parent, it's really easy to force your kids to do stuff. You're bigger than them. You control the purse strings. You possess the legal and moral authority to make them do what you think is best for them. But when you wield that power without so much as a conversation, you're teaching them that they have no power, no control, that their wishes don't really matter in your house, in this life.

You're also setting up a bad habit for yourself. You won't always have this power over them. You don't want to habituate a kind of disrespect for, or disinterest in, what they think they want. Because one day, they'll want to change their college major. They'll want to move across the country. They'll want to make some lifestyle change you disagree with. They'll want to tweak some long-standing family tradition. And you will be so used to thinking that you know better, that you are the decider, that you won't be able to handle it. Especially the part where they don't have to listen to you. But worse than that, your relationship with your kids won't be able to weather the fallout from your egotistical implosion.

Your kids don't always know what they want. But guess what? Nobody does. So you have to figure out how to be in charge without being a tyrant, how to generally know better without being a know-it-all. You have to learn how to use the gravity of your experience to move them gently in the direction they should go, instead of using the mass of your position as parent to force them that way.

This won't be easy . . . but such is the life of a parent.

July 23
How Often Do You Say No?

Even those of us who don't think of ourselves as strict parents should stop and think about just how often our kids hear us say the word *no*. As in: "No, stop that." "No, you can't go out tonight." "No, get off of there." "No, we have to go home." "No, I'm not buying you that." "No, that's not how you do that."

It's not that we're demanding; it's just that we care. This might keep them safe, but the downside is that from the perspective of a two-year-old or a twenty-year-old, it means that basically all they hear their parent say is no. No, no, no, no.

Harry Truman, father of a daughter, Margaret, had a clever quip about this: "I have found the best way to give advice to your children is to find out what they want and then advise them to do it."

His point is that nobody likes to be told what to do. And your job isn't to make them do all the things you want them to do; it's to help them do the things they want to do (safely and within reason, of course).

It's their life, after all. Learn how to say yes. Learn how to advise them on what they are going to do anyway—so that if you can't stop it, you can at least prepare them. Be someone who helps, not the kind of parent who only gets in the way.

July 24
You Have to Listen

The reason why we have two ears and only one mouth is so we might listen more and talk less.

—ZENO

Shortly after the release of his book *Parents Who Lead*, Dr. Stewart Friedman—an award-winning psychologist and a leading researcher on leadership and work-life integration—was asked what great new discoveries or insights he came across in the process of writing the book. "My favorite," he said, "was about how much parents have to gain by learning how to listen to their children about what they really need." Dr. Friedman elaborated:

> It's often quite surprising to hear what's actually on their minds and how you can be a better leader in your family when you know what's in the hearts and minds of those precious people who look up to you. One father, who was keen to impress upon his son the value of curiosity and study, asked him what he was interested in learning. To his utter delight, his son said, "I want to learn to vacuum." His son wanted to be useful; he wanted to contribute and have a purpose himself. You don't really know, in other words, what's inside until you pay attention, with dedication and compassion, like effective leaders do.

That little fellow is always trying to tell you things. Of course, it's not always explicit. Sometimes "I want to learn to be useful" comes out as "I want to learn to vacuum." Sometimes "I want to be a good friend" comes out as "Can you drive me to Bobby's house?" Sometimes "I want to be a writer" comes out as an awkward kid who doesn't want to watch sports with you.

Still, they are always trying to tell you something. And you'll hear them only if you're really listening.

July 25
Don't Help Them Become Who *You* Were

Tim Hardaway Jr. is the son of an NBA Hall of Famer. Growing up, it was hard being the son of someone who had played the game at such a high level, particularly while trying to master the same sport himself.

In the car on the way home from games, Tim Sr. would highlight the mistakes Tim Jr. had made, the shots he should have made, the plays he should have made. He'd say, "You're not performing at a high-enough level" and "Get better, or we'll stop you from playing the game of basketball forever." If Tim Jr. didn't want to watch basketball on TV, Tim Sr. would shake his head and say, "You don't love the game enough."

Tim Sr. would say that he put this pressure on his son because he loved him: "I wanted him to play like I had played, to take the game seriously like I took the game seriously, understand the game like I understood the game."

Sure, it "worked out" in the sense that Tim Hardaway Jr. is a great basketball player too . . . but is that because his dad said mean things to him? Or threatened him? Or could it have just as much to do with the fact that he's six foot five, has a six-foot-seven-inch wingspan, and played in college for John Beilein? And let's say it hadn't worked out or had just worked out less well. Don't you think both father and son, in retrospect, would have taken that trade if it meant they had a better relationship?

As we've said, our job is to help our kids become who they are. It's not to help them become who we were. It's not their responsibility to carry on your legacy, to play the sport you played, to wear the number you wore.

July 26
What Are You Making Them Do?

There's a line adapted from Aristotle but given to us by the historian Will Durant:

> We are what we repeatedly do. Therefore, excellence is not an act but a habit.

The real question as parents, then, is *What are we making our kids do?* Excellence isn't something we pursue as a destination. It's something we pursue in the doing. Day in and day out. In the little things as well as the big things. It's something that emerges when we turn that type of pursuit, through action, into a habit. And it's our job as parents to help our kids understand this. To help them realize who they are by what they do day to day, what they do this day, today.

We are what we do repeatedly.

July 27
Why? Why? Why?

> I would rather have questions that can't be answered than answers that can't be questioned.
>
> —RICHARD FEYNMAN

As a parent, there is no word you hear more. *Why?* Why not? Why can't I? Why do I have to? Why does it work like that? Why? Why? Why? Why? Why?

It's annoying, to be sure, but you must be sure to never discourage this. So much of what we take for granted as parents, and as people, is arbitrary and poorly supported. Perhaps that's because at a young age our own impulse to question and explore was suppressed. We were not taught to see that most of the rules and limitations of the world have no real basis in logic, or reason, or even morality.

When we asked "Why?" we were told, "Because." Full stop. We were not encouraged to challenge assumptions, to question the status quo, to *learn* why things are the way they are. And our limited access to wisdom and truth limited us in turn.

Let's not continue this tradition. Let's turn over a new leaf with this generation—the one *we* are in charge of raising into the best versions of themselves. We want our kids to make the world a better place; we want them to improve things; we want them to be better than us.

That can't happen if they are complacent, if they are credulous, if they don't think they are empowered to subject their reality to even the simplest interrogation and demand answers accordingly.

"Why?" is a great question. Help them see that.

And then help them answer it.

July 28
Give Them Space

If you're not careful, their whole lives get filled up.

Soccer practice. School. Cello lessons. Chores at home. You don't want them in front of screens all day; you don't want them to waste their lives or fall behind. You want them to make something of themselves.

But you have to be careful. Even two thousand years ago, Plutarch was warning parents to not overschedule and overplan their kid's lives. "Children must be given some breathing space from continued tasks," he wrote, "for we must bear in mind that our whole life is divided between relaxation and application."

Do you do your best work when you are exhausted and stretched too thin? Are you happy when your calendar is full? Aren't you tired of running them from place to place? Imagine how they feel! They don't even fully understand what stress is, what burnout is. So it's incumbent upon you to protect them from it.

Give them space. Give them the opportunity to relax. That's your job.

HELP THEM BECOME WHO THEY ARE

July 29
Do Not Get in the Way of Their Primal Inclinations

You want to show them your favorite movies. Your favorite bands. All the places you loved as a kid. The sports you love to play or watch.

This is special and wonderful, because you're sharing not just experiences or sights or sounds or tastes but parts of yourself. These things shaped who you are and how you became that person, and to share that is to give your kids a deeper look at the person raising them. But you should share with caution.

Just as you shouldn't overtly pressure your kids into a certain lane ("You need to become a doctor"), the author Robert Greene said, parents must be careful of the less overt forms of pressure—steering them to be interested in the things you are interested in, forcing them to participate in this activity or play that sport, calling the arts or entrepreneurship "risky" or artists and entrepreneurs "crazy." As Robert said:

> As a parent, you need to let go. You need to let your child blossom. You need to think of your child like they're a plant that you want to foster and grow in its most natural form and not hinder in any way. You have to let your child go in whatever direction he or she wants. When the child reveals a proclivity toward something, encourage them to go in that direction. Because that proclivity reveals something extremely powerful from within—it reveals what I call a primal inclination. Do not get in the way of their primal inclinations in any way, shape, or form. That's the most important thing you can do.

Throw away your expectations. Your responsibility is to encourage them to be who they are, not what you want them to be or who you wish you'd become. Don't force your interests on your child. Pay attention to their natural, primal inclinations, then foster their blossoming.

July 30
This Is Always in Their Control

We don't get to pick how tall our kids are, and neither do they. It's beyond their control whether they're big or small, whether they have the fastest reflexes or the strongest muscles or the quickest wit. They don't control whether the coach loves them . . . or is a jerk. They don't control most of what happens in the classroom, or in the locker room for that matter. As Cheryl Strayed writes in *Tiny Beautiful Things*, "You don't have a right to the cards you believe you should have been dealt."

So what do we tell our kids to focus on? What is always up to them?

What they do in response to those circumstances. What's up to them is whether they do their best or not. Whether they try hard. Whether they find a way to enjoy the process and live up to their potential.

So after practice, after the game, after the big test, you need to make sure that your questions and your criteria for judging them reflect that. Meaning not "Did you guys win?" or "Did you pass?" but "Did you have fun?" or "Did you do your best?" or "What do you think you could have done better to prepare?"

We don't control the hand we're dealt. Our biology isn't up to us, nor is our place in the world (geographically or socioeconomically). But our kids (or families) decide how we play that hand. We decide what we do about it. We decide whether we give it our all. We decide who we become.

Teach them that.

July 31
Prepare Them to Answer the Call

To each," Winston Churchill said, "there comes in their lifetime a special moment when they are figuratively tapped on the shoulder and offered the chance to do a very special thing, unique to them and fitted to their talents. What a tragedy if that moment finds them unprepared or unqualified for that which could have been their finest hour."

It's more accurate to say that life has many of these moments, many such taps on the shoulder: to serve, to take a risk, to run toward danger while others run away, to do a thing that people say is impossible.

Our kids will have many reasons to think what they're planning is the wrong thing to do. They will be pressured to put their dreams out of their mind. Fear will make itself felt. Will they let it prevent them from answering the call? Will they leave the phone ringing? Will their moment find them unprepared? Will their finest hour pass them by like a ship in the night?

What a tragedy that would be. As parents, we have to make sure that doesn't happen to our kids. We have to help them inch closer and closer to doing what they were put here to do, to being who they were meant to become. We are supposed to prepare them for when the phone rings, for when they get tapped on the shoulder, because the one thing we know for certain is that the call is going to come.

Will they be prepared to answer?

AUGUST

ALWAYS BE A FAN

(THE GREATEST GIFT YOU CAN GIVE THEM)

August 1
You Can Give Them This Gift

Jim Valvano wasn't yet out of high school when he first told his dad he had decided what he wanted to do with the rest of his life. He wasn't just going to be a collegiate basketball coach, he said: "Dad, I'm going to win a national championship."

A few days after Jim told his dad about his dream, his dad called him into his bedroom. "See that suitcase?" his father asked, pointing to the luggage in the corner. Confused, Jim replied, "Yeah, what's that all about?" "I'm packed," his dad explained. "When you play and win that national championship I'm going to be there. My bags are already packed."

"My father," Jim would later say in his legendary ESPY speech, "gave me the greatest gift anyone could give another person: *he believed in me.*"

Have you given this gift to your children? Our job is to spur our children to conceive of big dreams, to encourage them to go after them, to give them the greatest gift anyone can give another person: belief. If you don't believe in them, who will?

August 2
Just Be a Fan

Maybe your kid is into weird stuff. Maybe their heavy metal band sucks—or their talents as a rapper are almost offensive. Maybe you can't stand the shows they like, or maybe their dream is an unlikely one at best. Or maybe they are supremely skilled and have what it takes to go pro. Maybe with the right prodding and the right support they could be truly special, and you just need to make sure they don't slack off and miss the opportunities they need for that to happen.

But is that really your most important job? Your first job is to be a fan. Just a fan. Of them. Of their talents or lack thereof. Of their chances or lack thereof.

They don't need a drill sergeant in the living room. They don't need someone calling them out. They don't need someone telling them the hard truths. They don't even necessarily need your money to put them in that fancy league. They don't need you to berate their teachers and demand special treatment. They don't need you to be obsessed.

What they need is a fan. They need someone who supports them, who loves them, who is rooting for them. They need a fan with a healthy relationship to the game—not a stalker or a tyrant person.

Just be a fan. It's not that complicated.

August 3
What Are You Going to Focus On?

You can look at all the negative in the world. You can focus on the dark clouds above. Or you can look for the silver lining, the bright spots. We have that expression about whether the glass is half full or half empty. Well, what worldview are you going to teach your children?

Are you going to fill your house with doom and gloom? Or are you going to teach your kids to hope, to believe in their ability to make a difference, to find the opportunity inside the obstacles that life presents?

The author Alex Haley once said that he believed his job as a writer was to "find good and praise it." That fits in a parent's job description too. We're always going to have more success rewarding good behavior in our kids than punishing bad behavior. Looking for what we *want* to see in them and making that our focus is going to get us much further than seeking out conflict and engaging in criticism. This principle extends to our perceptions and portrayal of the world as well. It's better for everyone to talk up what we want to see instead of constantly bemoaning all the evil and wrongness that we can't seem to escape.

We have a choice: Inspire or disillusion. Empower or depress. What will it be?

August 4
Don't Be a Minimizer

> The parenting style that is good for grit is also the parenting
> style good for most other things: Be really, really demanding,
> and be very, very supportive.
>
> —ANGELA DUCKWORTH

E d Stack was a great kid. He worked quietly and loyally for the family business, Dick's Sporting Goods. He saved up enough money that eventually he could buy his father out and grow the family legacy. He tells the story of the first big-box store he opened. The company had previously operated stores that were a couple thousand square feet at most. This new store was twenty thousand square feet. It was transformative for the business—sales skyrocketed.

Reps from Nike were talking to Ed's father, the original founder, and said something about how proud he must be of his kid. To be succeeding like that. To be taking the store to the next level. As Ed explained, "My father, who could never really quite give you a compliment, looked at them and said, 'You're right, they did a lot of business. They did 25 percent more business than they thought they would the first month. So they're not really as smart as they think they are.'"

Sadly, who hasn't heard something like this from someone they desperately wanted to make proud? Those backhanded compliments. That way of cutting you down to size, of looking for some flaw, of seizing on your insecurities. What bullshit it is! Instead of taking the opportunity to show their love, they have to let their own fragile sense of self get in the way.

The minimum of being a good parent is *not being a minimizer.* Don't look for what's wrong, look for what's right . . . and celebrate it! Lift them up, don't cut them down. Root for them; that's what they want more than anything.

August 5
There Are Better Forms of Motivation

Across sports, politics, business, even the arts, we see a theme driving the most ambitious, the hardest working, the biggest risk-takers. Be they men or women, they all seem to be craving something, trying to prove something. The approval of their father. The love of their families. To shove it in the faces of the doubters. To get as far away as possible from the trauma.

It's hard not to see that this is real and productive fuel. As a parent, it should also be hard to see it, period. Because there are so many other forms of fuel out there that don't involve pain or what is, in many cases, a kind of abuse. Tiger Woods was set up to succeed in golf by his father's regimen of hyperattention as well as neglect. Did that help him? Sure. But given how incredibly talented and smart and hardworking Tiger is, don't you think he could have accomplished a lot without essentially being tortured with prisoner-of-war tactics?

You can subject your kids to hard and difficult things and it may help make them successful. These things may have even helped *you* be successful. Yelling. Blunt truths. Endless workouts. Emotional manipulation. These things work . . . but they also come at a steep emotional cost. Encouragement and genuine support, on the other hand, work equally well and have the added benefit of bringing you closer to your kids and making you both better people.

Choose the right form of motivation. Not the harshest.

August 6
Seldom Should Be Heard a Discouraging Word

> The innocent and helpless creature bestowed on them by heaven, whom to bring up to good, and whose future lot it was in their hands to direct to happiness or misery.
>
> —MARY WOLLSTONECRAFT SHELLEY

If you're not paying attention, it's easy to slip into a kind of casual, thoughtless negativity: *Why is your room so dirty? Why are you in such a bad mood today? Hey, stop doing that! Don't touch this. No, you can't watch TV right now. Why isn't your room clean? No, you can't have that. I'm disappointed with how you did on this test. That is just not realistic; shouldn't you think about trying something else? I don't think so. You already know the answer . . . and the answer is "no."*

This happens not because you're a bad parent but rather because you're a good one. You have rules and you enforce them. You have expectations and you push your kids to meet them. You know what's best. You want to keep them safe and you have a house to run.

But still, if you're not careful, it can come to be that almost every interaction you have with your kids is negative. It can start to feel, from their perspective, like an endless cascade of disappointment. And then, before you know it, you've become the voice of *discouragement* without even thinking about it.

Is that who you are? Is that the kind of relationship you want to have? If it isn't, then you need to pay attention. Watch your words. Count your *yeses* and *nos*. Be intentional about what you focus on. Let the little things go. Be positive.

August 7
Playing with Your Kids Is Everything

The years before the Civil War were rough on Ulysses S. Grant. He was struggling to make a life for his family. There was a sadness about his life, an endless drudgery of frustration and disappointment, of one failed career, one hardship after another.

There was only one respite to this. When Grant opened the front door to his house after work each day, his young son, Jesse, was waiting to challenge him to a fight. Jesse would boast he could beat his father. Grant, with faux seriousness, would look at the tiny boy and answer the provocation, "I do not feel like fighting, Jesse, but I can't stand being hectored in this manner by a man of your size." Jesse would then hurl himself at his father until he brought him down. On the ground, Grant would beg for mercy and shout that it wasn't fair to attack an opponent who had fallen.

In just a few short years, Grant's bulldog tenacity and toughness would shock—and save—the nation. It was Grant who broke the back of the Confederate army, fighting brutal battle after brutal battle. But those who knew him best knew that at heart he was a softy. That he loved his family more than anything.

It doesn't matter what you do for a living or how bleak things might be—playing with your kids is a wonderful thing. Play with them if they're young. Play with them if they're old, if you're old. Have fun with them. Be kids together. Play. Play. Play.

August 8
Don't Wait to Be Proud

It's a story as old as parenthood itself. The child tries and tries to win the approval of their parent, which never seems to come. There is pain, resentment, bewilderment. Only at the end, after much pain and resentment, is it revealed: The child had the thing they wanted all along. They just never knew.

This was the story of Claudia Williams, the daughter of Ted Williams. Only buried in a pile of memorabilia did she find a note left by her impossible-to-please father.

"To my beautiful daughter," it said. "I love you. Dad."

It's the story of the brilliant publisher Sonny Mehta. In Mehta's obituary, Roger Cohen wrote:

> When Mehta's father, a diplomat, died in Vienna, Mehta found in his desk a folder with every article ever published about him. The pride of his father, who had never complimented his son, was evident.

It breaks your heart. Why couldn't they have expressed this when they were alive? Was it a generational thing? Did they think it was helping to make their kids better, tougher? Why couldn't they have been more like Jim Valvano's father and given us the gift of being a fan?

We'll never know the answer to those questions. What we do know is we can't do this with our own kids. We can't wait to be proud. We can't keep our feelings for them hidden under piles of paper or in a drawer in our desk. We have to tell them now. We have to show them now. That we're rooting for them. That we love them. That we believe in them. That we're proud of them. Because we are. And they deserve to know it—before it's too late.

August 9
We're Not Raising Grass

In his induction speech for the Baseball Hall of Fame in 1984, Harmon Killebrew told the story of a time he was playing in the front yard with his father and his brother. His mom came out to tell them it was time for dinner and admonished them for tearing up the grass. "We're not raising grass," his father replied. "We're raising boys."

Success as a parent is not defined by having a car with spotless back seats. It's not having a perfectly decorated house filled with fragile things that never get broken. A kid's room should look like it was played in. A home should feel lived in. We should see their fingerprints everywhere—literally and figuratively.

Is your job really to raise a kid who never talks back? Who walks in lockstep or tiptoes through life? Or is it to raise a kid with their own opinions and their own dreams, with the confidence to articulate them and the ability to bring them to life?

The yard is there to be played in. The bike is made to be ridden, not kept in the garage in pristine condition. Your floors will be scratched. Food will be spilled. Messes will accumulate. Noises will be made.

Good. We're not trying to keep a spotless, quiet house. We're raising healthy, well-adjusted, happy children.

August 10
Engage with the Slime

For a long time, one of the arbitrary rules in Jeannie Gaffigan's house had to do with where, when, and how slime could be made. Maybe your kids are too old to care about slime, but it's not difficult to relate to Jeannie's dilemma. Sure, slime is fun for kids to make, but it's a pain in the ass to clean up, and who do you think is the one left with the scrubber and the paper towels in their hands?

At some point, though, Jeannie Gaffigan, a mother of five and the wife and longtime collaborator of the comedian Jim Gaffigan, had a change of heart about her rules—particularly after a battle with a life-threatening brain tumor: "I realized that I never asked, 'Can you teach me how to make the slime?' I never engaged with the slime. I engaged with the *control* of the slime."

Life is too short to nix your children's interests because you don't want to deal with a mess afterward. Think about it: How many negative rules do we make related to *things*? Food in the living room, shoes on the carpet, toys outside the playroom. These rules are often designed to make our lives easier as parents, but one of their unintended side effects is to make our kids' lives less fun.

At the same time, we also seem to have *fewer* positive rules for *ourselves*. Why not a rule about being interested? Why not a rule about playing and having fun together? Why not a rule about encouraging their fascinations rather than curtailing them?

Let's work with the slime, not against it.

August 11
What Kind of Voice Are You Giving Them?

You hear it all the time. It's been there all your life. That voice in your head. The one that tells you what's right, what you ought to do. This voice can also turn nasty, whispering that you're not good enough, that everyone sees through you, that you'll never measure up.

The performance psychologist Dr. Jim Loehr, who has studied countless athletes and elite leaders, says this voice is the key to success. "I began to realize," he said in an interview, "what really mattered in a really significant way: the tone and content of the voice no one hears. I came to understand that the ultimate coach for all of us in life is that private voice."

Where does it come from? Where did you get that voice originally? It came from your parents, mostly. As Loehr explains, we "know it begins to form as early as five years of age, and it comes principally from the authority figures in your life . . . however functional or dysfunctional."

This should sober us as parents. *We* are responsible for the voice that will live inside our kids' head for the rest of their lives. We decide whether that voice will belong to a wise and patient ancestor or a cruel and unpredictable ghost. We decide whether it will be a voice of conscience and kindness or doubt and insecurity. We decide that by *what we say to them, by what we show them.*

In each moment of every day.

August 12
Here's What Matters

The best way to make children good is to make them happy.

—OSCAR WILDE

The author Rich Cohen loves hockey. He loves watching his kids excel at it. Like any parent, the last thing he wants is for them to struggle or, worse, to be shortchanged—whether it's playing time or respect.

In his lovely book *Pee Wees: Confessions of a Hockey Parent*, Rich tells one story about a conversation he had with his son's coach. His son wasn't being given the time on the ice Rich thought he deserved, so he tried to make a case for it. The coach, on the other hand, had no patience. "Let me ask you this. Is Micah happy?" he said. "Yes," Rich replied. "Is Micah having fun?" "Yes," Rich had to admit. And that's when the coach got him with something every parent ought to be reminded of: "Then what do you care?"

If our kids are having fun, if they're happy, if they're learning, if they're building bonds with teammates, then nothing else matters. Our duty as parents is not to optimize our kids for success. It's to teach them how to be present, how to find things they love, how to be a good person, how to respond to the situations life puts them in. That's it.

Everything else? What do we care?

August 13
Be Careful of Your Implications

King George VI referred to his daughters as his "pride and joy." To be more specific, he referred to the two of them as "Pride" and "Joy." Princess Elizabeth was "Pride" and Princess Margaret was "Joy." Only with time did the two of them realize the sad implications of his remark—that he was proud of one and had fun with the other, and therefore found less happiness in the former and less pride in the latter. If only it were just a clever remark. If only there hadn't been real truth in it—if his actions hadn't confirmed it—there would have been little to infer.

It's so easy to joke: about our "easy" child and our "difficult one," about our "favorite," about our "special" one, about who or what "will be the death of us." God knows how many thoughtless asides about our kids have popped out of our mouths in casual conversation.

We have to consider the implications of the words we throw about like that. Because our kids are listening, and they *really hear us*. They are always trying to understand themselves and their place in the world. The things we say today, when they are young, will come back to them when they are older, and they will fit those words, for better and for worse, into the narrative of their lives.

August 14
Don't Merge Like This

Joan Didion didn't get into Stanford. She was crushed. Her father looked at her and shrugged. You might think that his lack of empathy added to her pain and frustration. But with time, she came to understand that her father had gotten the moment exactly right.

"I think about that shrug with a great deal of appreciation whenever I hear parents talking about their children's chances," Didion would write in a classic essay on college in 1968. "What makes me uneasy is the sense that they are merging their children's chances with their own, demanding of a child that he make good not only for himself but for the greater glory of his father and mother."

Her father shrugged because he had not placed any of his identity into what college his daughter got into. Perhaps he could have done a little better at understanding how much of *her* identity had been put into it. But then again, maybe that was the point. He wanted to show her how little it actually mattered—how her success or failure in life was going to be based on something far less superficial than college admissions.

And so it must go with us. We encourage our children. We want to set them up to succeed. But we can't merge their glory into our own. We can't let them think they have to impress us, make us proud, or worry that they have let us down or failed us. Certainly, we can't let them think that where they go (or don't go) to school has *any* bearing on who they are to us . . . or what they can do with their lives.

August 15
It Should Be the Easiest Thing in the World

Parenting is very hard. Keeping your kids safe. Keeping them fed. Keeping them in the best schools, making sure they get good grades in those schools. We have to do all this as we navigate a world where Murphy's Law is real, where bills have to get paid, where we have our own crap to deal with that no one is going to handle for us.

In that sense, parenting is an impossible job with impossible expectations. Yet in another, very real sense, being a parent is actually about the easiest job in the world. Because what do they really need? What is really demanded of you? *That you love them. That you accept them. That you support and encourage them. That you cheer for them. That you be their biggest fan.*

Nothing—literally nothing short of death—can stop you from doing those things. Seriously, how hard is it to believe in them? How hard is it to be encouraging? How hard is it to remind them that you don't care what's happened, what other people say, that you know they have goodness and potential inside them?

And here's the thing: death can't stop you from doing those things either, because if you do them now—if you give your kids what they need cheerfully, regularly, sincerely—it will stick with them as a voice in their heads for as long as they and their own children live.

August 16
They Need Somebody to Do This

You might not think of Muhammad Ali as someone who needed anyone to believe in him, but that's because you saw him only later in life. You saw the confident boxer, the brilliant self-promoter, the master of his craft, the fearless warrior.

But there was a time when he was a scared child, like every other kid. He was a young black boy named Cassius Clay in a segregated America, who struggled at Central High School in Louisville, Kentucky. His parents, worn down by life and work, expected little of him; the world, even less.

One person believed in Cassius Clay, however, and it was enough to change everything.

"Here he is, ladies and gentlemen!" his school principal, Atwood Wilson, would shout when he saw him, "Cassius Clay! The next heavyweight champion of the world. This guy is going to make a million dollars!" When some teachers wanted to fail Cassius, whose priority was athletics, not academics, Wilson intervened and gave a speech that few ever forgot. "Do you think I am going to be the principal of a school that Cassius Clay didn't finish?" he told them. "He's not going to fail in my school. I'm going to say, 'I taught him!'"

Every kid needs someone like this. Somebody who believes in them. Why was Muhammad Ali such a great fighter? Because somebody fought for him. You know who can do this for your kids? Who has to be that first, loudest, most resolute cheerleader for them? You.

August 17
Give Them Plenty of These

It never hurts to say a good word for your player.

—BILL RUSSELL

Queen Elizabeth II had a strange job. What were her daily duties? It's hard to say. It's easier to describe all the things she *didn't* do. She never passed laws. She never chose elected leaders. She didn't voice her opinion.

She did give out a lot of awards, though. Literally hundreds of thousands of them over the course of her seventy-year reign. She once said:

> People need pats on the back sometimes. It's a very dingy world otherwise.

Very true.

Nobody needs a pat on the back more than your kids . . . and there's nobody they'd rather get it from than you. Take an extra beat today to let your kids know what's special about them. Give them that pat on the back.

August 18
You Are the Toy

It is a happy talent to know how to play.

—RALPH WALDO EMERSON

Your son asks you to play trains, so you get the track down from the shelf. Your daughter wants to do a puzzle, so you start laying out the pieces. Then for some reason that is beyond the grasp of every parent who has ever lived, the moment you do what they say they want, they suddenly lose interest. Or they won't play by the rules, or they ask for something else, or now they want to move to a different room.

If you get exasperated—*What toy do you want?!*—you are missing the point. Or at least misunderstanding it. You see, *you are the toy*. What they want is to play with you—they don't want to be given a puppet, they want to pull your puppet strings.

When you understand this, everything is easier—no matter what age they are. Why is your teenager rebelling? In part, to get a rise out of you. Why is your middle-schooler being a smart aleck? To see how you'll respond. Why is your toddler calling for water from their bedroom, only to change their mind to juice, only to explain they meant the *other* juice, only to now ask to go to the bathroom. Because it's funny. Because it's a game. Because they're playing with the little bit of power they have in this strange, uncontrollable world: their power over the adults who have power over them.

So relax. Just go with it. Understand what's happening. It's not about the puzzle. It's not about anything. You are the toy.

August 19
You Must Have Their Back

When Sir Archibald Southby questioned Randolph Churchill's war record on the floor of Parliament, he hadn't meant anything personal. In fact, right afterward, he tried to shake Winston Churchill's hand, intending to explain it away as just politics.

No such thing existed to the Churchills.

"Do not speak to me," Winston Churchill told the man coldly. "You called my son a coward. You are my enemy. Do not speak to me."

Now, Randolph Churchill was not perfect, but that didn't prevent his father from standing up for him, from having his back. Nor should it ever prevent us. Winston Churchill's own father had not supported or believed in his son. Winston, deciding to do better, would not make that same mistake. He backed his son. He fought for him. He let Randolph know he could always be counted on.

We have to do the same. Our kids are going to screw up, but they need to know we'll never write them off. Our kids need to know that we'll take their side, that we'll fight for them, that we'll never let anyone wrongly abuse or attack them without hearing from us about it.

August 20
Encourage the Dream

It's not that parents don't believe in their kids. It's that they know the world is hard. They know that the odds are long. And most of all, nobody wants harm or crushing disappointment to come to their children. That's why we discourage them from dropping out, from trying to make it as a musician, from quitting their job to start a company. We're just worried.

Will Ferrell—one of the greatest comedic actors of all time, as we've talked about—certainly challenged his parents in this way. *You're going to become a sketch comedian? What?!?* Even his father, a working musician, had reservations about his pursuing such an uncertain, unstable career. Thankfully, he caught himself before Will came to him for advice. Putting his very natural, understandable worries on the back burner, Roy Lee Ferrell led with support and belief: "You know what? I think you have the skill, but it takes a lot of luck. If you don't make it, don't worry about it. You can just try something else."

Roy Lee was communicating to Will, from his own hard-won experience, just how hard and unlikely success was in one of those much-dreamed-of career fields. He was saying, *You're talented and I believe in you, but it's going to be really hard, so hard that if it doesn't work, you have to understand that it's just a reflection on the industry and not on you as a person.*

That is an incredible gift to give your children. Permission to try . . . along with permission to fail. The signal that you'll support them either way, that nothing changes based on the path they choose, the heights they reach, or the marks they fall short of.

August 21
Don't Care More Than They Do

In another great scene from Rich Cohen's amazing book on parenting through the lens of youth hockey, Rich tries to console his son after he doesn't make the team, in what was an extremely unfair process. Rich expected his son would be angry or at least aware of what had happened. He writes, "He was bugged but not devastated or even all that upset. Which upset me. Why did I care more than he did?"

This is a great question. *Why do you care more than they do?* Why are you spending so much time telling them they've been hurt (when they haven't been)? Why do you need them to take everything as seriously as you do?

When our kids get older, some of these things will become their problem. But for now? Let them have their childhood. They are young; they understand and feel things differently than you do. Don't assume that the "adult" way is better or necessarily more correct. There is a wisdom to their innocence—defer to it, or at least respect it enough not to corrupt it.

August 22
This Is a Tough Balance

As parents, we have to figure out the balance between supporting our kids and pushing them.

It's like those early days at the park when they find their way to the swing set for the first time. In the beginning, it's all about providing support while they get comfortable with the pendular motion of the swing. Then you start pushing a little more. But push too hard too soon and they can fly off the front or whip themselves off the back when the swing comes falling back toward the bottom. Eventually they get used to the ebb and flow of the swing, they find their grip confidently on the chains, they know how to anticipate the force of ever bigger pushes and the resulting swings in the other direction. And when that finally happens, that's when they start pumping their legs on their own, sending themselves as high as they can—higher than you ever thought they would be comfortable reaching.

As parents, that's the shifting balance we must find—and keep—at all times if we are to do right by our kids, because nobody improves in life simply by remaining where they are.

The founder of Dell Computers, Michael Dell, has a great mantra in his company related to this idea: "Pleased but never satisfied." Perhaps this is a way of thinking about ambition and progress and personal development that we can teach our kids and, with some sensitivity, also apply to our own parenting style. Remember: great coaches are harder on their teams when they *win* than when they lose. They are pleased but never satisfied. Because they know the team's true potential and they want to help them realize it. Just as you must with your kids.

August 23
They Don't Need a Lecture. They Need This.

> Which teacher is more worthy . . . the one who savages his
> students if their memory fails or their eye clumsily falters
> when reading, or the one who prefers to correct and teach
> with admonitions that bring a blush to the students' cheeks?
> Show me a brutal tribune or centurion and I'll show you one
> who makes soldiers desert—pardonably.
>
> —SENECA

As John Steinbeck was writing *East of Eden*, his son Tom was not taking school seriously. He was acting out. Steinbeck's wife thought Tom needed a lecture about this. Steinbeck, then in the middle of writing about two very different, unruly sets of sons, knew that wasn't quite right. "He needs more than that," he wrote in his journal. "He needs infinite patience and discipline."

Not only is that what your kids need, but it's what we *all* need. Patience and discipline. Kindness combined with firmness. In an *infinite* amount. Nobody wants to be lectured. Nobody wants to be nagged. What we need is to be understood and held accountable.

Think of your own troubles as a kid. When you were acting out, when you weren't taking school seriously, when you were getting into trouble, did getting yelled at help? What you really wanted—what you needed— was for someone to see *why* you were doing these things. You needed someone to guide you back to the right path and to help you realize the consequences of being off it.

Patience and discipline. That was what you needed. So give those things to your kids. They deserve it.

August 24
Be Something and Somebody

E. H. Harriman was a hell of a businessman and a surprisingly good father. He had a reputation as a rapacious industrialist, but at home he was tender and engaged with his kids. He was patient and he instilled in them good values.

Once, he wrote to his son's headmaster to ask how the boy was doing in his schooling. "Fair in his studies," came the reply, along with news that young Averell was "gaining steadily." Encouraged, he wrote to his son asking whether he might be able to "jack up" his efforts in English. "I know you can as well as some other subjects," he wrote. "It is encouraging to have you so improved, and I am sure you will catch on, and go on and on and be something and somebody."

That's a perfect phrase. He wasn't telling his son he needed to get perfect scores. He wasn't telling him that he was worthless for having come up short. Or that success was necessarily about being better than anyone else. Like Jim Valvano's father, what the elder Harriman was saying was that he knew what his son was capable of and, more important, what is expected of a person with his potential: to *be something and somebody*.

We don't necessarily need our kids to be financially successful or supremely powerful or famous. But we do expect them to make something of themselves—to *be somebody*, whether that's a respected member of their small church or the head of a legislative body. And we expect them to *do something*, because life is a gift.

To waste it? To do the minimum? No, that's failure for them and for us. So let's jack up our efforts and our expectations for them.

August 25
Are You Telling Them This?

A s a young novelist, Susan Straight was told by her mentor, the great James Baldwin, "You must continue to write. It is imperative." Imagine how different that was from the example she got from her own mother who, as we discussed, believed her own creative life was over the day she had kids.

The question we have to ask ourselves is: Which path are we choosing? Are we telling them that they must continue to fulfill their potential—that it's *imperative*? Or through our actions (or *in*actions) are we telling them the opposite? Have we unknowingly become dream killers, or are we actively becoming dream builders?

That's the question. And it is definitely imperative.

There is no benefit to quitting on oneself. Sure, you might have to face facts and choose one career path over another, but that's not the same as *stopping*. Making money from the thing you love to do is not as important as getting better at it, as maximizing your potential.

As parents, it is imperative that we root for them, that we be fans. We have to encourage them. We have to tell them to keep going. That there are more, better things ahead. The world is going to put up enough stop signs, erect enough obstacles, deliver enough heartbreak. We don't need to add to it. We need to do the opposite. We need to *believe in them*.

August 26
It's Your Job to Check In

Nobody steals a scene on *Seinfeld* quite like George's parents, Frank and Estelle Costanza. And naturally, nobody makes George more miserable than they do. They are a crazy, absurd set of parents.

In one episode, George has to make his weekly call to them, and it's a task he finds so onerous that he has to prepare things in advance to talk about. The twist, of course, is that George's parents dread the calls themselves. "And every Sunday with the calls," they finally complain.

In reality, this is precisely backward. Why is George checking in? That's his parents' job.

Your kids didn't choose this life; you did. What does that mean? It means as your kids get older there should be none of that "Why don't you ever call?" nagging. That's your responsibility.

That said, if you want the kind of relationship where your kids *do* call and check in and share what's going on with their lives, it starts when they're much, much younger. When you can't just expect them to open up and share with you. When you have to check in with them because *they don't know that they're struggling* or that there's anything worth sharing. Kids simply don't have the experience or the perspective yet to know one way or the other.

When it comes to stuff like this, "just being there" is not enough. You have to seek them out. You have to reach out. You have to gently pry them open. You have to help them realize their own feelings. You have to be more than there—you have to be proactive.

August 27
Other People Are Trying to Do This Too

The people you work with or for, or the people who work for you, also have a life outside of work. Like you, they are a mother or a father, a son or a daughter. Like you, they have kids and relationships and struggle to balance them all. Like you, they are trying to put family first and to be a fan.

The legendary NBA coach Gregg Popovich is a hard-driving boss, but he does his best to try to help the people who work for and with him. His former assistant coach Mike Brown tells the story of when he was going through a separation. His two sons lived with their mom in Colorado but were visiting him in San Antonio for a week. Brown took them to the airport before he had to catch his own flight for an away game with the Spurs. His boys were crying and begging to not have to get on the plane, to be able to stay with their dad. Brown called Coach Pop to tell him he was having some trouble and asked him to hold the team plane a few minutes. Pop told Brown to stay with his kids. "No, no, no," Brown said, "the kids will be fine."

"If you show up to this plane," Pop told him, "you're fired." "Come on, man! I'm going to be there." Brown said. "Remember, if I see you on this plane, you're fired." *Click.* Pop hung up on his assistant. Brown and his boys missed their flights and spent three more days together.

Can you imagine what it would feel like to have someone do that for you? Maybe not. But maybe you could make it feel a little more real by *doing it for somebody else.*

August 28
Don't Use Your Kids

Social media exploits one of the most vulnerable parts of our psyche: our need to be seen and heard and validated. The brilliant programmers of these networks have discovered how to reward this addictive impulse with Likes and comments and follower counts. They turned our greatest vulnerabilities into a game.

That's what parents should be worried about. When you're feeling insecure and want to be validated, resist the urge to just post more photos of your kid. Ask yourself: *Is this really what my kid wants? Is this really healthy or appropriate? Or is exploiting their cuteness just a cheap way to get attention and feel better about myself?*

Being a fan is not about showing them off or trying to impress people—at dinner conversations or on social media. It's not bragging about where they go to college or how cute they looked dressed up for their birthday.

Our job is to take care of them, not exploit them. Don't turn your kids and the precious experiences you have with them into fodder for this insatiable maw.

August 29
Teach Them to Be a Good Sport

How someone handles winning and losing reveals so much about their character. The earlier kids are taught this, the more prepared they will be for the real world (which includes plenty of both).

In his essay "On Anger," Seneca lays out some specific advice for fathers when it comes to teaching kids how to be good sports. He writes:

> In contests with his comrades we ought not to allow him to become sulky or fly into a passion: let us see that he be on friendly terms with those whom he contends with, so that in the struggle itself he may learn to wish not to hurt his antagonist but to conquer him: Whenever he has gained the day or done something praiseworthy, we should allow him to enjoy his victory, but not to rush into transports of delight: for joy leads to exultation, and exultation leads to swaggering and excessive self-esteem.

This is important. We want our kids to possess the will to win, but not so much that it possesses them. We want them to feel good when they win, without being so dependent or addicted to that feeling that they are crushed when, inevitably, they lose. We don't want their success to fuel their ego, or their shortcomings on the field to lead to insecurity or self-loathing.

It is, like all things, about balance. And most of all, about being respectful, being responsible, and enjoying the process more than the results.

August 30
This Is What It Takes to Thrive

Several years ago, the writer Malcolm Gladwell pointed out how surprising it is that even in the NBA, which is filled with objectively talented and elite athletes, it sometimes requires a team change or a head coaching change (or a mental-skills professional) for a player to thrive. They might have bounced around to two or three places, had multiple disappointing seasons, and then suddenly, when the environment around them is right, when they have the support they need, *bam*, they're *great*.

His point was this: if even athletes being paid millions of dollars to perform need this, how can we possibly just *expect* kids to succeed in any old classroom we drop them into? We are so quick to write kids off—even our own kids—as not good at math, as a so-so student, as having trouble focusing or whatever. So quick!

But of course, environment is everything. The right supporting cast is everything. Timing is everything. We have to be patient. We have to be flexible. We can't stop rooting for them, believing in them. We have to take a page from these sports teams that, understanding they have a very valuable asset on their hands, do not despair when things don't immediately click. No, when things aren't working, they invest more. They don't blame the star. They blame the system . . . and then try to fix it. And the fans cheer like crazy the whole time.

Well, our kids are even more priceless than any basketball player. And their education is even more important than playing a game well.

August 31
Being a Fan Isn't Easy

I t was a time when women did not have jobs, let alone become *published authors*. Not respectable women, anyway. And yet there Jane Austen's father was, submitting Jane's writings to a publisher. "As I am well aware of what consequence it is that a work of this sort should make its first appearance under a respectable name I apply to you," he wrote to the well-known publisher Cadell, according to Claire Tomalin's book *Jane Austen: A Life*.

Being a fan of your kids is not just rooting for them at the occasional soccer game. It's not just telling them they're special. It's also putting yourself out there, taking risks for them. It's being willing to defy conventions, to encourage *them* to defy conventions if they feel their calling demands it.

You tried your whole life to raise a kid who is comfortable with themselves, who is confident, who is competent, who could be successful. When your efforts begin to bear fruit, real challenges will sprout up alongside. As they push the boundaries of their comfort zone, they may well push you out of yours. But that's good! That's what we want!

We have to believe in our kids. To be their fans. To be willing to risk with and for them. If we don't believe in our kids, who will? Be a real fan. It's not easy, but where would the world be if great parents had always taken the easy route?

SEPTEMBER

RAISE A READER

(LESSONS IN LEARNING AND CURIOSITY)

September 1
This Is the Great Leveler

Not all of us are able to give our children riches. Or powerful connections. Or even superior genetics. Does this mean our kids are at a disadvantage? That they're screwed? Nope. Because there is a great leveler out there—one that we can show them and that they can use at any time.

The famous Princeton basketball coach Pete Carril would tell his young athletes:

> My father came from the province of León in Castile, Spain and worked for thirty-nine years in the open-hearth for the Bethlehem Steel Company. Every day, before he left for work, he would remind my sister and me how important it was to be smart. "In this life," he would say, "the big, strong guys are always taking from the smaller, weaker guys but . . . the smart take from the strong."

It's simple fatherly wisdom: use your brain. It's the secret weapon of underdogs everywhere, available to all and always free.

September 2
This Is How You Teach Them

> They say I tell a great many stories. I reckon I do; but I have learned from long experience that *plain* people, take them as they run, are more easily *influenced* through the medium of a proud and humorous illustration than any other way.
>
> —ABRAHAM LINCOLN

If the Bible is any indication, Jesus rarely seemed to come out and say what he meant. He preferred, instead, to employ parables and stories and little anecdotes that made you think. He tells the story of the servants and the talents. He tells the stories of the Prodigal Son, the Good Samaritan, the mustard seed, and the lost sheep. Turns out, that's a pretty effective way to get a point across and make it stick.

And so it will be with your kids. We learn through stories—whether it's the story of Cincinnatus or a story about the time when you were their age. We learn when people share moments of vulnerability, of their hard-won experience. We don't like it when people *tell* us the point; we like it when they *show* us.

So stop thinking about giving them all the answers and start thinking about stories to tell that make the answers self-evident. It's the best way to teach.

September 3
Introduce Them to the (Friendly) World of Ideas

> Our first job, our first responsibility, is instilling a sense of
> learning, a sense of a love of learning, in our kids.
>
> —BARACK OBAMA

The Marine general and former U.S. secretary of defense Jim Mattis has talked about his idyllic childhood in Pullman, Washington. There he spent time outdoors, explored, got in trouble, and had an all-American childhood. He talks lovingly of a house filled with books, run by parents who encouraged their children not only to read them but to question and interact with them as well. He recalls, "They introduced us to a world of great ideas—not a fearful place, but a place to enjoy."

What a thing to say! A target for each of us to aim for with our own children.

You must teach your kids to be curious, to be open, to be willing to explore. Your job is to teach them how to make their own informed opinions, how to decide for themselves, how to be comfortable with uncomfortable topics. Ideas are our friends. They will serve your children well, and your children will serve them well, if you teach them early and often.

The world is a place of great ideas. There is nothing to be afraid of . . . except fear and ignorance.

September 4
Teach Them Early—When You Still Can

> To learn is simply to allow something to be done to you, and
> to be quickly persuaded is natural for those who are less able
> to offer resistance.
>
> —PLUTARCH

We have to start teaching our kids the important things early, even when it seems like they are way too young, because if we wait, they'll be able to fight us off. They'll have the words and the resolve to resist the lessons that we know they will need in life for the struggles they can't see coming.

We have to get them while they're still young and impressionable. We have to push past their reservations. Of course they would rather play video games. Of course it's more fun to goof off. But now is the time. Before they can fight us off with their full determination. Before the cement is completely dry.

278   RAISE A READER

September 5
Do You Do This over Dinner?

He who cannot put his thoughts on ice should not enter into
the heat of dispute.

—FRIEDRICH NIETZSCHE

Some families watch TV at dinner. Some families eat separately. Some families talk idly about their day. Dinner at Agnes Callard's house is different. She and her children *debate*.

Because Callard is a philosopher, many of their debates are philosophical. If a conjoined twin committed a crime, should both twins be punished? Is it possible for the other twin to be completely innocent? But some of the topics are silly, such as the debate, led by her then seven-year-old, on what would be the ideal type of glove.

It wasn't the content of the debate that mattered, of course—it was the activity. It was that they did it as a family. And like most great parenting strategies, this wasn't some forced or formal activity. It wasn't an obligation or a chore. These debates began as discussions between her and her husband that her kids wanted to join. They evolved over time. The rules are ad hoc; the tradition is organic. But in the end, it shaped the course of her family and their intellectual lives.

Can you say the same about your dinners? Maybe you should talk about it, then. Maybe even debate it.

September 6
How to Get Them to Read (or Do Anything)

> A reader lives a thousand lives before he dies. The man who never reads lives only one.
>
> —GEORGE R. R. MARTIN

In her classic poem, "Tula ["Books are door-shaped"]," Margarita Engle describes books as "door-shaped portals," which is as apt as it is beautiful. Books carry us across oceans and centuries, she writes, with the extra benefit of making us feel less alone. Stephen King's line was that books are "uniquely portable magic."

We want to give our kids access to this magic; we want them to walk through these portals. *We want them to read.*

Reading anything is better than watching so much TV or playing with the iPad or texting endlessly on their phone, after all. But are we doing enough to motivate them to pick up a book? Are we providing a good example?

How often do your kids catch you reading? How often do they see you with a book in your hands? You want them to read, but do you read regularly to them? You tell them that books are important, that books are fun, but where is the evidence?

If you want your kids to read more, if you want them to walk through those magical door-shaped portals, show them what a reader looks like. Talk to them about books. Make books a central part of your house . . . and your lives.

September 7
The Lives of the Greats Remind Us

Why do we tell stories to our kids? Why do we tell them about history? Teach them about Martin Luther King Jr., George Washington, Porcia Cato, Cincinnatus, Florence Nightingale, Jesus, Marcus Aurelius? Because it matters.

As Longfellow wrote,

Lives of great men all remind us
We can make our lives sublime,
And, departing, leave behind us
Footprints on the sands of time.

We are trying to teach our kids the most important and pressing lesson of all: *that they can make a difference, they can change the world.*

We tell our kids stories to inspire them. That's what bedtime reading is about—not just tiring them out so they'll go to sleep. The point of history class isn't to berate them with the evil deeds of old dead white guys. We want them to know: People can have an impact. People can lead wonderful lives. People can leave their footprints on the sands of time.

Not just people, not just heroes or the dynastically wealthy, but *your kids* too. They can do this. And in helping them realize that, *you* are making your own impact.

September 8
Are You Bringing This Home?

> A child learns more in one split second, carving a little stick,
> than in whole days, listening to a teacher.
>
> —SIMÓN RODRÍGUEZ

Orville and Wilbur Wright were bicycle salesmen from Ohio. They weren't engineers. They didn't go to college; they didn't have any technical training. Meanwhile, there were teams of engineers from the top universities working on the same problem. One was funded by a grant from the U.S. War Department.

How could the Wrights have possibly bested those deep pockets to become the inventors and pioneers we know them as today?

"It began for them with a toy," David McCullough writes in *The Wright Brothers*, "a small helicopter brought home by their father, Bishop Milton Wright, a great believer in the educational value of toys. . . . It was little more than a stick with twin propellers and twisted rubber bands, and probably cost 50 cents."

It might not seem like a toy could change a child's life, but of course it can. As Simón Bolívar said many years earlier, a child can learn as much from a stick as from any teacher. Toys are more than just things to play with. They are worlds to discover. They are things to be responsible for. They are things to take apart and put back together. They are laboratories for life.

We spend a lot of time introducing our kids to the world of ideas. Let's also carve out some time to bring home cool toys. Toys with educational value. Toys that teach them about other cultures. Toys that get them interested in flight or science or math or history or technology. Toys that are, in and of themselves, vessels for ideas.

Who knows what might come from their exploration of fun.

September 9
Teach Them to Notice

> Pay attention. It's all about paying attention. It's all about taking in as much of what's out there as you can.
>
> —SUSAN SONTAG

When former diplomat and secretary of defense Robert Lovett was a kid, he and his dad took similar routes in the morning and evening to work and to school. And the fact that they left both places at slightly different times allowed Lovett and his dad to play an interesting game.

At night after dinner, according to biographers Walter Isaacson and Evan Thomas, Lovett's dad would ask questions about what he had seen. "'How many horses were pulling the cart?' he would ask about a midtown construction project. 'How many girders were in the cart?' 'How were the horses hitched to the cart?'" There would be a few quarters as a reward if young Robert was right, but he could be docked a quarter from his winnings if he got anything wrong.

This was more than just a silly activity they did together, although such things are wonderful. What his father was teaching him was the *art of paying attention*. Robert was learning to notice, to focus on the details and not to take his surroundings for granted, to be *present*. It was a skill he used to great advantage as he rose through the diplomatic ranks of the State Department.

Of course, you don't have to play the same game, but you can find your own way to reward and inspire your kids to pay attention. The quarters and the pats on the back they might win will be nice in the moment, but they will pale in comparison to the value of the real gift you'll have given them, which will last them a lifetime.

September 10
"Beautiful" Is What They Say It Is

There is an old LEGO ad from the early 1980s. It has a little pigtailed redhead holding her LEGO creation. What is it? Honestly, it's hard to say. It's basically random blocks snapped together. One of the LEGO men has a tree on his head. Needless to say, no architect would sign off on this project. But the smile on this cute little kid's face says it all.

"Have you ever seen anything like it?" the copy on the ad reads. "Not just what she's made, but how proud it's made her. It's a look you'll see whenever children build something all by themselves. No matter what they've created . . . LEGO Universal Building Sets will help your children discover something very, very special: themselves."

As parents—as adults—it can be so easy to step in and tell your kids how things are supposed to go. *Trees don't go on people's heads! A window doesn't make sense there! But where will they sleep? Dogs and cats aren't friends! There is no air in space!* We think that we are helping or that we are teaching. But really we are stepping on their ability to create and imagine. We may well be depriving them of that beautiful look of pride that the little girl in the ad has—the one that comes from doing something all by yourself. And discovering yourself in the process.

Playtime is for play. It's supposed to be silly. It's supposed to be fun. There are no rules. None of it matters . . . unless they want it to matter. So give them some space. Encourage them. Just watch. Let them be beautiful.

September 11
This Is How You Make Them Smart

I have no special talents, I am only passionately curious.

—ALBERT EINSTEIN

There is a story about Sandra Day O'Connor in Evan Thomas's great book *First*. "During one of Washington's every-seventeen-years eruptions of dormant cicadas," he writes, "O'Connor collected a batch of the large, dead insects and sent them in a shoebox to her grandchildren in Arizona."

Her clerk was baffled. O'Connor explained: "One of the most important things to me is that my children and grandchildren are curious. Because, if you're not curious, you're not smart."

We don't have control over what kind of brain our kids are born with. We don't even really control what kind of college they get into. Are they a math kid or an artist? Right-brained or left-brained? That's not up to us. But what we can influence is whether they're curious. We can encourage this instinct—asking them questions and rewarding them for asking their own. We can cultivate this instinct until it becomes a personality trait—finding all sorts of interesting things and showing them to our kids. And we can demonstrate it—pouring fuel on the sparks of curiosity they exhibit by engaging with the things we're curious about too.

We can't make them a specific kind of genius. But we can make them smart . . . by showing them how to be curious.

September 12
This Is Something to Invest In

> When I have a little money, I buy books; and if I have any left,
> I buy food and clothes.
>
> —ERASMUS

You work hard for your family. You know how you sweated for each dollar, which can make those dollars hard to spend. Especially if you have an eye toward investing—every dollar expended now comes at the cost of returns in the future.

That's one way to think about it, but it's not the *only* way. Marcus Aurelius wrote that what he learned from his great-grandfather was to "avoid public schools, to hire good private teachers, and to accept the resulting costs as money well spent."

What Marcus was talking about is *investing* in your children's education—whatever form you decide it will take. A tutor to teach them Spanish a couple times a month? A piano instructor? A yearly pass to the museum downtown? The gas and the commute to the magnet school on the other side of town instead of the closer but less rigorous one? Private tuition? One parent working less so you can homeschool?

None of this is cheap. But don't think of it as an expense. Think of it as an investment. It's the most important investment you can make—it's an investment in their knowledge, in their education, in their future. It's making them better. It's worth what it costs.

September 13
You Have to Unlock This

It wasn't until law school that future secretary of state Dean Acheson was fully unlocked as a human being. There, he said, with the help of his professors, he was introduced to a "tremendous discovery," as he called it:

> The discovery of the power of thought. Not only did I become aware of this powerful mechanism, the brain, but I became aware of an unlimited mass of material that was lying about the world waiting to be stuffed into the brain.

It was this discovery that propelled Acheson to become not just one of the top legal minds of his time but eventually the country's principal diplomat. Yet it's also a little sad. He went to Groton School, Yale College, and Harvard Law School. His parents were smart too. But somehow nobody had been able (or interested?) to get him to realize *the power of thought* until he was in his midtwenties? Unreal!

Just as we have to help introduce our kids to the world of ideas, we also have to help them discover the incredible power of thought. We have to give them a sense of the limitlessness of human potential trapped in those three pounds of soft tissue between our ears. We have to show them what a powerful mechanism they have been given; then we need to show them how to use it.

We need to unlock their brains . . . as early as possible.

September 14
Not Just to Read, but to Read Critically

> To read attentively—not to be satisfied with "just getting the gist of it."
>
> —MARCUS AURELIUS

An illiterate world is not a good one, but a world where people unthinkingly believe and accept everything they read is not that much better. So it's great that you're teaching your kids to read, but are you teaching them to read *critically*?

They need to know: Authors can be wrong. Authors can be questioned. A book is not a one-way conversation. It's a dialogue between the reader and the writer, between the past and the present. Show them how to take notes, how to disagree, how to question what they see on the page, and how to participate in the dialogue that has begun in the pages they are holding.

They need to know: No one book is definitive. No one school or system has all the answers. Show them how to read books from opposing thinkers. Read one book together . . . then read something that presents a different point of view. Talk about the importance of debate, how to compare and contrast. Teach them to be more than a reader, teach them to be a wide-ranging, critical reader. A questioner. A reviewer. A *thinker*.

September 15
Protect This Impulse

The famed French photographer Henri Cartier-Bresson was a pain in the ass to his teachers. He was bored by what they were teaching in school. He didn't pay attention. He was constantly getting caught reading something that had nothing to do with his schoolwork, books that were often inappropriate for his age.

One day, as he was about to start sixth grade, he was caught by the principal reading Mallarmé or Rimbaud, two beautiful French poets. At first, the principal seemed like he'd finally had enough. "Let's have no disorder in your studies," he barked, using the informal *tu*. Every other time Henri had been addressed this way, it had been followed with punishment. But then the principal's voice turned to kindness. "You're going to read in my office," he said, and led the boy there, where Henri returned over and over again as a precocious, curious reader for the rest of his school days.

It was this conversation—this little bit of intellectual guardianship and protection of his curiosity—that helped Henri carve out the foundations and freedom that would lead him to become one of the greatest photographers in history.

We have to remember that our job as parents, as educators, is not to keep our kids in line for its own sake. It's not to crush their initiative because it's disruptive or uncomfortable or difficult for us. We have to encourage them. We have to make space for our kids.

If they want to read? By God, let them! If they want to skip ahead or deviate from the conventional path? Cheer them on! Who knows, they may have just found their way . . .

September 16
It's About the Right Moment

> There is a select group of writers who are accessible to anyone, at whatever age or stage of life—Homer, Shakespeare, Goethe, Balzac, Tolstoy—and then there are those whose significance is not properly revealed until a particular moment.
>
> —STEFAN ZWEIG

Maybe they can understand *Ender's Game* at eleven, or maybe it won't be until they're seventeen. Maybe they can get the message of *The Great Gatsby* in high school, or maybe it's something you'll have to read as a kind of family book club later on. Maybe they'll take to poetry early, or maybe they won't. Maybe they'll love *The Little Prince* or *Charlotte's Web* as much as you did, or maybe tonight is just not the night.

Stefan Zweig was twenty when he first picked up Michel de Montaigne's *Essays*—an incomparable book—but he had "little idea what to do with it." It wasn't until the last year of his life, after two world wars and a forced exile, that Zweig picked up Montaigne again. This time, the connection was instant. The impact was enormous. Because the moment was right.

Remember, our goal here is to *raise* readers. But as with gardening, there is a time and a season for certain things to take root, and until you get there, the thing you'll need most is patience.

September 17
You Gotta Give Them Access

> The story of Theodore Roosevelt is the story of a small boy
> who read about great men and decided he wanted to be like
> them.

—HERMANN HAGEDORN

Theodore Roosevelt certainly came from a privileged family. They were rich, they were social elites, they had a mansion in Manhattan. Yet, as Doris Kearns Goodwin wrote, his main advantage was actually pretty simple:

> Few young children read as broadly or had such access to books as
> young Roosevelt. He had only to pick a volume on the shelves of the
> vast library in his family's home or express interest in a particular
> book and it would magically materialize. During one family va-
> cation Teedie proudly reported that he and his younger brother
> and sister, Elliott and Corinne, had devoured fifty novels! Thee
> [Theodore's father] read aloud to his children in the evenings after
> dinner. . . . Above all, he sought to impart didactic principles of
> duty, ethics, and morality through stories, fables, and maxims.

It would be wonderful if we could hand our kids a famous last name, a legacy admission to Harvard, or a trust fund, but that is difficult to do. What you can do—what you *must do*—is give them access to a library. To unlimited numbers of books. Bring them up in a house that, if it lacks rich heritage or fame or noble lineage like the Roosevelts', is at least rich in a love of reading.

September 18
The Two Most Important Skills to Teach Your Kids

L ooking back on his surprise path to the presidency, one of Gerald Ford's main regrets came from the course of study he took in college. He would write in his memoirs that if he could go back, the two main things he would have studied were writing and public speaking. Writing well and speaking confidently and articulately before an audience were the two main skills he used in every facet of his life as a leader, and they were the two things he—like most students—got the least instruction in.

With all that has changed since Ford went to college (class of '35), how little has happened to disrupt that. Nothing remains more important than effective communication.

Kids learn dance in PE but pubic speaking and debate are optional, extracurricular activities. How nuts is that? Kids are evaluated on standardized tests . . . as if effective communication can possibly be captured via multiple choice. In fact, the questions and passages on standardized tests are often the epitome of poor writing and ineffective communication!

If schools aren't going to do it, we parents have to. It's on us to teach our kids these important skills—to make sure they're able to express themselves on the page and in person. We've got to give them the opportunities to get up and address an audience—and encourage the confidence required to be comfortable doing so.

Whatever happens in the future, communication will be key (and king). It's your job to make sure they're ready.

September 19
Let's Get to the Bottom of It

> How could youths better learn to live than by at once trying
> the experiment of living? Methinks this would exercise their
> minds as much as mathematics.
>
> —HENRY DAVID THOREAU

The author Susan Cheever tells a story of Henry David Thoreau, who before he became a great writer was a teacher. The school he taught at was close to a river, and it was a source of endless fascination to the kids, mainly what made so many of the interesting sounds that came from the water.

"It has been disputed whether the noise was caused by frogs," one student reflected later on. "Mr. Thoreau, however, caught three very small frogs, two of them in the act of chirping. While bringing them home one of them chirped in his hat."

Isn't that lovely? He didn't just dismiss their question with an obvious answer. He showed them how you go to the source of things—he showed them the importance of following your curiosity. Thoreau was full of demonstrations like that. For instance, he gave each student a small plot of land and taught them how to survey together, how to grow plants, and how to observe what was happening on their plots.

Yes, we're busy. Yes, we know stuff. But we can't just tell them what we know. We have to show them. We have to roll up our sleeves, take off our hats, and get to the bottom of stuff together.

September 20
Provide Them with This Unusual Advantage

More than three decades after their famous first flight, a journalist asked Orville and Wilbur Wright how they did it. How did two brothers with "no money, no influence, and no other special advantages" do what specialists with all those advantages couldn't do?

"It isn't true," Orville corrected, "to say we had no special advantages. We did have unusual advantages in childhood, without which I doubt we could have accomplished much." What was their unusual advantage? "The greatest thing in our favor," Orville explained, "was growing up in a family where there was always much encouragement to intellectual curiosity. If my father had not been the kind who encouraged his children to pursue intellectual interests without any thought of profit, our early curiosity about flying would have been nipped too early to bear fruit."

We have to do this too. We have to cultivate their curiosities, whatever they may be. We have to encourage their interests, without any thought of whether or not they might be able to profit from them.

We don't have to be special, or specialists, to give them this unusual advantage.

September 21
Raise Them to Be a "Why" Child

I n F. Scott Fitzgerald's short story "Head and Shoulders," the young prodigy Horace explains:

> I was a "why" child. I wanted to see the wheels go around. My father was a young economics professor at Princeton. He brought me up on the system of answering every question I asked him to the best of his ability.

A "'why' child"—what a delightful phrase! Isn't that who we're trying to raise? A child who knows how to figure things out. A child who isn't content with taking things at face value, who isn't satisfied with simple explanations.

Can this be annoying? Absolutely. It can even get them in trouble. But curious is better than complacent, and annoying is better than ignorant.

To be sure, there will be times when you're too tired to answer their questions. There will be other moments when you feel their questions are inappropriate. But in those moments, you must pause and breathe and remember that you have to seed this habit. You have to make sure you water it too—and do your best never to stamp it out.

The more questions they ask, the better. Not just for you or for them but for the world they live in.

September 22
Show Them What They'll Get Out of This

The way to teach a kid to love books—as the great lover of books Robert Greene has said—is by appealing to their self-interest. *Show them what they will get out of books.* Tangibly. Immediately. Better yet, *find them a book that will have a big payoff for them.*

President Joe Biden has talked about how reading earlier in his life about the orator Demosthenes and his speech impediment helped him overcome his own stutter—you think an experience like that, early on, doesn't turn a person into a reader for life? Find them books that will entertain them. That will help them get their crush to like them. That will make them laugh. That will piss their teachers off. That will help them learn a new skill or solve a problem or feel less alone.

Focus on the ROI—because that's what books are, investments. You put down a few dollars, commit several hours, and you get something back. To get your kids to read, you have to be a reader, of course, but you also have to show them what they will get out of books. Or else why would they bother?

September 23
Never Make Fun of Them for This

Your kids will do all sorts of ridiculous things. They will trip and fall, and yes, you will sometimes laugh. You will tease them about this and that. They'll make hilarious mistakes. They'll look back on their own childish ridiculousness with amusement. Your family will have all sorts of inside jokes.

This is fine. This is wonderful. It's what binds people together—the ability to bust each other's balls, to share memories and experiences.

One biographer of Harry Truman noted that the former president "mispronounced a reasonable number of words, which in the beginning puzzled me. Then I realized that while he had often read them, he had seldom, if ever, spoken them aloud, not even in many cases heard them spoken aloud."

It's essential that your house and your relationship be a safe place for the mispronunciation of words. Do not make them feel self-conscious about reading, about tackling topics outside their comfort zone. This is how they grow. Tease them and have fun about many things. But mispronouncing a word? Respect it. Encourage it . . . and if you want to fix the problem, start by expanding your own vocabulary!

September 24
Are You Showing Them How to Be a Student?

> Live as if you were to die tomorrow. Learn as if you were to
> live forever.
>
> —GANDHI

If you think back to when you were a kid, what appeared to you to be the best part about being an adult? No more school. Our parents didn't have to carry around heavy books or do homework. We never saw them applying to get into this school or that one. It's sort of sad that, by and large, we show our kids that education stops. That while adulthood isn't always fun, one perk is that you no longer have to go to class. That graduation is a final destination.

It doesn't have to be this way. There's the story of Epictetus teaching one day when a student's arrival caused a commotion in the back of the room. Who was it? Hadrian, the emperor. Hadrian's example clearly had an impact on his successor and adopted grandson, Marcus Aurelius. Late in his reign, a friend spotted Marcus heading out, carrying a stack of books. "Where are you going?" he asked. Marcus was on his way to a lecture on Stoicism, he said, for "learning is a good thing, even for one who is growing old. I am now on my way to Sextus the philosopher to learn what I do not yet know."

If you want your kids to value learning, if you want them to never stop furthering the education you've been investing so much time and money and care and worry into, then we have to show them what an adult committed to lifelong learning actually looks like. We have to show them we have not graduated, we are not on summer break, we have not arrived at the final destination of education.

Wisdom, they must learn, is an endless pursuit.

September 25
Make Sure They Spend Time around Old People

In his book *The Vanishing American Adult*, former senator Ben Sasse pondered what might strike a person from the distant past as odd about our modern society. Aside from the technology, he said, they'd notice the extreme *age segregation*. Invariably today, we spend time almost exclusively with people our own age.

Our kids go to school with other kids. We work with other adults. Our own parents and grandparents are shunted off to retirement communities and old folks' homes and cruise ships. The average age in the U.S. Senate, where Sasse worked, is around sixty-one. There are only ten senators, as of this writing, who are younger than him. The closest they get to young people is summer interns, pages, and junior legislative aides.

When was the last time you stayed under the same roof as someone twice your age? How many conversations do you have with people who grew up without the things you completely take for granted?

In Lori McKenna's song "Humble and Kind," she talks about visiting "grandpa every chance that you can." But it actually requires more than that, more than just seeing your own family. You have to make sure your kids aren't stuck in a bubble, living their lives away from anyone but other children.

Instead, you have to expose them to wisdom. Expose them to people who remember the good and the bad things that humans did in the recent and not-so-recent past. Expose them to people who have learned painful lessons. Expose them to people who have accomplished incredible things.

Otherwise all that wisdom might be lost, and so might your children.

September 26
It's About Learning, Not Memorization

To know by heart is not to know.

—MICHEL DE MONTAIGNE

I t's time for us to review your multiplication tables, you tell them. Let's look over your vocab flash cards. Or maybe you're one of those parents who make their kids recite poems or plays, who sign them up for speech competitions. Maybe you're drilling them for a spelling bee right now.

It's all making them smarter, you tell yourself. But is it? Or is it just teaching them how to *act* smart?

We're not trying to raise robots. We want kids who can *think*, who can figure stuff out. Who cares what they can recite? We want them to know *what something means* as much as we want them to know *what it is*. We want them to love learning, not trivia! So make sure your priorities are aligned. Make sure the activities you design actually get you closer to that goal. Make sure you're focused on the right stuff.

Teach them to *know*. That's what counts.

September 27
What Game Are You Teaching Them?

There are two types of games in this life: finite and infinite. Finite games are things you do once and then they're over. An infinite game is more like life itself—it goes on and on and everything is interrelated and independent. The former is zero-sum, the latter is non-zero-sum.

Tobias Lütke, the founder of Shopify, tries to live life as an infinite game. He also tries to make sure he doesn't send mixed messages to his kids. We talk to our children about education as an infinite game, he has said. We say it's about the love of learning, it's a lifelong pursuit, it's about developing into the best person you can be . . . but then we send them off with strong expectations of winning the finite game of first grade.

This sounds familiar, right? We've caught ourselves comparing our kids' grades with other kids'. We've talked to other parents about what grade level they're reading or doing math at and what percentile they're in statewide. We've obsessed over GPA and standardized test scores as if they were keys to the kingdom . . . of what exactly? Then we grill our college kids about whether they found their major yet, about whether the major they picked is going to snag them a high-paying job or not.

You want kids who are in this for life. You want kids who don't think in zero-sum terms. Teach them to play the infinite game. Teach them by playing it yourself.

September 28
They Must Be Surrounded by This

> No man has a right to bring up his children without sur-
> rounding them with books.
>
> —HORACE MANN

Do you know Lewin's equation? You're experiencing its implications as you read this:

$$B = f(P,E)$$

Behavior (B) is a function of a person (P) and their environment (E). Our habits, our actions, our lives, are determined by our surroundings.

What does this mean for us as parents? Well, we're largely the architects of our kids' environment. We all have different means and ends, but within those means we control what we surround our children with. The influences. The colors. The moods. The people. The interactions. And of course, the most important thing there is to a child's intellectual development: the books.

If you want them to be readers, you have to design the environment of a reader, as an architect does. You have to surround them with books. Good ones. Silly ones. Short ones. Long ones. Used ones. New ones. You have to display them prominently in your house. You have to take your kids to libraries and independent bookstores. Otherwise, how else could they possibly become readers?

September 29
Don't Baby Them When It Comes to Books

Modern books for children are rather horrible things, especially when you see them in the mass.

—GEORGE ORWELL

Not long ago, kids were taught Latin and Greek so they could read the classics . . . in their original languages. Think of *Aesop's Fables*. Think of children being read *Plutarch's Lives* by their parents. This is heavy stuff. And purposefully so. When you read old schoolbooks, what you're really doing is acquainting yourself with the obscure yet illustrative figures from the ancient world, while also displaying a willingness to wrestle with timeless and morally complex topics.

These days, the children and young adult sections of bookstores overflow with infantilizing escapism, fantastical melodrama, and just plain absurd nonsense. The curmudgeons among us want to blame millennials and Gen Z for this. Their laziness and faltering tastes are why we're awash in this stuff.

But do you really believe our kids are dumber than the kids of Orwell's time? Or back before that? Of course not! They're kids. *We're the problem.* Parents. Adults. Educators. Publishers. As a collective, we've stopped believing our kids are capable of reading challenging books. So we provide them with "kids' editions" and silly picture books instead of helping them build their reading muscles. Then we wonder why they can't handle heavy stuff.

Well, stop it. Push them. Push yourself. They aren't babies. Or at least they shouldn't be after they've learned to read for themselves.

September 30
Do They Have a Project?

Mastery doesn't come from rote recitation. It comes from falling in love with something. It comes from hard work, sure, but only when the hard work is aligned with a passionate love of a subject or a craft or a field. Forget credentialing; give them something to sink their teeth into!

As Paul Graham wrote:

> If I had to choose between my kids getting good grades and work-ing on ambitious projects of their own, I'd pick the projects. And not because I'm an indulgent parent, but because I've been on the other end and I know which has more predictive value. When I was picking startups for Y Combinator, I didn't care about applicants' grades. But if they'd worked on projects of their own, I wanted to hear all about those.

If you want a kid who has real skills and real passion in this world, you'd be well served to do the same.

OCTOBER

STRUGGLE AND EMERGE

(HOW TO RAISE THEIR RESILIENCE)

October 1
A Child's Life Should Be Good, Not Easy

The Stoic philosopher Seneca got front-row seats to one of the worst parenting jobs in history. In 49 AD, he was recalled from exile to tutor a twelve-year-old named Nero. The ancient historian Cassius Dio tells us that the boy's mother, the empress Agrippina, had the entire empire under her thumb and used her power to make sure her boy never had to struggle for anything. She was what we today call a snowplow parent. And in clearing the path of every conceivable impediment and obstacle, Agrippina created a monster, one of the worst human beings in history.

It's little mystery why we see Seneca write over and over again about the importance of struggling with and overcoming adversity. The job of "the good parent," he says, is to "out of love for the child, [act] as a trainer, endlessly manufacturing trials for the child." The job of the good parent is to make their child's life good, not easy.

There is a great Latin expression, "*Luctor et emergo.*" It means "I struggle and emerge" or "I wrestle with and overcome." The gods, Seneca writes, "want us to be as good, as virtuous as possible, so assign to us a fortune that will make us struggle." Without struggle, he says, "no one will know what you were capable of, not even yourself."

It is hard *not* to be a snowplow or helicopter parent. We love our kids so much; we want nothing but the best for them. We can't bear the thought, let alone the sight, of their struggling. But we have to let them scramble through the brambles and the pitfalls of growing up. We have to remind ourselves day after day: *a child's life should be good, not easy.*

October 2
You Can't Prevent Them from Making Mistakes

In the novel *Siddhartha*, the title character tries desperately to convince his son of the importance of the simple way of life, having learned the wisdom of it through painful experience. Like you, like all parents, he watches as his son ignores his warnings, despairing as he goes the wrong direction. Confiding his frustration to his friend, Vasudeva, Siddhartha is hit with this question:

> "Do you really believe you have committed your follies so that your son may be spared them?"

It would be wonderful if our kids didn't have to learn through trial and error, if they could simply accept our advice and start where we left off, rather than touch the proverbial hot stove for themselves. But we should be wise enough as human beings by now to know that is simply not how life works. Much of what we learn has to be learned on our own. Some mistakes have to be made to be fully understood. Don't your own experiences teach you that, anyway? How many of your parents' warnings did you really heed?

You can't prevent your kids from making mistakes. You have to give them the space to learn on their own. But you can take solace in the knowledge that you've instilled the character, the awareness, and the willingness to ask for help that they will need in order to bounce back from the mistakes they will inevitably make.

October 3
This Is the Main Lesson

> The chief task in life is simply this: to identify and separate matters so that I can say clearly to myself which are externals not under my control, and which have to do with the choices I actually control. Where then do I look for good and evil? Not to uncontrollable externals, but within myself to the choices that are my own.
>
> —EPICTETUS

There is a lesson underneath nearly everything we want to teach our kids. It is a heady one . . . and yet also a very simple one. The lesson you have to teach happens to be the core of Stoic philosophy, and also the key to success in life: *We don't control what happens in life. We control how we respond.*

Your daughter thinks a teacher is unfair and doesn't like them? Okay, that very well might be true. So what is she going to do about it? The coach says your son is too short to play basketball? Same thing. Screwed up and failed a math test? There's a bully on the playground? Only got into their safety school? Same. Same. Same.

Teach your kids not to wallow in these misfortunes but to focus on *what is next.* Guide them to put their energy toward their response. Because that's what's up to them. That is the superpower they have. If you teach them that, they have it.

October 4
Make Them Do Their Own Stuff

Sit and pray your nose doesn't run! Or, rather just wipe your
nose and stop seeking a scapegoat.

—EPICTETUS

There is a great story about a young Spartan woman, Gorgo, who would one day become queen. Despite her royal status, like all Spartans she was raised to be self-sufficient, with no frills or needless luxury.

So imagine Gorgo's surprise when she witnessed a distinguished visitor to Sparta have his shoes put on by a servant. "Look, Father," she said innocently to her father, King Leonidas, "the stranger has no hands!"

Sadly, for some of us, it could just as easily be deduced that our kids have no hands. And no brains. We put on their clothes for them. We make their decisions. We clear the road in front like a snowplow. We hover like a helicopter, just in case something goes wrong. We do *everything* for them.

Then we wonder why they are helpless. We wonder why they have trouble with anxiety or low self-esteem. Confidence is something you earn. It comes from self-sufficiency. It comes from experience. When we coddle and baby them—when we take away their hands—we deprive them of these critical assets.

It's not right. It's not fair.

October 5
Don't Be Like This

In early 2021, the musician John Roderick was rightfully criticized by parents all over the world for missing the point on how to teach kids.

His daughter was hungry. He was busy. She wanted to cook some beans. He wanted her to figure out how to do it on her own. As he worked on a jigsaw puzzle, she struggled to open the can of baked beans with a can opener. She struggled and struggled and struggled. "Will you please just open the can?" she said. He wouldn't—wanting this to be a lesson. She kept trying, he kept making suggestions (and tweeting about it). This went on and on and on and on for *six hours*, until she finally opened the can.

Roderick was dubbed "Bean Dad" for his efforts. There's a difference between being a supportive parent and being a bean dad. There's a difference between letting your kid wrestle with difficulty so they can be better for it and letting them fumble with a can so you can tweet a story.

No, our job isn't to open every can for them. Nor is it to let them struggle in the dark for six hours. Step in, show them *how* to be self-sufficient. Show them how the damn can opener works! Start the can for them the first time and let them take it from there.

Be a guide; don't be a bean dad.

October 6
Help Them Forge This

> Just as in fair weather, then, one ought to prepare for the storm, so also in youth one should store up discipline and self-restraint as a provision for old age.
>
> —PLUTARCH

Theodore Roosevelt spent almost every day during the first twelve years of his life struggling with horrible asthma. The attacks were an almost nightly near-death experience. He was bedridden for weeks at a time. Born into great wealth and status, he could have remained weak and would have been taken care of throughout his life. Then one day his father came into his room and delivered a message that would change the young boy's life: "Theodore, you have the mind but you have not the body, and without the help of the body the mind cannot go as far as it should." Roosevelt's younger sister, who witnessed the conversation, recalled how the young, fragile boy looked at his father and said with determination: "I'll make my body."

It was the beginning of his preparation for and fulfillment of what he would call "the Strenuous Life." He worked out every day thereafter. By his early twenties, his battle against asthma was over. Roosevelt had worked that weakness out of his body.

Not everyone accepts the cards they are dealt. They remake their bodies and their lives with activities and exercise. They prepare themselves for the hard road. Do they hope they never have to walk it? Sure. But they are prepared for it in any case.

Are your kids? Nobody is born with a steel backbone. It has to be forged. Your job is to help your kids forge theirs.

October 7
Teach Them to Handle Things

Robert Lovett, the U.S. secretary of defense under President Truman, once said, "You may think this is a small thing, but you'd be amazed at the number of people [I] met in Washington during the war who had never learned to handle anything by themselves."

If you want your kid to stand out, if you want your kid to succeed, teach them how to handle themselves, how to *solve problems.* That's what will make them one in a million. There are plenty of Ivy League kids who struggle to make good decisions, to take care of business, to think and speak clearly. There are geniuses out there who, quite frankly, will say and do things that make you wonder how they manage to cross the street without getting hit by a car.

This isn't to say you should lower your sights. It's to remind you to make sure you're aiming at the right thing. Degrees, fancy credentials, all the right experiences? What does it matter if they aren't self-sufficient, if they can't get things done?

October 8
You Have to Let Them Struggle

No parent wants to see their kids suffer. It's almost more painful for you than it is for them to trip over their words, to scratch their heads over their homework, or to bumble their way through the early years of their career. But if they never struggle, they can't grow, they can't learn, they can't get better.

Thomas Edison, a genius and a business success if there ever was one, had trouble with exactly this issue. He was so brilliant, so headstrong, so clear about what he wanted, that he could not quite give his sons room to develop and learn. He couldn't quite figure out the line between boss and father.

His wife wrote him a great letter once that stands as advice to all parents:

> You've made a success of your life, built up tremendous industries successfully so you have nothing more to prove to the world that you are capable—All know it—*Can't you be happy in just letting the boys struggle along*, with you to guide them. . . . Forget a little bit that you are Charlie's manager and be a father—a big father!

Of course, it's wonderful that you care, that you'd die for them if necessary. But you have to forget a little bit—as Edison had to—just how much you feel for them, so that they can learn. And in this way, you'll save them so much more suffering in the future.

October 9
You Have to Come Up with Challenges

A good half of the art of living is resilience.

—ALAIN DE BOTTON

O f course, you want tough kids. Kids who are active and resilient, who are healthy and competent. You want them to be able to overcome obstacles and to defend themselves, and with all that to always be prepared for the ups and downs of life.

But you can't just *want* tough kids. You have to *make* tough kids.

Theodore Roosevelt was famous for taking his kids on long walks and leading them over boulders and through thick woods. He wanted to get them used to exerting themselves and solving problems. Cato the Elder, the great-grandfather of the towering Stoic Cato the Younger, a man who rose through the ranks to become one of ancient Rome's most politically influential citizens, did the same thing. He trained his son Marcus "in athletics, taught him how to throw the javelin, fight in armour, ride a horse, use his fists in boxing, endure the extremes of heat and cold, and swim across the roughest and most swiftly flowing stretches of the Tiber."

You make kids tough by challenging them and teaching them the rewards of those challenges. You make them tough by toughing things out, together.

October 10
Yet Don't Be Too Tough

Many a tough parent has had to come to terms with the fact that each child is different and needs different things. Cato the Elder had to do just that with the challenges he designed for his son Marcus. As Plutarch writes, he had to account for the fact that Marcus was his own person:

> Since his body was not strong enough to endure the extreme hardship, Cato was obliged to relax, a little, the extraordinary austerity and self-discipline of his own way of life.

As it should be! We raise tough kids by teaching them—lovingly, patiently, understandingly—how to grow past their limits. Still, we acknowledge and respect those limits. We create challenges for them, but *we* are not the challenge. No, we are their ally. We are on their team. We love them. We're working with and for them, not against them.

October 11
Be Like This

Do you remember the viral video of a little four-year-old Iranian boy named Arat Hosseini trying to do box jumps? Arat tries and fails nine times. Then, his dad, Mohamed, enters the frame and gives his son a pep talk. On the very next attempt, Arat lands the jump. On top of the box, he double fist pumps before jumping into his father's arms.

This is what *"Luctor et emergo"*—"I struggle and emerge"—is all about. It is not about pointless struggle. It's about being by their side, encouraging them, picking them up when they fall, telling them what they need to hear *when* they need to hear it. It's being like Mohamed the box-jump dad, not John Roderick the bean dad.

October 12
Teach Them That They Decide the End of Every Story

When Vice Admiral James Stockdale was shot down over Vietnam, he was taken prisoner by the North Vietnamese. He spent nearly eight years being tortured and subjected to unimaginable loneliness and terror. He had little choice in the fact that he was shot down or that he was taken prisoner. When asked how he made it out alive, he said:

> I never lost faith in the end of the story, I never doubted not only that I would get out, but also that I would prevail in the end and turn the experience into the defining event of my life, which, in retrospect, I would not trade.

What Stockdale told himself—and what helped him endure this terrible ordeal and others—was that he possessed an incredible power. He could decide how he was going to use this experience in the rest of his life, however short or long it would be.

Teach them that. Teach them to see hardship as fuel. Teach them to see an opportunity where others see an obstacle. Teach them that despite everything outside their control, they retain an incredible power: the power to choose what they do with what happens to them. They get to decide what role an event will play in their life. They have the power to write the end of their own story.

October 13
Make Them Prove It

In his wonderful book *Outdoor Kids in an Inside World*, Steven Rinella tells a story about taking his kids camping in Montana. One of his kids confidently claimed to have spotted a scorpion. When Steve didn't believe him, the child got increasingly upset, convinced that he had, in fact, seen one. "I told him the only way he would change my mind," Steven writes, "is by bringing me a scorpion, which seemed like a perfectly safe and reasonable thing to say since we all know there are no scorpions in Montana."

Every parent who has challenged their kids on those impossible kinds of claims knows what happened next. Within *minutes*, the kids were back with two scorpions on a rock. "A quick Google search revealed that we were beholding two specimens of Montana's only scorpion species, the northern scorpion, which is mostly found around rimrock areas in the Yellowstone Basin. It was news to me."

We all learn the hard way to be credulous of what our kids claim. Even if they are wrong a lot, the one time they're not, it will cost you. But that doesn't mean they should have it easy. Make them do the work. Make them prove it. Make them track the scorpion down. Make them find some evidence, give a detailed description, build the case. Better yet, do it together. You're teaching them to show their work, to support their position, to convince and persuade . . . and you're keeping them busy in the process.

October 14
Pain Is a Part of Life

> Even though you have these powers free and entirely your own, you don't use them, because you still don't realize what you have or where it came from. . . . I am prepared to show you that you have resources and a character naturally strong and resilient.
>
> —EPICTETUS

Oh, how you wish you could guarantee they will never suffer. Of course, you know that's not possible. As the character in Hermann Hesse's *Siddhartha* says, we cannot spare our kids the suffering we have gone through in our lives. We cannot prevent them from suffering altogether. Because suffering and pain are parts of life.

As a parent, the goal is to raise kids tough enough—*loved enough*—to deal with what life is going to throw at them. We don't *want* them to suffer, but when suffering comes (and it is definitely coming), we want them to be able to endure its initial shock, navigate its ups and downs, and then learn from its consequences.

Think about that today. Think about toughening your kids up; think about preparing them for an uncertain future. Because that is the one thing we know for certain. Things are going to be tough. Things will go wrong. More pandemics and emergencies and recessions and heartbreak lie ahead. Our kids are going to have to be ready for it . . . and it's on us to make sure they are.

October 15
Courage Is Calling

In 2006, Benjamin Mee bought a zoo. Literally *a zoo*. It was broken down and in desperate need of a caring owner. Mee and his family were struggling too. Things hadn't been going well for them either. But Mee explains to his son—in a scene immortalized by Matt Damon in the movie version of Mee's book, *We Bought a Zoo*—that our lives are defined by the moments when we put ourselves out there:

> You know, sometimes all you need is twenty seconds of insane courage. Just literally twenty seconds of just embarrassing bravery. And I promise you, something great will come of it.

This idea of breaking courage down into little pieces is a very good one for us parents to pass on to our own kids. A person isn't brave, generally. We can be brave only specifically in the moment. This is as true for us and our kids or Benjamin Mee's son as it is for the most decorated soldiers who have ever served in the military.

If you read the citations for many Medal of Honor recipients, for instance, the action that rises to the level of heroism is almost always just a moment. It's usually not fighting off twelve insurgents for five hours—it's sprinting across an open plain for twenty seconds, exposed to enemy gunfire on three sides, to come to the aid of a fallen comrade.

Just literally twenty seconds of insane, embarrassing bravery. That's what courage is. So teach them how to find those few seconds of courage. Tell them something great will come of it. Promise them.

October 16
There Is Good in Everything

Parenthood can feel like one tough situation after another. One kid is sick. The other is struggling in school. You just got a call from your neighbor telling you that your son was caught throwing rocks at their house yesterday. Your daughter is being bullied. It looks like the whole family is going to be *super* late to today's soccer game.

Ugh. It's frustrating. It's overwhelming. It can feel so negative.

What we need to remember in moments like this is that line from Laura Ingalls Wilder:

> There is good in everything, if only we look for it.

If we, as parents, look at everything being thrown at us as problems, as a burden, we are going to get burned out . . . fast. But if, instead, we can see the good in each of these issues, if we can focus on the opportunity within each obstacle, not only will we be more likely to make it through, but we'll be better parents for it.

October 17
Help, but Don't Make Them Helpless

There is so much to do. Your kids have to get dressed. They have to eat. They have go to school. They have to do well in school. They'll need jobs. They'll need to figure out how to find a home, find a spouse, navigate the difficulties of the modern world.

There is so much to do . . . and they are so bad at all of it. So how does a parent get involved without crossing the line? How do we know where to help, what to handle for them, what to tell them they don't have to worry about? Of course, there are no rules. No one can give you a perfect list: Pay for their college, but not their car. Cook them food, but don't do their homework for them. Clean the kitchen, but not their room.

So maybe instead we should look for a good principle to follow instead. Perhaps we can adapt Plutarch's line about leadership:

A parent should do anything, but not everything.

A great leader is never above rolling up their sleeves. Like a great parent, they'll do *anything* for their family or their organization. But they also know they can't do *everything*. It's not good for them or for anyone else.

October 18
Teach Them That It's Figureoutable

> The impediment to action advances action. What stands in
> the way becomes the way.
>
> —MARCUS AURELIUS

There's a story that occurs constantly in the biographies of creative and brilliant people. It goes something like this: As a kid they have a question—maybe it's about how car engines work, or what Antarctica is like. It doesn't matter what the question is about, really—history, science, animals—because their dads all have the same response. They say, "I don't know, but let's go figure it out!" So they go to the library or the hardware store or the computer and they dig around until they find the answer.

What this experience did for the young versions of these notable figures was instill in them a few essential lessons that would then set them on their paths: (1) their parents actually listened and cared; (2) curiosity is the starting point of a great adventure; and (3) there are places, like the library or the internet or some wise old neighbor, where answers can be found.

Most important, though, they learned something well expressed in the title of Marie Forleo's book: *Everything Is Figureoutable*. Problems can be solved. Ignorance can be eliminated. Answers can be tracked down. The unknown can be made familiar. Things can be discovered.

Show them how this works. Point them to the library or the laptop, the telephone or their science teacher. Teach them that everything is figure-out-able. Big and small.

October 19
Teach Them That It's Figureoutable, Part II

When Charles Lindbergh was thinking about attempting the first transatlantic flight, he ran into an issue: he honestly didn't even know how long the distance was.

There is an incredible exchange in his memoir about the flight, where in the early preparation Lindbergh is talking with a mechanic about his plan to go from New York to Paris by a certain route.

"How far is that?" one of them asks.

"It's about 3,500 miles. We could get a pretty close check by scaling it off a globe. Do you know where one is?"

"There's a globe at the public library. It only takes a few minutes to drive there. I've got to know what the distance is before I can make any accurate calculations. My car's right outside."

Lindbergh was a guy who knew how to solve his own problems by *figuring stuff out*. Lindbergh and his partner end up taking a piece of string, stretching it from New York to Paris across the curve of the globe, and then measuring it against the key. They got it pretty damn close too, close enough for him to survive the flight.

We don't have to solve our children's problems for them. We don't have to teach them how to memorize things. What we have to do is teach them how to help themselves. We have to show them that everything is figure-out-able.

October 20
Be Careful How Helpful You Are

In 2016, Jeannie Gaffigan found out she had a tumor in her brain the size of a pear. It was quite possible she would die, but if she didn't, her recovery would be long and painful and she might never be the same. It was an incredibly difficult time for the Gaffigan family. In an interview, she explained just how afraid she was that her family would not be able to function or survive without her:

> I was, like, being wheeled into the OR being like, "My computer password is," you know, "The Fresh Direct password is." I was like, there's just too much to impart. And as I was recovering, I realized that doing everything for people completely robs them of their ability to function. And so there were two things there. It taught me I was overcontrolling my life, my people, and my kids. And secondly, it should be that they're just fine on their own. They don't need the boot camp that I was running.

Of course, the lesson here is not that you or your kids' coparent is not important. That would be absurd. What Jeannie realized is that by holding on too tight, by being *so* helpful, she was actually holding them back. "There I was, useless," she said, "and everybody was okay. Everyone was fine. They were better. And Jim—stuff came out of him that he never had before. And things blossomed in my kids, and I watched it from afar. They didn't need me, but they kind of did."

October 21
Make Them Find Out for Themselves

I t would be easy to give them all the answers. It's even fun to give them the answers. It would make things go faster and more smoothly and let you get back to what you were doing. But you can't. You just can't.

We've said before that the goal is to raise kids who know how to figure things out. What does that mean? It means you have to *let* them figure things out.

John Stuart Mill would recall that in his own unique childhood education, which was supervised by his father, "anything which could be found out by thinking I was never told, until I had exhausted my efforts to find it out for myself." It's not that his father never helped him—like some homeschooling bean dad—it's that he encouraged his son to take a crack at it first. More than encouraged—he let him struggle with it, let him *not know* until he either learned or learned how to learn. The boy had to try and fail before he came to the rescue.

Luctor et emergo, remember? I struggle and emerge? We have to make them understand that they have what it takes to do this on their own, and if they don't, the best way to get it is to develop it by experience, by curiosity and exploration. We hold some of our answers back not because we don't love them but because we love them so much. We let them struggle *because* we believe in them and because we believe even more in what will come out the other side.

October 22
How You See It Matters

> Choose not to be harmed—and you won't feel harmed. Don't
> feel harmed—and you haven't been.
>
> —MARCUS AURELIUS

There are things that nobody ever wants to happen—especially to their kids. Whether it's breaking an arm or being bullied, life visits things upon us. Things that frustrate, things that hurt, things that cause problems.

While we'd never choose for these things to happen, we have to remember that when they do happen, we still do retain some choice: as James Stockdale did upon his descent into the North Vietnamese jungle, we choose how we see these difficult events. We choose the story we tell ourselves about them.

The power of this idea—whether it was embraced or rejected—revealed itself in the attitudes of parents during the pandemic. Too many parents chose to see that their children had been harmed, be it by distance learning or by not seeing their grandparents. Of course, these events were undesirable. And there *were* consequences. But "harmed"? This is a subjective word. This is a choice.

Will your children be affected by things that happen? By having to change teachers midyear because of a move? By having glasses? By a divorce? By their learning issues? Yes. It would be dishonest to claim otherwise. But *negatively* affected? That's up to you. Because how you decide to see it and, more important, how you choose to respond are going to determine how your children perceive these events as well.

October 23
Don't Start This for Them

General H. R. McMaster and his millennial daughter jokingly refer to her peers as the "start-my-orange-for-me generation." Meaning the kids she grew up with can't even peel an orange without having their parents get it going first. And now as adults they suffer for it. Because for as long as they've been conscious of it, their parents have been doing stuff like that for them. Whether it was science fair projects started the night before or arguing with teachers over (bad) grades they'd rightfully earned or funding the down payment for a house they couldn't afford, McMaster's daughter was surrounded by learned helplessness.

There are lots of reasons for this snowplow, helicopter parenting style: narcissism, fear, insecurity, economic uncertainty, and, of course, real love. Regardless of the emotion behind it, the effect is the same.

Our goal is to raise self-sufficient kids. So let them peel their own oranges. That doesn't mean just let them struggle like the bean dad; it means *teach them*. It means encourage them. It means set expectations for them. It means let them go off on their own.

October 24
They Can Still Be Successful

Yes, it's true: many of the most successful artists and entrepreneurs and world leaders came from horrible circumstances. Adversity shaped and formed them, even fueled them to greatness.

Does that mean that, because you remain happily married and you are able to put your kids into good schools and new clothes, they are somehow disadvantaged? Hardly!

"It has been suggested that an unhappy childhood is necessary," the dancer and writer Agnes de Mille wrote in her biography of Martha Graham. "Possibly. Yet many childhoods are unhappy without producing anything attractive, one almost-certain result being trouble in life."

The reality is that successful people come from all sorts of backgrounds. Franklin Delano Roosevelt had loving parents. Churchill did not. They both reached the same heights . . . and though they both struggled to do it well, they each sought to provide good, stable, and loving homes for their own children.

Creating a happy childhood for our kids is the whole point of what we're trying to do here. Don't second-guess yourself. Their lives should be good. Just remember that good is not the same as easy!

October 25
Nobody Likes What Is Spoiled

> There is a certain beauty in the child, the beauty of inno-
> cence and docility. But there is nothing beautiful about a
> spoiled child.
>
> —DOUG McMANAMAN

There is nothing more lovely and more wonderful than a child. Their laugh. Their joy. The cute things they say. But like every sweet thing, it can easily turn sour.

You're not doing your kids any favors by giving them everything they want. You're not helping them by removing every difficulty and preventing all adversity. You're not making their lives easier by fighting all their battles. You're not rewarding them by overindulging them.

No, you're spoiling them. And you're not doing much of a service to the world in the process, either. Instead, you are setting your kids up for a very tough and unpleasant time in this life. You are, in fact, making them very weak and very unpleasant.

Don't spoil them. All things in moderation, even as you love them as much as humanly possible. It's a difficult balance, to be sure, but the stakes are too high not to get it right.

October 26
Don't Deprive Them of This

All of humanity's problems stem from man's inability to sit
quietly in a room alone.

—BLAISE PASCAL

Our instinct is to make sure every second of our kids' time is filled.
They've got school. And swim practice. And guitar lessons. And
scheduled playdates. We tell them to go play outside. To read or do their
homework or practice their instrument. We ask them what they want to
do next. We are always forcing or encouraging them to do something,
anything.

This is usually all very well-intentioned. But it is depriving them of a
very important skill in life: the ability to be alone. To sit with their own
thoughts. To entertain themselves. To get comfortable with boredom.

Some kids are extroverts. Some are introverts. But *every kid needs to
know how to be alone and to be happy in that space.* There are lots of opportunities for you to help them develop this ability, depending on their
age and personality, of course. When they start stirring in the morning,
don't rush in. When they're quietly playing in their room, take a step back.
Let them be bored. Let them lie around for a little while after school or on
the weekend. Let them have some time with themselves so they might
cultivate some independence.

It's a critical part of life (as every adult knows). Those who lack the ability to sit quietly in a room alone are miserable and prone to addiction and
overstimulation. So teach them now. Or, more accurately, give them the
space to teach themselves.

October 27
Let Them Know About Your Battles

Major Taylor was the greatest cyclist of his generation. Born black in America in 1878, if Major was to fight his way to the top of his sport, he would have to fight his way through brutal racism and unfairness to do it. The dual battles took their toll on Taylor. In the end, he lost not only his fame and fortune but the family he loved too. He died alone, penniless, and estranged from his young daughter, Sydney.

As Michael Kranish writes in *The World's Fastest Man*, for many years Sydney just thought her father had failed her, and naturally, she was angry at him. "Sydney had been bitter at what she interpreted as her father's rigidity and aloofness. Only later, she said, did she truly understand the strains he had faced—the physical one of racing for decades, and the mental one of battling racism. The combination, she believed, had slowly killed him."

Sydney didn't know her father's battles. Those battles weren't his fault . . . but his failure to talk to her about them was. We all struggle. There has never been a parent (or a human being) who didn't have their own battles. If we don't explain this to our children, if we can't be vulnerable or honest with them, there will forever be an unbridgeable gap between us. We will lose time and connection that we can't ever get back.

All of us will lose what Sydney and Major lost: a chance to support each other, to understand each other, to learn from each other's struggles, and to be loved and fully appreciated by each other.

October 28
You Can Survive Anything

It was the best of times, it was the worst of times.

—CHARLES DICKENS

We doubt ourselves as parents. Not just sometimes but all the time. We wonder if we're doing enough, if we're doing things right, if we have what it takes to raise good kids.

Well, we can put that to rest. The COVID-19 years have settled the matter.

You have been through the wringer. You have been through the crucible. *And you're still here.*

You got through it. You did your best. You may have stumbled but you never gave up. You might be exhausted from it—how could you not be—but you have also gained incredible strength from it.

Seneca talks about how the real object of pity is the person who has never been through adversity. Those of us who have? It wasn't easy, but at least we know now what we're capable of.

If you ever wondered if you have what it takes . . . now you have proof. You do.

October 29
You Have to See It This Way

I f you haven't heard the famous Jocko Willink "Good" speech, you should listen to it as soon as you have a chance. Because his Navy SEAL mentality doesn't just apply to warfare; it doesn't just apply to entrepreneurship or leadership. It is also a prescription for parenting. In fact, we might easily adapt it as a personal mantra to some of the daily troubles we face as parents day in and day out.

Oh, my kid woke up sick this morning? *Good*, we'll spend the day at home together.

The take-out order got canceled last minute? *Good*, we'll have breakfast for dinner.

You caught your kid lying? *Good*, now you have an opportunity to talk about honesty.

Pulled over for speeding? *Good*, show your kids how you handle owning a mistake.

Business in trouble? *Good*, talk to them about grace under pressure.

Flight delayed? *Good*, have fun in the airport as a family.

Traffic? *Good*, you get more time with them.

They are struggling in math class? *Good*, time for you to brush up on your algebra.

Your kids are counting on you. You don't get to despair. There's no time to complain. No one is going to come take this problem off your hands. It's on you. It's what you were given by fate or chance, and now you've got to work with it. You've got to *make* something of it.

You have to *make it good* . . . for them.

October 30
Give Them This Great Power

When she was about thirteen years old, Condoleezza Rice came home heartbroken because a classmate had gotten up and moved seats, refusing to be seated next to a black girl. You might have expected her parents to comfort her, to tell her that America still had a long way to go, and to assure her that she was just as good as everyone else. Indeed, they may have done those things, but her father also chose in that moment to give his daughter some pretty counterintuitive advice: "It's okay that some close-minded person doesn't want to sit next to you, *as long as they are the one that moves.*"

Instead of making his daughter feel like a victim, he *empowered* her. He gave her a great gift in that moment—it was a gift of dignity and strength. Yes, he was telling her she couldn't control what other thoughtless or mean people did. She could, however, decide not to let it affect her, not to let it change how she lived her life or how she went about her own school day. If some racist kid (with racist parents, obviously) wanted to change where they sat, that was their choice. But she didn't have to bend or be changed by it. She didn't have to let it get to her.

They can move. She didn't have to do a thing. That was her power. Your kids should know they have that power too.

October 31
Don't Be One of Those Parents

A helicopter parent hovers. They refuse to let their kid out of their sight. They follow them on the playground so they never fall down. They don't let them ride their bike to a friend's house so they never get lost. They make all their kids' decisions for them. They check in constantly with their teachers to make sure everything is going according to plan. *Their* plan.

A snowplow parent doesn't hover; they drive out in front of their kid, clearing the road of every conceivable impediment and obstacle between adolescence and . . . retirement? Their kid's, not their own.

Coach doesn't think their kid is good enough to be the star player? They'll start their own team. College applications? They've got it handled—even if it means bending the rules or breaking the law. At great pain and expense, their kid will never have to struggle, stumble, or be rejected.

Needless to say, neither of these approaches is likely to produce what every good parent wants: self-sufficient, happy, and well-adjusted children. Even though many helicopter and snowplow parents come from a good place—they love their kids so much that they want nothing but the best for them—they are actively doing harm.

Your job is to be *there* for your kid, not to be their *everything*. Your job is to teach your kid, not to prevent them from ever failing. Yes, you have to keep them safe, but not at the cost of keeping them sheltered. Not at the expense of life itself.

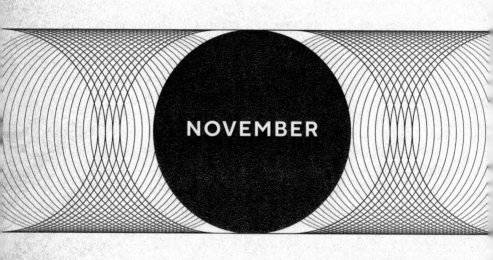

NOVEMBER

GIVE THANKS AND BUILD BONDS

(LESSONS IN GRATITUDE AND CONNECTION)

November 1
Parenthood Is a Bond We All Share

All of our fellow animal creatures, as Aristotle observed long
ago, try to stay alive and reproduce more of their kind.

—MARTHA NUSSBAUM

You love your kids more than anything. They are so special to you. Your eyes close when you think about them. Your heart softens. There is nothing you wouldn't do for them. There is no one who means more.

Think about them for a second. Do you feel that radiating warmth? Do you feel it washing over you? You just want to hug them, right? Maybe you even want to cry. That's what being a parent is.

Now take a minute to consider the many people with whom you share that feeling. Consider how basically every single person, even murderers on death row, even the rude person who just shoved you in the supermarket, even the billionaire you think is destroying our political system, has that same feeling about their kids. Run it backward and forward too. Cleopatra felt that way about her daughter. Frederick Douglass felt it about his sons. So too did billions of ordinary people in small towns and caves and ships on stormy oceans.

Being a parent is something special. It's also something that is nearly universal. We might be kinder and more forgiving and find more common ground if we could just remember that a little more often.

November 2
You'd Trade Anything for This, Yet . . .

When Kobe Bryant took off in his helicopter from downtown Los Angeles on January 26, 2020, he was a five-time NBA champion. He was a two-time finals MVP. He was a two-time Olympic gold medalist. He had won an Emmy and an Oscar and he was a *New York Times*–bestselling author. He had earned hundreds of millions of dollars in his career and raised a venture capital fund of more than $100 million.

Yet it goes without saying that he would have traded all of those things for just one more day as a dad to his four girls. And you would do the exact same thing.

Who wouldn't?

We know this. If asked, we would say it. You would say it, right? Yet . . . yet . . . yet . . . look at your choices. You'd give up so much for one more bedtime with your kids, and here you are, on your phone while they're in the bath. No amount of money could compensate you for one more morning with them, and here you are, grouchy because it's early, put out because you're sitting in traffic as you drive them to school.

You have, right now, in your grasp, the thing that Kobe Bryant would have traded *anything* for. *Do. Not. Waste. It.* Be grateful for it.

November 3
This Is Something to Be Glad About

I t can be hard to express your feelings as a parent sometimes. Not so much because parents are expected to bottle up their emotions but because the emotions that come with being a parent can be so overwhelming and complex. It's a rush of a million feelings: love, joy, fear, absurdity, exhaustion, responsibility, motivation, and primal attachment.

No one prepared you for any of this . . . and it's unlike anything you've ever dealt with before. How do you express it? How do you let your family know what they mean to you? How they have you wrapped around their finger, how they are your everything?

Maybe this exchange from *The Boy, the Mole, the Fox and the Horse* will suffice.

> "Sometimes I want to say I love you all," says the mole, "but I find it difficult."
>
> "Do you?" says the boy.
>
> "Yes, so I say something like I'm glad we are all here."

I'm glad we are all here. Isn't that the perfect way to capture how you feel? Joy and gratitude that you're together, that this is happening. That's something to be glad about. That you have each other. That we're all here, right now, despite it all.

November 4
You've Been Graced

Charles de Gaulle had a hard life. He was a POW in World War I. He had to flee France in order to save it in World War II. He endured protests and assassination attempts. He also had a daughter named Anne, who was born with Down syndrome. In 1928, when she was born, this was not something people knew how to deal with—disabled children were often sent away to institutions. Parents were made to feel ashamed, as if they were responsible for having, in the language of the day, a "retarded" child.

But not de Gaulle and his wife, Yvonne. They embraced their daughter. They built their lives around the challenging but rewarding experience of raising her. "Her birth was a trial for my wife and myself," he said. "But believe me, Anne is my joy and my strength. She is the grace of God in my life. . . . She has kept me in the security of obedience to the sovereign will of God."

Each of our children is different. Each comes with their own limitations, challenges, and personality. Whether they are seriously handicapped, have a minor learning disability, or bring into our lives this or that, it doesn't matter. We have been graced. They are a blessing, an opportunity for us to change and grow; they give us joy and something to throw ourselves into.

November 5
Are You Teaching Them Gratitude?

Your kids should be grateful. Not to Mom and Dad, of course; you're just doing your job. You're *legally and biologically* obligated. Your kids should be grateful for everything. We all should. It's amazing that any of us are alive at all. The odds are astronomically small that we are here, that we are *us*.

So it's important that you teach your kids about gratitude. Jason Harris, the CEO of Mekanism—an award-winning ad agency—and the author of *The Soulful Art of Persuasion*, has an interesting practice for *persuading* your kids to have a more grateful outlook about life. As he writes:

> Every Sunday night we write down in our book three things for which we are individually grateful. I know this is not an earth-shattering idea.... But this practice has made a world of difference for me and my kids. It resets you and gets you prepped for the week ahead.... What's helpful about writing these reflections in a notebook is that you can consult previous entries and jog your memory on truly trying days.... Keeping thoughts of gratitude on the surface of your mental life can help you realize that whatever might be going wrong today, on balance we all have a ton to be positive about.

Beautiful. And how much more beautiful would the world be if more of us took up this practice with our own kids?

November 6
It's Always a Blessing

A writer—and, I believe, generally all persons—must think that whatever happens to him or her is a resource.

—JORGE LUIS BORGES

The thing about being a parent is that it gives you superpowers—or at least *a* superpower. Nothing too special. You can't fly. You can't stop bullets with your chest. But you are able, at least with the right frame of mind, to be serene and happy in the kinds of situations that make everyone else miserable.

A delayed flight. A sick day. Traffic. A pandemic. These are things other people dread. Parents certainly don't look forward to them either, but they always have this: they understand it's more time they get to spend with their kids.

All the inconveniences of life are, through the lens of our superpower, an opportunity to hang out with the people we love most! Who can beat that? In fact, delayed flights and traffic or a rainy day are some of the best opportunities, period . . . because now your kids are trapped! Who cares if they don't want to spend time with you? You've got them where you want them.

So don't complain about the inconveniences. Enjoy them. They're a blessing. Now you get to spend more time with your kids.

November 7
There Must Be Hope

> But you have to have hope. You have to be optimistic in order
> to continue to move forward.
>
> —JOHN LEWIS

A lot has happened in your life. It's rightly made you cynical about some things, be it politics, relationships, or other people. A lot has happened in history too, and anyone who has ever read a book will have trouble shaking the fact that a lot of lies have been told, a lot of horrible rigging of the system has happened, and a lot of that contributes to the mess we're in now.

But guess what? You have kids now and you don't get to be a cynical, angry person anymore. Because *you're responsible for the raising of the next generation.*

It is imperative that we give our children hope. That we explain the world to our kids in a way that empowers them with agency, that shows them progress is (and has been) possible. That as awful as things are, as the poet Maggie Smith says, the world still has *good bones.* Like a good real-estate agent, she tells us, we have to convince our kids that they could turn this into something beautiful. You have to show them that they can make a difference, then equip them with the skills, the resources, and the responsibility to do so.

You have to teach them that no one and nothing is irredeemable.

November 8
You'll Want Them to Come to You with Problems

Do you want to be the kind of parent whom your kids turn to when they have a problem? You want them to come to you with their fears, with their secrets, with their dilemmas, don't you?

Well, then you better make yourself the kind of parent who has *earned* that honor, who has *earned* that respect. Because it's a privilege and not a right. Need proof? Think about your own parents and how many things you kept from them. Even more, *why* you kept those things from them.

Sure, some things we hide because we know it's stuff we're not supposed to be doing. But a lot of it is stuff we could have used their advice on, that we ached to connect over—yet we knew we couldn't. They would rush to judgment. They wouldn't let us explain. It would trigger their anxiety or their temper or their moralizing reminders. And we already had enough problems!

You want them to come to you? You want to help them? Then show them you're worthy of their trust. Teach them that reaching out is worth doing. Teach them that they'll get a fair hearing. Prove to them that you make things better, not worse.

November 9
You Will Want a Crowded Table

> What a great spectacle it is when a husband or wife with many children are seen with these children crowded around them!
>
> —MUSONIUS RUFUS

It's helpful to sit back and really think about what parental success looks like.

First, of course, it's having healthy kids who survive to adulthood—that's obvious.

But second, when you flash way forward into the future, what is it? It's that beautiful phrase captured in the title of the Highwomen's hit "Crowded Table." At Thanksgiving. On birthdays. At some summer house on the beach you all rent as a family. That is, having kids whom you get to see, whom you have a good relationship with, whom you want to spend time with . . . for the rest of your days.

If you want a garden, the song reminds us, you're going to have to sow the seed.

And if you want a crowded table, you'll need to make the right decisions now so they'll *want* to make the decision to fly from their homes to yours when they're older and have families of their own. You'll have to plant a little happiness, give a little love, if that's what you want to reap.

You'll need to set the table today to have the one you'll want tomorrow.

November 10
How Timeless This Is

What's so wonderful about being a parent is how it connects us to every father and mother and family that came before us. There is a line in one of Seneca's essays: "illi in litoribus harenae congestu simulacra domuum excitant hi ut magnum aliquid agentes . . ." ("while children at the beach bring toy houses to life out of heaps of sand, as though engaged in a grand enterprise . . .").

That's the kind of timeless observation that a writer at the beach with their kids would make. Seneca was spending time with family and he was struck by the innocence and the metaphor of kids building sandcastles . . . *just as your kids build sandcastles.* And with that, two thousand years of distance evaporates. A father in ancient Rome, exactly the same as a father in Pensacola over spring break or a mom at a public beach in Africa's Ivory Coast.

It can be humbling and comforting to take the time to think of these moments. As you try to rein in your difficult teenager, as your three-month-old falls asleep in your arms, as you nurse your daughter with health problems through her recovery—the fact that this kind of thing has been happening throughout human history should be heartening. They made it; you're going to make it.

What a tradition you are part of. Think how many parents have come before you and will come after. We all struggle. We all triumph. We all smile watching our kids play in the sand.

Parenthood, this timeless enterprise.

November 11
There Is Nothing Better Than This

> Love is the only legacy that matters. Let's not point our love
> in the wrong direction.
>
> —DONALD MILLER

Falling in love with your spouse is great. Making a lot of money is awesome. Crushing it at work is the best. It's nice to have a big house or to go out and have a wonderful night with friends. But there is nothing quite like coming home to your kids. Having them rush into your arms for a hug. Feeling them fall asleep on your chest on the couch. When they climb on your shoulders. When they talk to you about something they're excited about. When you hear them coming around the corner, excitedly saying your name, and they jump into your bed.

Nothing's better, as Bruce Springsteen put it, than *blood on blood.*

There is a lot of great stuff in life, but nothing is better than family. That's what he's saying. The blood relationship is not what he's talking about. He's talking about the bond. The people you'd do anything for.

So the question to think about today is: If this really is the best and most important thing in your world, are you really building your life around it? We pull extra hours at the office to get promoted. We take risks to make investments with our money. We make plans to see friends or have fun. But do we actively sacrifice and scheme so that we might have more of that one pleasure that tops them all? Do we actively prioritize the thing that truly matters most? Those moments when *blood is on blood*, when family is together?

November 12
This Is Why You're Here

> Whoever wants to become great among you must be your servant, and whoever wants to be first must be slave of all. For even the Son of Man did not come to be served, but to serve, and to give his life as a ransom for many.
>
> —MARK 10:43–45

Sometimes you get a glimpse into the lives of childless people and feel a tinge of jealousy. How much more time they have. Even the acronym DINK can make your mouth water a bit: *dual incomes, no kids.*

And yet? You know you made the right choice, not just because you love your kids but because kids give us the most important thing in the world. They give us purpose—a reason why we're here. That verse from the Gospel of Mark should land deeply with any parent.

We are here to give them a good life . . . and in so doing, make our own lives worth living. So there is no need to feel jealous. If there is anyone to envy, it's you.

November 13
You Should Like Being Their Chauffeur

W*hat am I,* many a parent has asked their kid, *your chauffeur? What do you think I am, an Uber driver?* It's understandable—it can be a pain to drive your kids around. To school. To a friend's house. To soccer practice. Sometimes it can feel like this is all parenting is—driving a little person around . . . for free.

But instead of seeing this as an obligation, see it as a gift. For a bunch of reasons. First off, twenty minutes in the car can be something you share and remember forever.

Second, how often do you get this kind of captive audience? You guys are stuck together! This is wonderful. This is what you wanted, right? An opportunity to connect? To bond? To have fun? So use it!

Third, as many parents with older kids will tell you, something changes when kids are in the car with you. Suddenly, you're not the parent. You're just a companion. Kids will share and say things in the car they wouldn't say anywhere else. Or better, if their friends are with them in the car too, you fade into the background and suddenly get to watch how your kid is with other people. You'll learn things about your own son or daughter that you'd never know otherwise. You'll get a glimpse into who they are in a way they could never articulate to you directly.

The point is: driving your kids around is a privilege. It's an opportunity. Don't complain about it. If anything, volunteer to do it!

November 14
You'll Want Them Close

J ohn Jay O'Connor III grew up in San Francisco. His family was local royalty. He went to college at Stanford, just down the road, and returned there for law school as well. So how did the O'Connors end up in Phoenix? It wasn't because he wanted to be close to the family of his new wife, Sandra Day O'Connor—who lived as far east as one could get in Arizona, on a ranch in the middle of nowhere. It certainly wasn't because Phoenix was a bustling metropolis or a paragon of culture—not in the late 1950s, anyway.

The answer was simple. He didn't want to be very close to his family. As he later reflected: "My mother was a very critical woman, and I did not want to listen to her time and again."

We all want great things for our children . . . but most of all, especially when we're older, we're going to want them to be close to us. How can we increase our chances of that? How can we do our best to ensure the existence of that lovely, crowded table we talked about the other day?

By being pleasant to be around. By not making our anxieties and fears our kids' problem. By loving them as much as we push them. By helping them be who they are . . . not what we think they should be. By asking ourselves, every time we feel like criticizing or judging or starting an argument, *Is this worth what I am about to withdraw from our relationship?*

By putting them first, but not putting everything on them, we might one day find them as close to us at our table as they are close to our hearts.

November 15
No, This Is the Special Part

In her wonderful book *On Looking*, Alexandra Horowitz takes a series of walks in different environments. What does a geologist see on a city block? What does a naturalist see walking through a park? What does a dog see on a short walk around the block? But the most interesting walk was the one Alexandra took with her nineteen-month-old.

The idea was to really try on her son's perspective on the world. So they walk out of the apartment, down the hall to the elevator, into and then and out of the elevator, and across the lobby to the front door, where they would start the walk. And as Alexandra went to check in with her baby boy, she suddenly realized . . . *that the walk had begun all the way back inside the apartment.*

To a kid, the world is a very different place from the one we live in and walk through and, if we're being honest, take for granted. This has more to do with their size and their inexperience than anything else, but that doesn't invalidate their opinions and impressions. If anything, it opens a new window for us to look at the world through, as it did for Alexandra. It reminds us of how we felt about new things when we were their age. It is an antidote to cynicism and world-weariness.

As parents, we have to appreciate the fact that our kids can help us see the world maybe better than we can help them see it. They can help us see that anything can be special and fun, that a walk doesn't have to be outside, that dinner can be anywhere and a cardboard box can be more fun than the Christmas present it was carrying. We have to encourage this spirit. We have to make sure we don't crush it with subtle corrections and insistence on the "official" way things are or should be. Most of all, we have to learn from their perspective and add it as much as possible to our own lives.

November 16
They Help You Notice Things

I t was painting that finally helped Winston Churchill slow down and learn how to *see*. He had been so busy, so ambitious, that he had not cultivated the eye or the discipline to slow down and really look at the world. Artistic hobbies can do that for you.

Parenting can have the same effect. Nothing cultivates your eye quite like games of "I Spy" in the car. Helicopters have been flying overhead your whole life, but it was only when your son or daughter became obsessed with them that you started to really *notice*. Do you think Sandra Day O'Connor went out and gathered cicadas before she was a parent and grandparent? No, it was the act of sending them off to curious children that got her to appreciate this gross but fascinating bit of nature.

The things our kids like, the joy we take in their joy—it forces us to slow down. To notice. To develop an eye. Because we want to point things out. We want *them to see*. So we pay closer attention than ever before. We keep our eyes peeled wider than ever before. We slow down in a way that, if left to our own devices, we never would.

And for that we must be grateful.

November 17
Let Them See You in Your Element

> I loved going with my father to the legislature. I would sit in the galley for hours watching all the activity on the floor and then would wander around the halls trying to figure out what was going on.
>
> —LYNDON JOHNSON

What do you think drew Steph Curry to basketball? It was the time he spent in arenas watching his dad play. The lights before the team ran through the tunnel. The cheers of the crowd. The pounding of the music. The sound of the buzzer. Seeing Dad *do his thing*. Even Curry's obsession with popcorn hints at a kid who spent countless afternoons and evenings in NBA arenas, soaking in not just the sights and sounds but even the smells and the tastes.

This is an old story, one as old as parenthood itself. It's why blacksmiths had sons who became blacksmiths, why as soon as women were allowed to have careers, the daughters of teachers followed their mothers into the classroom and soon enough into more and more elite professions.

So let your kids see you work. Expose them to the good and the bad of it, even the boring parts of it. You have no idea what parts they'll find exciting. You never know what you might be opening their eyes to. Don't pressure them to go into the "family business," of course, but give them a chance to see how that business runs. Let them see you in your element.

November 18
This Is the Highest Praise

In the book *My First Coach* by Gary Myers, Tom Brady's father, Tom Brady Sr., was told some of the things his son had to say about how much he enjoyed being with his dad growing up. Tom Sr. was visibly taken aback by the remarks. They were that yearned-for confirmation that every father desires. As he said:

> I think every father relishes time with their sons, and you never know if the son relishes time with his father. For me to hear he respects me, as much as I respect him, is the most satisfying feeling that I could ever have. I remember when he was still in high school and I would go in to wake him up in the morning so we could go play golf. It was always the greatest joy for me that he wanted to play golf with me. Years later, he made the comment that, "I never wanted to stay out late on Friday night because I wanted to play golf with my dad Saturday morning."

If there is one way to judge, in the end, whether you've done this thing right, that is it. It's the ultimate test of a parent's worth: Did you build the kind of relationship where your kids want to spend time with you? This isn't something that you just throw up your hands and hope for. It doesn't just happen because your personalities magically align. It's something you have to work for—you have to *create* the alignment. You have to build the relationship.

November 19
Look for the Double Opportunity

Bill Simmons is a busy man. He's a writer, a podcaster, a CEO, a documentary film producer, a husband, and a father of two. His eldest, Zoe, played on a big-time travel soccer team. So every weekend for months during soccer season, Simmons drove for hours around Southern California to various tournaments. If you know anything about Los Angeles, you know that traffic is a frustrating, nerve-racking hell on earth.

And yet Simmons wouldn't trade it for anything. As he would say, the drive to and from tournaments meant he had his daughter trapped in a confined space for a couple hours where he could check in with her. How's school? Friends? Boyfriends? How are you feeling about things going on in the world?

As parents, the one thing that is always in short supply is time. And Bill Simmons's time is as thinly stretched as anyone's. Which is why he learned how to double up on it. As we should too.

The jogging stroller lets you exercise . . . while spending time with your kid. The drive to school . . . is a chance to have that conversation you needed to have with your daughter. All the chores that need to be done around the house . . . are a way to teach your kids about responsibility. As a parent, you always have to be looking for the double opportunity. Time is at a premium. Resources are scarce. Don't waste any of them.

November 20
You'd Do This Only for Them

The comedian Hasan Minhaj tells a story about taking his young daughter to school picture day. She had a runny nose and was having trouble wiping it. The next thing he knew, he found himself sucking the snot out of his daughter's nose with a Starbucks straw. As the sheer foulness of the moment hit him, so did another thought: *I would never do this for my wife.*

We'd do a lot for a spouse, for our parents, even for a stranger in need. We would do *anything* for our kids, because they didn't do anything to deserve being thrust into existence, completely helpless in the beginning, entirely dependent on us for years. They didn't choose to be here on this earth. They didn't choose us to be their parents. We chose to have them. We made them. They are not just part of our lives; they are part of us. They are *of* us.

There is something about this relationship that softens the hardest head and warms the coldest heart. And while the relationship will change over time—Hasan will not be sucking snot through straws a few years from now—what will not change is the urge and the willingness to do anything for our kids.

November 21
Do Not Be Afraid

> The world is a narrow bridge, and the important thing is not
> to be afraid.
>
> —HEBREW PRAYER

Do you know what the most repeated phrase in the Bible is? It's "Be not afraid." Over and over again these words appear. They're a warning from on high to "be strong and of good courage," as we hear in the book of Joshua. "Do not be afraid nor be dismayed."

A similar chord is struck in much of ancient Greek mythology. Some version of "Be brave," "Have courage," "Don't be scared," appears more than a dozen times in the *Odyssey*. It doesn't matter which religion or philosophy or great mind you turn to, you will find courage in the same place the Stoics held it: at the top of the list of virtues.

It is impossible to be a good parent without having courage or cultivating courage in our kids. After all, it is the environment we create for them, the values we teach them, the rules we give them, and the bonds we forge with them that will give them the courage to do and be the things they were destined to accomplish and become.

Remember Barack Obama's observation:

> What makes you a man is not the ability to have a child, but the courage to raise one. As fathers, we need to be involved in our children's lives not just when it's convenient or easy, and not just when they're doing well—but when it's difficult and thankless, and they're struggling. That is when they need us most.

None of this parenting stuff is easy. A lot of it is scary. But it is essential. And it matters whether you have the courage to step up and do it every day for the rest of their lives.

November 22
Everybody Is Going Through Something

At five years old, the future NFL linebacker Ryan Shazier started losing his hair. It turned out to be a rare autoimmune disease called alopecia and, as you can imagine, not exactly an easy thing for a kid to go through. He was teased. He was looked at strangely. He felt different.

But one day, his parents helped him realize something. They said to him: everyone is going through something; the only difference is that *what you're going through is visible*. Other kids had learning disabilities or were going to bed hungry at night or had parents who were getting divorced. All those struggles were hidden—perhaps intentionally, out of shame and fear—but that didn't mean they weren't real. It didn't mean that anyone had it better or worse than Ryan. In fact, it meant they were actually all in the same boat.

Did Ryan suddenly stop getting teased? Did it suddenly not hurt to get teased? No, but it did help. It gave him perspective and patience and hope.

This is something we have to teach our kids. Life isn't easy. No one is dealt a perfect hand. Some troubles are visible. Some aren't. But we're all struggling with something. When our kids understand this, they'll feel better about those difficult moments. And they will be armed with the empathy they need to be kinder and more understanding of other kids too.

November 23
What Are You Even Fighting About?

There is no family immune to conflict. The problem, then, is not that conflicts happen; it is how we handle them when they occur, how we let these disagreements and miscommunications take on a life of their own. As Bruce Springsteen sings in "Tucson Train":

We fought hard over nothin'
We fought till nothin' remained

But more hauntingly, he talks about how long he ended up carrying that nothin'—something we're all guilty of. So much of the stuff we get upset about doesn't even matter . . . and then because we get upset about it, we end up saying things that do matter and can never be unsaid. We fight over nothing and destroy everything we care about most.

You will want a crowded table when you're old, we've said. Well, that's going to require some delayed gratification now. Some restraint now. It means letting things go. It means admitting you were wrong. It means telling your kids, your spouse, your own parents, that you're sorry. It means accepting apologies from them too. It means showing them how to patch things up with their siblings, with other people.

We can't let arguments take on lives of their own and risk their taking the joy out of our lives. Life is too short, family is too precious, to destroy over nothing.

November 24
Look for the Excuse

When he was a young teenager, Lewis Puller Jr. got himself an afternoon paper route. It was one of those things that his parents insisted on so he could learn responsibility and hard work and all that. And it was certainly good for that.

It was also good for something even better. One day, Lewis's bike got a flat tire, so his dad (Chesty Puller, the most decorated marine in U.S. history) drove him on the route. The next day, it rained, so Chesty did it again. On the third day, Lewis's dad got the car and drove him again anyway—even though he didn't need to. It was just the excuse he was looking for to spend time with his son.

These are the excuses we have to look for as well. Yeah, you could have dinner delivered . . . but going to pick it up is something to do together. Yeah, you could put them in the carpool . . . but driving the carpool is a chance to see them *with* their friends. You could buy their clothes online . . . or take them shopping, just the two of you. You could run on the treadmill . . . or strap them in the bike trailer instead and go for a ride. You could tell them they have to go to bed . . . or you could stay up and watch TV together.

Look for the excuse. Find the opportunities.

November 25
Don't Let Them Sneer

The poorest way to face life is to face it with a sneer.

—THEODORE ROOSEVELT

It is so easy to fall into the clutches of forces like contempt and wallflower nihilism and superiority. But this kind of cynicism, a wise man once said, is really a kind of cowardice. It voids creativity, collaboration, and connection. And we model it almost unthinkingly. Little comments under our breath; making fun of stuff that makes us uncomfortable; rationalizing our avoidance of things we'd rather not do or deep down know we don't do well. These choices are passed on so easily to impressionable children who are always watching.

Our kids came into the world with fresh eyes, a full heart, and so much energy. Don't deprive them of these forces. Lift them up. Let them be earnest. Let them care and try. Better yet, let them infect you with their sincerity and the clarity of their passion.

Whatever you do, don't let your cynicism infect them.

November 26
Let Them Take You Down a Peg

A proud man is always looking down on things and people; and, of course, as long as you are looking down, you cannot see something that is above you.

—C. S. LEWIS

In the midst of the Civil War, Abraham Lincoln went to visit the defenses that ringed Washington, DC. As he inspected the front lines, a Confederate sniper took a shot at him—and, thankfully, missed. A soldier nearby shouted at Lincoln, "Get down, you damn fool!"

It was a pretty remarkable moment in presidential history. As Gerald Ford observed, "Few people, with the possible exception of his wife, will ever tell the president he is a fool." The office has the effect, he said, of increasing one's sense of self-importance.

One of the great things about being a parent—if you do it right—is that it's very humbling. No one knows how to cut you down to size quite like your kids. They don't care how rich, how important, how respected you are. To them, you're a goober. To them, you're unfunny, old, and hopelessly uncool. You're someone they can make fun of. In fact, you're who they practice their sense of humor on. They're not impressed with how much you paid for the hotel room—they want to know if there is a swimming pool. They don't care how trendy a restaurant is—they hate that it doesn't have chicken fingers. They don't want you to drop them off in front of school, and they don't think you're clever. They suspect you don't have any idea what you're talking about.

"No man is a hero to his valet" goes the old expression. Plenty of parents are heroes to their kids, of course, but no one is exempt from their children's uncanny ability to size them up and cut them down from time to time. And that's a good thing.

GIVE THANKS AND BUILD BONDS

November 27
This Is a Family Motto

It was one of *those* nights. The boys would not go to sleep. They had that contagious energy that so often keeps brothers awake. The first time their father came in to tell them to go to bed, they didn't listen. The second time either. More giggling. Fighting. Playing games. Messing around. Getting into mischief.

Finally, the third time, famed college football coach Jack Harbaugh was readying to yell—just like the father in the movie *Step Brothers*—"RUMPUS TIME IS OVER!" And yet he didn't. Instead, he just looked at the boys, the future NFL coaches John and Jim Harbaugh, caught as they were in the middle of their fun, and said, "Who could possibly have it better than you two? You share, you laugh, you're brothers, you tell each other stories, you share your dreams. Who could have it better than you two?"

The boys answered in unison: "Nobody, Dad, nobody." It was this question that became the Harbaugh family motto, and one worth aspiring to in every family, rich or poor, big or small.

Who has it better than us?

November 28
Family Doesn't Hold You Back

I t's a pernicious belief that goes a long way back—back even to the Buddha himself, who had to leave his family to find enlightenment. The writer Cyril Connolly once said that the enemy of art is the "pram in the hall," that kids hold artists down.

While there is no question that raising kids is hard, that it takes enormous amounts of time and energy—especially in a world where so much of the burden unfairly falls on women—real artists and entrepreneurs and leaders know the truth. Kids are not a burden or an impediment to success. They help us. They give us purpose and clarity and, most important, balance.

The great Lin-Manuel Miranda and his wife had their first child just two weeks before the first rehearsals of his smash play *Hamilton*. You might think that this was a disruption or a distraction, but in fact it was the opposite. Miranda told the filmmaker Judd Apatow in the book *Sicker in the Head* that *Hamilton* might not have succeeded without this life event, and Miranda himself might not have been able to withstand the success either. Having an infant at home wasn't a distraction; it forced him to *ignore* distraction. "I had to say no to ninety percent of it," Miranda says of all the offers and party invites that came his way, "because . . . I had to sleep eight hours and I knew I was gonna wake up twice and change diapers. My family really saved my ass, because I think that's how you lose it."

So actually maybe family does hold you back . . . from getting in trouble. From biting off more than you can chew. From thinking you're bigger or more important than you are. It holds you down . . . to reality, to what actually matters. It makes you realize that you're loved, that you're enough. And as it happens, all of this can make you *better* at what you do.

November 29
It's an Honor to Do This

They say that the reason people have long shaken hands with their right hands was to signal that they came in peace and were not dangerous. They say that when dogs roll over and show you their belly, it's an indication of trust and deliberate vulnerability. Funnily enough, it's the same thing when they look at you while they go to the bathroom—they are exposed but are looking at you because they know you'll protect them.

These might not feel like particularly meaningful gestures of respect and love, but they are. It's an honor to get them, even though we regularly overlook their significance. The same is true of so many things that our kids do. Think about how vulnerable and small they are . . . even as they get older. Think about how helpless they are on their own.

The way they'll let you pick them up and throw them, the way they like to crawl into your bed, the way they call for you at night, the way they feel safe enough to cry around you. These things are an honor. They are incredible gestures of vulnerability and trust and love.

And you earned them . . . though you can never fail to keep earning them. This is something you cannot let down and cannot take for granted. They are a little fellow following you. They are looking at you with wide eyes and an open heart.

Live up to the honor they bestow on you with their trust and love.

November 30
You Got What You'll Want

There have been some iconic father-son moments in sports history. Tiger Woods hugging his son Charlie after winning the Masters. Drew Brees lifting up his son Baylen after winning the Super Bowl. Michael Phelps running to kiss his son Boomer after making Olympic history. Tom Brady screaming his son's name as he ran off the field after clinching his tenth trip to the Super Bowl. There are mother-daughter moments, too. Serena Williams's daughter, Olympia, taking pictures of her mom from the stands at the US Open. Paula Radcliffe training for the New York City Marathon (which she won in 2007) while pregnant.

Why do these moments give us the chills? Because we know the feeling. It doesn't matter what happened at work. It doesn't matter what we've just done or been through. The first thing on our minds is our kids. We want to hold them. We want to tell them we love them. We want to share with them.

And here's the other thing about those moments. Yeah, sometimes we wish we had gone pro. Yeah, it'd be nice to make millions. To be famous. To reach the pinnacle. But the real prize? These athletes all reach for one thing . . . and it's not the trophy. They want what you already have.

Sure, pursue your dreams. Strive to be one of the best at what you do. Aspire to be great and successful and all that. But don't ever forget that when or if you get there, you're only gonna want what you already have. You can say hi to your son or daughter right now. You can tell them that you love them right now.

It'll feel just as good as a trip to the Super Bowl—to you and to them.

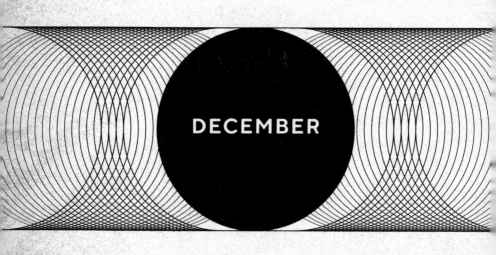

DECEMBER

TIME FLIES

(YOU COULD LEAVE LIFE RIGHT NOW)

December 1
Cherish the Garbage Time

We save and plan for elaborate vacations. We anticipate for months and months. And when it inevitably isn't as special or elaborate or photo-worthy as we'd hoped, we feel awful, like we're not enough, like we haven't done enough.

Yet the comedian Jerry Seinfeld, who has three kids, questions the "quality time" that so many of us chase.

> I'm a believer in the ordinary and the mundane. These guys that talk about "quality time"—I always find that a little sad when they say, "We have quality time." I don't want quality time. I want the garbage time. That's what I like. You just see them in their room reading a comic book and you get to kind of watch that for a minute, or [having] a bowl of Cheerios at 11 o'clock at night when they're not even supposed to be up. The garbage, that's what I love.

Special days? Nah. Every day, every minute, can be special. All time with your kids—all time with anyone you love—is created equal. Eating cereal together can be wonderful. Blowing off school for a fun day together can be wonderful—but so can the twenty-minute drive in traffic to school. So can taking out the garbage or waiting in the McDonald's drive-through.

Cherish the "garbage time." It's the best kind of time there is.

December 2
You Are Constantly Losing Them

> I saw the faces of those little boys who aren't here anymore,
> the ones who lived with me in the dreamtime of early child-
> hood.
>
> —CAITLIN FLANAGAN

Every parent's deepest fear is losing their child. And the terrible, beautiful tragedy of parenthood is that, indeed, we are constantly losing our children. Day by day by day.

Not literally, of course, but in the sense that they are growing, changing, becoming something new, something more independent. On a daily if not an hourly basis. Professor Scott Galloway has talked about the profound grief he felt looking at an old picture of his eleven-year-old. Yes, it was true that his eleven-year-old was now a great fourteen-year-old, but the eleven-year-old was no more.

Such is our fate. Such is the life we signed up for. We want them to grow. We can't wait for them to start walking, to start school, to experience all the wonderful things that life has in store for them. Yet this also means that they'll never again be what they are right now—that what they are right now is ephemeral and fleeting for us at best.

Blink, get distracted, take it for granted? It's gone. You've missed it.

December 3
Think the Unthinkable

It's fitting that one of the most important things you can do as a parent would require you to think about a thing that's very nearly impossible for a parent to even consider. It comes to us from Marcus Aurelius by way of Epictetus:

> As you kiss your son good night, says Epictetus, whisper to yourself, "He may be dead in the morning." Don't tempt fate, you say. By talking about a natural event? Is fate tempted when we speak of grain being reaped?

Of course, this is not an easy thing to do. It goes against all our impulses. But we must do it. Because life is fleeting and the world is cruel. Marcus lost eight children. *Eight!* Seneca, we gather, lost one early too. It should never happen, but it does. It heartbreakingly, world-wreckingly, nobody-deserves-it does. And it's not that we hope Marcus Aurelius's and Seneca's philosophical training prepared them for the pain of losing a child (nothing can prepare you for that). What we hope is that this exercise meant they didn't waste a single second of the time they did get with their beautiful children.

A parent who faces the fact that they can lose a child at any moment is a parent who is present. They don't rush through bedtime. They see it as the gift that it is. They don't hold on to stupid things. A great parent looks at the cruel world and says, "I know what you can do to my family in the future, but for the moment you've spared me. I will not take that for granted."

December 4
Don't Let Them Do This

They say it all the time. *When will this be over? Are we there yet? Why is this taking so long? Do we have to?* It's whiny. It's annoying. You ask them to stop. But in getting upset, you miss the real opportunity to teach them and to explain to them what they're really saying.

In his book *Travels with Epicurus*, the writer Daniel Klein recalls a formative moment:

> I remember one long-ago evening, on an overcrowded train to Philadelphia, hearing a young woman moan to her mother, "God I wish we were there already!" Her white-haired mother replied eloquently, "Darling, never wish away a minute of your life."

They're kids, so they don't understand how short a time we actually have on this planet. Even you, as an adult, sometimes forget it. That you get only eighteen summers at home with your kid. That you drop them off at school only a little more than a thousand mornings. That you'll get only so many breakfasts together, so many trips to the store, so many waits in the waiting room at the doctor's office.

To wish that away? To waste those moments, those minutes? To want it to be over soon? What a tragedy. We can't take any time with our kids for granted. And we have to teach them now, before they regret it, not to waste a minute of this life that we have.

December 5
Tempus Fugit

> This is our big mistake: to think we look forward toward death. Most of death is already gone. Whatever time has passed is owned by death.
>
> —SENECA

Every time you pick them up to trim their nails. Every time you take them to get a haircut. Every time you take a load of outgrown clothes to Goodwill or to a friend's house. Every time you have to buy them a new pair of socks or shoes, be sure to acknowledge the moment.

Notice what has led up to this. Whether it's a few weeks between nail trimmings or six months for a new pair of bigger shoes—what has happened is a piece of their childhood has elapsed. That time has passed, and it's gone forever.

Now ask yourself: Did you spend it well? Did you *live* it? Were you who and what they needed you to be?

The Stoics remind us that death isn't just some inevitable event in the future. It is happening right now. Every time they wear out a coat, every time they outgrow a pair of shoes or a pair of pants. Those moments mark movement. They are the score marks of the homemade growth chart on the kitchen doorframe. They tick off opportunities for time together that never come back.

December 6
What Would You Do Less Of?

The height of cultivation always runs to simplicity.

—BRUCE LEE

We spend so much time on stuff that doesn't matter. Maybe it's doomscrolling on our phone or answering emails. Maybe it's arguing with your spouse, with your kids, with strangers on the internet.

You hate these things but you let them fill up so much of your life. Marcus Aurelius, frustrated with some obnoxious thing that was consuming his days, once asked himself, "You're afraid of death because you won't be able to do *this* anymore?"

That's the thing about *tempus fugit* (time flies). It's so clarifying. If you had unlimited time, maybe you wouldn't mind spending two hours a day in traffic. Maybe you wouldn't need to steer clear of the cesspool of Twitter or the bottomlessness of your inbox. If suddenly death were real to you—if you were given a few months or years to live—what would you immediately spend less time doing? What is the "this" that Marcus Aurelius referred to that you would cut out?

December 7
You Can Find the Time

> I didn't see why it had to be either/or. . . . If you have a job in the daytime, you write at night. It's all a question of how much you want to do it.
>
> —MARGARET ATWOOD

We think we're too busy. We think it's impossible. We're parents now. There's no way we can start that company. There's no way we can finish that project. We have to be realistic. We've got to put it aside for now. *There just isn't enough time.*

As a young, struggling novelist, the writer Susan Straight would walk her daughter in the heat of Riverside, California, until she fell asleep. For naps. At night. It was the only way she could get her down. And the second her daughter drifted off, Straight would stop wherever they were, sit on the curb next to the stroller, and write in her notebook. She finished an entire novel that way. Even as passersby would offer her money, thinking she was homeless, she kept at it. Little did they, or she, know that the novel would go on to win major literary prizes and launch a wonderful career.

We talked in November about how parents have to look for the double opportunities—the ways to spend time with your kid *and* do what you need to do. Part of that is also looking for the moments inside the moments, when we can find the time, squeeze it like an orange for all it's worth, and get our work in too.

We can do this. We have to do this. It's not impossible. It's been done by people who had it harder than us. Toni Morrison did it. Susan Straight did it. You can do it. Whether it's writing or going back to law school or training for a marathon, you can find the time.

You don't have to give up. You don't have to be realistic. Just be creative.

December 8
It's the Thousandth Time That Counts

I would have given anything to keep her little.

—JODI PICOULT

C'mon, Dad, again! One more time! Can we keep going a little longer? Let's start over! I don't want to stop!

You've heard all these things more times than you can count. The request for one more book before bed. One more time riding on your back. To watch that funny video one more time. To sing that song once more from the beginning. To hear the story over again. To jump in the pool one more time . . . and then one more time after that . . . and one more time after that.

No matter how patient and indulgent you are, there will come a point when you'll want to say no. When you'll feel like you *have* to say no. Because you've got to go. Because this can't possibly be interesting to anyone. Because it feels irresponsible.

Maybe that's all true. But you know what? Say yes. Even if it's the thousandth time. In fact, say yes *because* it's the thousandth time. Because that's the time that counts.

You never know when you'll get another time. None of us know how long we've got. None of us know how many more times we have. So say yes. Make this thousandth one count like it was the first.

December 9
What Will You Regret?

> To have a child is the greatest honor and responsibility that
> can be bestowed upon any living being.
>
> —CHRISTOPHER PAOLINI

On their deathbeds, parents think about a lot of things. They think about the world they're leaving to their sons and daughters. They think about how they parented. They think about the mistakes they made. They think about what they did right. They are warmed by the thoughts of their children, and if they are lucky, they find themselves surrounded by them.

The question for you to think about today, on a day hopefully quite far from that moment, is: What decisions are you making *now,* and how will you think about them *then*? Think about what most parents regret as they come to the end of life: They wish they'd expressed their love for their kids more. They regret not spending more time with their kids. They regret not telling them often enough how proud of them they were. They regret taking things too seriously. They regret letting petty differences or petty problems loom larger than the love that they felt in their hearts. They regret not being present, spending all that energy trying to organize perfect "quality" time when there was so much ordinary, wonderful garbage time to be had. They regret spoiling their kids, not teaching them the right lessons, not having the conversations that needed to be had.

Well, you're lucky. Because you're not on your deathbed right now. It's not too late. Nor is it ever too early. *Today* you can adjust and change to make sure you don't have those regrets—or at least you can seek to minimize them.

December 10
Why Are You Rushing?

The trees are coming into leaf. . . . Their greenness is a kind
of grief.

—PHILIP LARKIN

We're always in a rush. We have to get them ready for school. We have to get them off to bed. We have to get to the airport. We have to get back inside. We have to finish up dinner.

We are, as parents, it seems, perpetually short of time and always eager to get to the next thing. But it's worth stopping and thinking today about what we are actually rushing *to* and what we are rushing away *from*. You're wrapping up bedtime quickly—why? So you can sit and watch Netflix after they're asleep? You cannot stand for them to be late to school—why? Fear of other parents judging you? You want to be to the airport how early? And for what reason? Because it recommends doing so on your ticket?

When we rush, we should know that we are hurrying through life. We are zipping through their childhood—the exact thing that we will stop and miss at some point not long from now. How much of this will seem important then? How much would we give to get back a few of the minutes that right now we seem to want to be over as quickly as possible?

So slow down. Savor it.

December 11
The Present Is Pleasurable Enough

> This is the real secret of life—to be completely engaged with what you are doing in the here and now.
>
> —ALAN WATTS

After a long and arduous hunt in 1888, Theodore Roosevelt finally got the bull caribou he had been tracking. "It was one of those moments," he later wrote, "that repay the hunter for days of toil and hardship; that is if he needs repayment, and does not find life in the wilderness pleasure enough in itself."

A hunter who enjoys only bagging their quarry is likely to be a disappointed hunter, nine times out of ten. More important, they are a blind and deaf hunter who needlessly misses out on the majesty of life outdoors. And the parent who thinks this is an occupation you "win," who believes parenting is measured mostly by those special, big moments, is missing a lot of majestic life as well.

It's not about the future, about getting through the terrible twos or terrible teens to some idyllic end result. The next milestone is not there to assure us the days of toil and hardship were worth it. We can't forget to notice and appreciate the little pleasures of the experience, the right here and now.

Find pleasure enough in what's present today.

December 12
You Have the Time

> You see how much time you have only when you stop think-
> ing you have none.
>
> —GUSTIE HERRIGEL

Every parent feels short on time. You have work, your marriage, your relationship. You have your kids and soccer practice and lunches to pack and baths to give. You have all those important conversations to have, rules to set down, homework to check, and curfews to enforce. Plus, you have your own health and your own interests to service.

Who has the time? you have probably said to yourself. *How can I get it all in?*

You have to stop with this idea that you are rushed, that it all needs to be squeezed in—because it's the urgency and franticness that are actually speeding things up. That was Gustie Herrigel's powerful insight.

You see, it's your desire to "squeeze it all in" that's filling your to-do list and making you miss opportunities. You won't need to schedule as much quality time with your kids if you realize that it's *all* quality time. You won't need to go to the gym as much if you realize that running around the yard is exercise. You won't need to do a whole lot of things when you realize they don't really matter. And when you drop them, you'll have more space and more freedom.

December 13
Love the Little Moments

> Enjoy the little things, for one day you may look back and
> realize they were the big things.
>
> —ROBERT BRAULT

The morning rush before you get them ready for school. The time you spent waiting at a traffic light. When you were both hungry, so you stopped for fast food. When they messed up, but instead of getting mad you sat down as a family and talked. That weekend afternoon where you watched a movie on the couch.

These seem like little, inconsequential, ultimately forgettable moments. The background noise of life. Quintessential garbage time. But that's misleading. Just as one man's trash (or garbage time, in this case) is another man's treasure, so can these little moments—if you decide to see them properly and soak them in—become the big moments, the important time.

Don't take it for granted. Don't let your mind or your attention drift. Don't get too anxious (or ambitious) about the future at the expense of the present. Just be here now. Be with them.

Treat the little things as big things. Because in truth, that's what they are.

December 14
Is It Really Time to Go?

> Whatever [my son is] doing right now, that's the most im-
> portant thing. So I encourage him to keep doing it as long as
> possible. I never say, "Come on! Let's go!" . . . Of course my
> adult mind wanders to all the other things we could be doing.
> But I let it go, and return to that present focus.
>
> —DEREK SIVERS

Even the most patient of us gets bored. Or has somewhere to be. Or really doesn't see what makes *this* flower—the four hundredth one drawn in a row—so special. So we want to prod our kids along.

Dinner's almost ready. We're going to be late. The game's about to start. It's really hot out here.

We have to work to override these instincts. Because the truth is, most of the stuff we're rushing to is not that urgent. There is a certain amount of Zen in that, which is valuable to us for its own sake. But with regard to our kids, it's also teaching them a valuable skill. Shouldn't we want them to develop the ability to focus and pursue their curiosity? Isn't it worth it for them to get a little dirty or for you to show up to the birthday party a bit late because they were really, intensely *alive* for a few minutes?

Encourage your kids. Resist the urge to hurry. It's not really time to go. You're exactly where you—and they—need to be.

December 15
Every Moment Is the Same

> Always hold fast to the present. Every situation, indeed every moment, is of infinite value, for it is the representative of a whole eternity.
>
> —GOETHE

With bills to pay or traffic to wait through, a colicky baby or a resentful teenager, it can be hard to feel that the moment right in front of you is a gift. But indeed, these are wonderful moments. We must, as Goethe put it, hold fast to them.

That's what parenting is. It's right now. It's whatever you're doing in this moment. Always.

Driving them to school. Folding laundry. Getting some quiet time before they wake up. Putting them back to bed when they wake up in the middle of the night. Sending them to their room. Taking away their phone because their grades have slipped. This is all it. This is all part of the job. And every one of these moments is wonderful. Every one of these moments is a gift.

All of it is right now. It's being presented to you at this very moment.

December 16
You Must Amend Your Life

This great Robert Southwell poem is a haunting reminder to all parents:

> My ancestors are turned to clay,
> And many of my mates are gone;
> My youngers daily drop away,
> And can I think to 'scape alone?
> No, no, I know that I must die,
> And yet my life amend not I.

Do you parent according to the unpleasant fact that we will not be here forever, or are you more like Southwell? Are you in denial, struggling to accept the only fact that matters and to amend your life accordingly?

When you wake up each morning, when you walk through the front door each night, forget what you were bothered about at work. Forget what is happening in the news. Forget what you and your spouse are fighting about. *Be* with your kids. *Be* with your family.

Life is short. Your family is what matters. Your kids are what matters. So forget all the things you'd like to do "someday." *Do them with your kids now.*

December 17

This Could Be the Moment

The simple things are also the most extraordinary things.

—PAULO COELHO

You're busy. It's just a trip to the store. Your kids have been a pain all day. You're trying to get ready to give them a special surprise. And because of what you're trying to do, get through, or plan, you're not thinking about right now. You're thinking about later. Is that so bad? In theory, of course not. The problem is that, in reality, this moment may be *the* moment.

Think of your own childhood. Think of what stands out. Is it the big moments? The big conversations? Or is it ordinary experiences, ordinary interactions—ones your own parents don't even recall—that have somehow wormed into your memory?

Like when your dad skipped work and took you to a random midweek baseball game. When Mom made breakfast for dinner—your favorite—for no reason in particular. Or conversely, when they spoke to you sharply, when you saw them do something bad, when you were made to feel a certain way you'd never felt before.

Every moment is a chance to parent. Indeed, you are shaping them in every moment, whether you intend to or not. Every moment could be the moment. So you can't rush through them, you can't assume they don't matter, you can't lower your standards for yourself. Because this could be the last, best moment you get.

December 18
Try to See It This Way

At the end of *Death Be Not Proud*, John Gunther's memoir about his son's life, Gunther's wife, Frances, writes, "Johnny lay dying of a brain tumor for fifteen months. He was in his seventeenth year. I never kissed him goodnight without wondering whether I should see him alive in the morning. I greeted him each morning as though he were newly born to me, a re-gift of God. Each day he lived was a blessed day of grace."

Hopefully, thankfully, most of us will not have to go through what that family did. But we can and we must try to practice what they practiced. *Because you never know.* Wouldn't it be better to see each day this way, that each day with them is a gift, a lucky break, a midnight reprieve, as opposed to a chore?

Act tonight as if it were your last time together. Soak it in. Appreciate it. Be everything they need. And then in the morning, arise and be surprised, grateful, blessed, by the grace of another try. Then live accordingly.

December 19
Do Your Future Self This Favor

At some point you will look back at this moment in your kids' lives with the misty wistfulness of nostalgia. It doesn't matter what the future holds for them, or which paths they take; you will look back at this time with a sense of longing.

It's just a fact. Because they'll never be two again. Or twelve. Or twenty-five. You get only so many bedtimes, so many baths, so many drives to school, so many vacations, so many evenings on the couch, so many times in the garage trying to fix something they asked for your help with. In the end, we will all wish we could go back in time to get just one more of any of those moments.

Well, that can't happen. But there is a way that we can travel to the future, or at least speak *to* the future. As the great author of children's books Adam Rubin has said: we can, by the choices we make today, tell our future selves *that we did everything we could.* That we soaked it in. That we didn't rush through it. That we told them what they meant to us.

Do your future self the favor of a lifetime. Don't take this moment for granted. Don't let your temper rule. Don't be stubborn. Don't value the wrong things. Love now, while you can. Embrace the moment while you can. Don't rush away from it while it's still here.

December 20
They Could Be Your Last Words

On January 8, 2022, about to go onstage to perform stand-up, Bob Saget—legendary comedian, longtime host of *America's Funniest Home Videos*, and Danny Tanner on *Full House*—got a text from his daughter. We don't know what she said, but it wasn't urgent.

He could have easily said to himself, *I'll respond later. I'll call her in the morning.* We've all done it. We're running late. We're processing emails when they call from the other room. We're about to go into a meeting when they text us. We're tired and we rush through our good-nights.

We tell ourselves that we'll respond in a little bit. We tell ourselves that we'll have another chance, that there will be other phone calls, other texts, more good-nights. But that's not always true.

Saget took a second to send what neither of them could have known would be his last text. "Thank u," he wrote. "Love u. Showtime!" Hours later, he'd be found dead, tragically, in his Orlando hotel room at age sixty-five.

No one knows what their last words will be. No one knows how much time they have. So let's use the time we have, before we lose the time we're never guaranteed. Let's make sure we tell our kids how we feel about them while we can.

December 21
They Learned This Lesson For You

There are people who have seen their children die.

—MARY LAURA PHILPOTT

The comedian and actor Rob Delaney's son, Henry, was healthy and beautiful, but then he got sick. Delaney and his wife, Leah, didn't know what to do, so they took Henry to the doctor. It took a long time but, eventually, the doctor found that Henry had a brain tumor. They operated on it and he got better. But sadly, the tumor took Henry's life at just two years old.

On Marc Maron's podcast, Rob shared how his perspective changed following Henry's death:

> I hold my children, and I hold my wife, and I know that they will die. And I know that it could happen before I die. So I know that our time together is finite. It will end. And so I appreciate them so much more. I marvel at the fact that these particular collections of cells coalesced around these souls for a temporary period, and I'm so lucky to get to be here at the same time as the little collection of cells and bones and nostril hairs. And so I really make the most of it in a way I didn't before. And I wish that that skill didn't come from something so painful. But it did. That was the price tag for me to receive that gift. And now I have it, and I appreciate it.

When we appreciate how little time we have with our loved ones, we can make the most of that finite amount of time. Families like the Gunthers and the Delaneys, as well as quietly grieving families all around you, have learned painful and powerful lessons. We can't take their pain away, but we can heed it. We can do our best to appreciate it from afar, what they paid for it, and apply its wisdom in our own lives.

Remind yourself this morning and every morning: this will end. *Tempus fugit. Memento mori.* Then go marvel at the collections of cells coalesced around the souls of those you love. Make the most of your time with them.

December 22
What Is More Important?

> Life is short. Do not forget about the most important things
> in our life, living for other people and doing good for them.
>
> —MARCUS AURELIUS

Your kid wants to go swimming, but you have to make this phone call. Your kids want to wrestle, but you have to cook dinner. Your kids want you to come tuck them in, but it's a tie game with forty-two seconds left in regulation.

We pick these things because they're urgent. Because they'll only take a second. But mostly, we pick them because we can get away with it.

If something seemingly more urgent or out-of-control were to intervene, you would push the phone call. If you were stuck in traffic, you would order delivery. If the boss called and *needed* something, you would find out later who won the game. Yet here you are, telling your kid (and their earnest request to spend time with you) that they are not as important. Here you are choosing *it* over your kid.

Most of whatever we're doing can wait. Not indefinitely, of course. No one is telling you to put it off forever. But this moment right now, you won't get back. Take it. Play. Sit with them. Talk with them. Pause the TV. Save the draft and come back to it. Let dinner get cold. Tell so-and-so you'll have to call them back.

Your kids are more important.

December 23
You Can't Put Things Off

Do you know what one of the last things Abraham Lincoln ever said was? As he sat in the box at Ford's Theatre, waiting for the play to start, Lincoln turned to his wife and said, "How I should like to visit Jerusalem sometime."

Within minutes, an assassin would fire a bullet into his brain. Within hours, he would be dead.

Just as you have your many reasons for why you are waiting to do this or delaying doing that, Lincoln had his. And yet life has a way of stripping all our reasons bare, of humbling our plans and assumptions. We must live, as Marcus Aurelius said, as if death hangs over us. We must parent this way, too. Because it does hang over us. We cannot put off until tomorrow, he said, what we can do today—whether that's being good (our highest priority) or telling people we love them or taking them to the places we've always wanted to see.

December 24
It's Not About the Stuff

> I've never met a thirteen-year-old who said, "My dad was never around because he was always working, but I have a sweet mountain bike so it was all worth it."

—JON ACUFF

You work very hard and are able to provide. Not just the basic necessities but all sorts of extras. Because of you, your kids have a swimming pool. They have nice vacations. They have a big TV downstairs with lots of channels. They have all this and more.

And yet it doesn't matter.

It's not the swimming pool they want; it's *you* in the swimming pool with them. It's being in the motel room eating snacks, together, wherever you happen to be, that they really want. The TV is great, but not as a substitute for Dad.

The stuff you get them is great. It is not, no matter how nice it is, a substitute. It is not the point. They'd rather play in an inflatable pool from Walmart with you than play alone in one with a slide and a waterfall. They'd rather live in an apartment and have family meals together than feel lonely in the best neighborhood in town.

They want *you*. They want *fun*. And you should want those things too, because there is no telling how much longer you'll have them to yourself, or they'll have you in their lives.

December 25
This is a Gift You Can Give Yourself (And Your Family)

When you were younger, for Christmas, all you wanted was presents. Now that you're older, now that you have kids, all you want is *presence*. All you want is for your kids to be present over the holidays.

Paul Orfalea, the founder of Kinkos, is worth hundreds of millions of dollars. When asked about his wealth, Orfalea didn't talk about buying expensive stuff or building a great company or taking exotic vacations. He said, "Do you know what success is? Success is when your children want to be with you when they're adults. How many people have all the material stuff, and their kids don't come home for the holidays? Come on."

Success, as we've talked about before, is having a crowded table. At the end of your life, success as a parent will be a family that comes together, that spends time together, that wants to be around you.

So here on Christmas, and throughout this holiday season, take some time to think about what it will take to have that. Think about the choices you're making with your kids now so that they'll choose to fly from their homes to yours when they're older and have families of their own. Think about the gifts you have to give them today—your love, your support, your presence—to receive the gift of a crowded table in the future.

December 26
Forever Young

One of the reasons some kids are so unprepared for the real world is that parents see the sweetness and innocence of a kid and think, *I want to keep them like this forever.* They felt like their own childhood was too short, and so they seek to extend childhood for their children for as long as possible.

It's an understandable impulse, but it's also a kind of contradiction. Instead of enjoying how special their kid is in that moment, the parent is thinking both about the future (their own) and about the past (their own) and trying to figure out how to protect their kids from them. Instead of being present, instead of seizing and drinking in *right now*, they are futilely trying to hold back a tide that no one—not even the most dedicated father—can stop: time.

Today and always, we should remember that line in the famous William Blake poem:

> Hold Infinity in the palm of your hand
> And Eternity in an hour

If you want your kid to be forever young, enjoy this moment here in front of you. Experience it fully right now. Don't give even a thought to what lies around the bend. Because you know what you'll find? That right now just keeps on going . . .

December 27
This Is When It Matters

The Europeans of the past had some *weird* parenting practices. Michel de Montaigne's parents sent him to live with villagers as an infant. Jane Austen's mother breastfed each of her kids for the first month, then handed them off entirely to someone else. Aristocratic parents delegated to nannies and tutors and governesses until the kids were old enough to participate in adult conversations.

What most of us understand now, either culturally or intuitively, is that every minute you have with your kids matters . . . but the younger they are, the more those minutes matter. There's an old expression: "Give me the first six years of a child's life and you can have the rest."

Imagine *generations* of parents who did exactly the opposite of this. No wonder the past was so horrible . . . and people did such horrible things to each other. The first thing their parents did to them was horrible! They severed the first, most important bond a child has—the familial bond.

And think about what this cost them! Yes, kids are difficult when they're young, but it's also when they're the most fun, the most innocent, the absolute cutest. So why are we so busy? Why are we working so much? Trying to have it all—cramming in all the old things we used to do before we had kids while we ask our parents to watch our children for us? We tell ourselves that when our kids are old we'll make more time for them, we'll have more freedom—and besides, they'll appreciate it more when they're older.

No! Now is when it matters most! Now is when it counts! The earlier the better!

December 28
This Could Be That Day

It was just another day on vacation for the Roosevelts in 1921. Franklin Delano Roosevelt, then thirty-nine years old, in the prime of his career and life, spent the morning sailing around Campobello Island with Eleanor and his two older boys. They had quite an adventure. Seeing a small fire on another nearby island, they rushed and put it out as a family. When they got back, FDR and his sons raced each other more than a mile to a swimming hole. And then later they jumped into the Bay of Fundy together.

For FDR, a busy man, these days were too few. This one, in 1921, took on a special significance after the fact, because, as Doris Kearns Goodwin writes in her book *Leadership*, within forty-eight hours, "paralysis had spread to [FDR's] limbs, thumbs, toes, back, bladder, and rectal sphincter. Pain shot up and down his legs." His life would never be the same. Never again would he race his boys on foot. Never again could he play and sail and dive with them without intense physical pain. In fact, he very nearly died.

The hard truth is that today could be that day for us. We have no idea what viruses or diseases are already making their way through our bodies. We have no idea what awaits us at the top of the stairs or around the corner or across the street. So we must enjoy every moment with our kids. We must give everything we have to being a parent and relish the joy they bring us.

December 29
This Is the Eulogy You Get to Hear

I t was an early summer night in 1967. The Stafford family was all together. They'd had dinner. They'd laughed. They'd caught up on their day. And then the parents headed to bed while the kids kept the evening going.

It's a scene out of millions of family vacations and reunions and Thanksgivings and Christmases. In his diary the next morning, William Stafford—the poet—would recount how wonderful it had been. "Last night the kids in our living room stayed up to talk after Dorothy and I came out to bed," he said, "and they were talking about us, or about to do so— benevolently. I happened to think: this may be the only, and is probably the best, memorial service I will ever get."

At the end of your life, success as a parent will be a family that comes together, that spends time together, that wants to be around you. But Stafford's realization is a powerful one. Those evenings together? That's the funeral you get to attend. The family dinners, the long conversations— these are the eulogies you get to hear.

Cherish this while you can. Cultivate it while it's still possible. It's what makes life worth living.

December 30
What Can You Do?

When she was a soon-to-be empty nester mother of two, Mary Laura Philpott wrote her belated reflections on what it must have been like for her father, who worked high up in the federal government during the Cold War preparing for how to protect the president during a nuclear attack on the Capitol. She tried to imagine how he must have carried on with his work knowing that he was, in fact, preparing for the very end of the world and almost certainly of his own DC-based family.

This paragraph is worth reproducing in full:

> What do we do, then, if we cannot stop time or prevent every loss? We carry on with ordinary acts of everyday caretaking. I cannot shield my beloveds forever, but I can make them lunch today. I can teach a teenager to drive. I can take someone to a doctor appointment, fix the big crack in the ceiling when it begins to leak, and tuck everyone in at night until I can't anymore. I can do small acts of nurturing that stand in for big, impossible acts of permanent protection, because the closest thing to lasting shelter we can offer one another is love, as deep and wide and in as many forms as we can give it. We take care of who we can and what we can.

All you can do is keep on keeping on. Love. Try to be present. Do your best. Protect them. Take care of them. Ignore everything else.

December 31
Begin Anew, While You Can

Each haircut, each set of outgrown clothes, each round of spring cleaning, each start of a new sports season is marking a passage of time. It's moving us closer to that thing we dread: our kids growing up, our kids leaving, our final parting.

But the point of this message is not to depress you. It's not intended to take the joy out of spring. On the contrary, it's to help you enjoy it now, while it's here. It's to remind you of how important it is . . . and what a wonderful opportunity it presents.

As Philip Larkin writes in his beautiful poem "The Trees," about the annual message the earth gives each spring:

> Last year is dead, they seem to say,
> Begin afresh, afresh, afresh.

The past is past. The last year is gone forever. The length of the future remains, as ever, uncertain. But now is now. The new season is here. Let us put our mistakes behind us. Let us work against distraction, addiction, and busyness. Let us rededicate ourselves to the reason we are here—to parenting, our most important job. Let us begin afresh, afresh, afresh.

Let's enjoy this spring with all it presents. Because when spring dies and turns to summer, so do we a little, so does one of only so many seasons we have with our kids.

Tempus fugit.

Interested in more timeless parenting advice?

Visit

dailydad.com/email

to sign up for a daily email
to continue the journey.

Also by Ryan Holiday

Also by Ryan Holiday and Stephen Hanselman

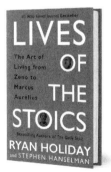

ryanholiday.net
dailystoic.com